icle=Examiner

AY, APRIL 19, 1906.

AND FIRE:
CO IN RUINS

MBLOR AT 5:13 O'CLOCK YESTERDAY MORNING, THE SHOCK LASTING 48 SECONDS,
MASS OF SMOULDERING RUINS. AT SIX O'CLOCK LAST EVENING THE FLAMES SEEM-
R FURY HAD SPARED DURING THE EARLIER PORTION OF THE DAY. BUILDING THEIR
THE DAY WANED, LEFT THE BUSINESS SECTION, WHICH THEY HAD ENTIRELY DE-
ELL THEY HAD MADE THEIR WAY OVER INTO THE NORTH BEACH SECTION AND
THE BAY SHORE, OVER THE HILLS AND ACROSS TOWARD THIRD AND TOWNSEND
R PATH. THIS COMPLETED THE DESTRUCTION OF THE ENTIRE DISTRICT KNOWN
THE CHANNEL CANNOT BE TOLD AS THIS PART OF THE CITY IS SHUT OFF FROM

IR BLANKETS AND SCANT PROVISIONS TO GOLDEN GATE PARK AND THE BEACH TO
RECKED SECTION PILED THEIR BELONGINGS IN THE STREETS AND EXPRESS WAG-
IONS. EVERYBODY IN SAN FRANCISCO IS PREPARED TO LEAVE THE CITY, FOR THE

LED INTO HEAPS. FACTORIES AND COMMISSION HOUSES LIE SMOULDERING ON
"CALL" AND THE "EXAMINER" BUILDINGS, EXCLUDING THE "CALL'S" EDITORIAL

200,000,000. THESE FIGURES ARE IN THE ROUGH AND NOTHING CAN BE TOLD UNTIL

RED, EITHR BURNED, CRUSHED OR STRUCK BY FALLING PIECES FROM THE BUILD-
, IMPROVISED AS A HOSPITAL FOR THE COMFORT AND CARE OF 300 OF THE INJURED.
ATH IN THE HORROR.
AS PLACED UNDER MARTIAL LAW. HUNDREDS OF TROOPS PATROLLED THE STREETS
IRE AND POLICE DEPARTMENTS. THE STRICTEST ORDERS WERE ISSUED, AND IN
T THEIR DEATH BY RIFLE BULLETS WHILE AT WORK IN THE RUINS. THE CURIOUS
HE CROWDS WERE FORCED FROM THE LEVEL DISTRICT TO THE HILLY SECTION BE-

HE LINES OF FIRE DEPARTMENT WOULD HAVE BEEN ABSOLUTELY USELESS AT ANY
MORNING IT WAS SEEN THAT THE ONLY POSSIBLE CHANCE TO SAVE THE CITY LAY
BE HEARD IN ANY SECTION AT INTERVALS OF ONLY A FEW MINUTES, AND BUILD-
LAMES JUMPED AND ALTHOUGH THE FAILURES OF THE HEROIC EFFORTS OF THE PO-
DESPERATION THAT WILL LIVE AS ONE OF THE FEATURES OF THE TERRIBLE DISAS-
ON.

THE GREAT
EARTHQUAKE
AND FIRE

EX LIBRIS

P. R. Hansen

THE GREAT EARTHQUAKE AND FIRE

▲▲▲

▲ SAN FRANCISCO, 1906 ▲

JOHN CASTILLO KENNEDY

William Morrow and Company, New York, 1963

CONTENTS

SAN FRANCISCO

the area destroyed by the great fire

April 18-21, 1906

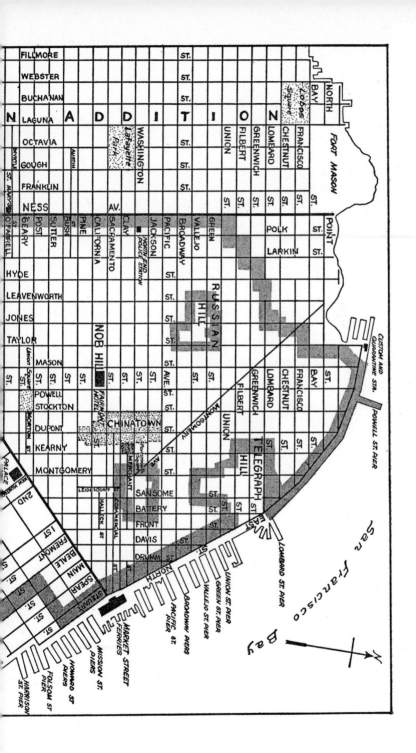

ONE

"San Francisco is a mad city, inhabited for the most part by perfectly insane people whose women are of a remarkable beauty."

—Rudyard Kipling

▲▲▲

San Francisco was a wicked city in 1906, and there were those who said after the disaster that it had only got what it deserved. The news was greeted in Benton Harbor, Michigan, for example, with a celebration that included a brass band. They'd known it was coming, those Flying Rollers of the House of David announced. Not only had they known it, they were responsible for it. They'd sent their missionary, Mary McDermitt, out there to convert the heathens of San Francisco, and while she had preached in the streets, San Franciscans had gone on their gay, happy way, ignoring her. That was too much for Mary, and using powers possessed by any prophet of the Flying Roller sect, she had called down an earthquake on them. It had better be a lesson to San Francisco, Prince Benjamin, patriarch of the sect, thundered. There wouldn't be much time, either, because the world was going to end in 1916.

San Francisco was a good deal on people's minds in those days. Back East, Bishop Hamilton warned his flock that it was "a city of saloons and anarchy, where Methodism flourisheth not," and, not knowing that Mary McDermitt had already settled things, called on the faithful from Lawrence, Mass., to Trenton, N.J., to contribute their pennies toward sending another missionary to San Francisco.

San Franciscans were used to that. They paid no more attention to it than they did to the predictions of disaster in *Zadkiel's Almanac for 1906.* "In San Francisco Mars and Saturn are on the fourth angle, or lower meridian," the Almanac pointed out. "In the vicinity of that great city underground troubles—probably a serious earthquake—will be destructive about Christmas day or the latter half of February. The winter will be stormy and cold. Otherwise the quarter will be a prosperous one." Maybe a few superstitious ones waited nervously until February was over, but then everybody scoffed. Winters were always cold and stormy in San Francisco, times were always prosperous, and there hadn't been any earthquake, although it wouldn't have proved anything if there had, since San Francisco was always having earthquakes. Quite a few people could still remember the big one of '68. That was why, ignoring the six times the city had been destroyed by fire, ninety per cent of the city's buildings were now built of wood: brick buildings were too vulnerable to earthquakes.

Times were prosperous and the city was booming. There were 450,000 people now, so many people that new subdivisions were being laid out all the way to the Pacific Ocean. There was even one paved street in the "Sunset" district west of Twin Peaks, where there had never been anything but sand lots before. By now San Francisco was so far ahead of Los Angeles' 204,000 that that city, which San Franciscans usually viewed with mixed feelings of condescension and alarm, would never be able to catch up.

San Francisco was an ugly city, most visitors thought, with its motley collection of shacks and dilapidated houses that dated back to the fifties and its newer houses, square and graceless, heavily ginger-breaded and invariably bay-windowed. Ugly, and inconvenient too: City of a Hundred Hills, they might call it (there were actually forty-four discernible hills within the city limits), that hardly disguised the inconvenience of the street system, which had been laid out in rigid grid pattern as though the hills were not there at all, leaving streets to swoop up and down sheer hillsides and sometimes dwindle into mere stairways. Nevertheless, it had a charm and a style all its own that grew out of these hills, out of a history that dated back to the founding of Mission San Francisco de Asís (Mission Dolores) in 1776, and most of all, out of its people. For, more than most cities, San Francisco had sprung from adventurers, gamblers, seafaring men, gold seekers, drifters; it had been leavened with Russian traders and Spanish dons, English thugs and Chinese laborers and Italian immigrants. The mixture that resulted was vigorous, independent, crude, cosmopolitan.

This year, of all years, there was an infectious fever in living in San Francisco. Not since the fabulous years of the nineties had life been so good, so happy, so exciting. They could find time to think of others who were in trouble, of course, and to give generously. Right now a fund was growing in the city for the fifty thousand homeless survivors of Vesuvius, which had begun to erupt April 6. It was easy to give when things were going so well here.

It had been a brilliant social season from the moment Ned Greenway, the little champagne salesman who ruled San Francisco society, opened the season with his first Friday night ball. Prospective debutantes had learned to their dismay that this year, for the first time, his Friday Night Cotillion Club would admit only girls whose mothers had been members, but even those excluded admitted that the decision represented an advance for San Francisco. It brought the city up to the rank of Charleston and its St.

Cecilia Ball, which was a rank that all too newly rich San Francisco devoutly longed to hold.

The carefree, happy season had reached its peak on April 17. The weather, which for the last few days had been cold and dreary, was suddenly warm and radiant. All over town there was a fiesta feeling: at the Columbia Theatre, where Victor Herbert's new musical extravaganza, *Babes in Toyland,* was playing; at the Mechanics' Pavilion, where there was to be a "stirring grand march on rollers" (this Mechanics' Pavilion, within a dozen hours to be a makeshift hospital, a morgue, a heap of ashes); at the Grand Opera House on Mission Street, where Caruso and Fremstad were to sing *Carmen.*

The Opera House was an exciting place to be this evening. It was one of the oldest theaters in San Francisco, and it had known hard times. It had closed in 1885, when business began to move off Mission Street, and after standing empty for years had stooped to vaudeville and then to "independent" theatrical companies touring in defiance of the theater trust. That was all behind it now. The last four years had seen Mission Street revive, new buildings rise, and a return of business. Once again refurbished and gilded, its chandelier, the largest in the west, glittering with light, its three massive tiers crowded, it housed the opera.

The Metropolitan Opera Company had actually opened the night before with Goldmark's *The Queen of Sheba,* but it had been a spiritless, ill-inspired performance, not at all to San Francisco's taste. All society looked forward to tonight's performance, and it was unanimously agreed that the opera season "really began" tonight. For if there was a role that the city took to its heart, which it really understood, it was the wild and passionate Carmen. Why, a new Carmen here would attract five times the interest of a new Hamlet!

It was a capacity house, with a small fringe of standees. A

fussy little fire sergeant rushed back and forth importantly, elbowing through the indulgent crowds, determined to preserve "the letter and the spirit" of the fire laws. Young John Barrymore, glad to be finished with his small part in *The Dictator*, which had recently closed, settled down in his seat and began to make discreet advances, while her escort's attention was distracted, to the young woman fortune had placed next to him. Society matrons lingered to see and be seen. Society reporters breathlessly took notes of who was wearing what.

"Glitter gowns" predominated among the well-dressed dowagers, but there were surprisingly few "pneumonia corsages" tonight—surprising because, ordinarily, "the higher the prices the lower the neckline" and tonight's prices were high: seven dollars for a seat, sixty-six for a box. (Seats at the Majestic Theatre where the "riotously funny farce," *Who Goes There*, was playing were only twenty-five, fifty and seventy-five cents.) If there were some women, society reporters noted disapprovingly, wearing the same dresses tonight they had worn Monday night, if some dowagers, not too long out of the laundry or the boarding house, were having trouble keeping their "ta-raras" straight, it was still a night of spectacular dresses, all glitter and diamonds.

There in a proscenium box was Mrs. William Tevis, in an elaborate gown of white satin, with insertions and corsage decorations of lace, embroidered in pearls, with a diamond dog collar and a diamond tiara. There was Mrs. M. H. de Young, wife of the *Chronicle* publisher, in another box, in white brocade, with a coronet of diamonds. And Mrs. Frederick Kohl, in a gown of black lace, spangled, a two-inch-wide dog collar of diamonds and pearls, an assorted lot of "shimmering things on the corsage line," the inevitable diamond tiara and a brilliant American Beauty rose. But most spectacular of all, in a box that must have glowed even after the lights went down for the performance, was Mrs. James Flood. Old Mary Leary Flood could remember when they'd sold the family cow to pay her way from Ireland to the United States, and she had helped her husband tend bar at the Auction Lunch Saloon on Washington Street, before he'd hit it rich on the Comstock. Diamonds gave her a comfortable feeling, and she had plenty of them: tonight she was wearing a diamond tiara, diamond dog collar, diamond shoulder straps, *and* diamond stomacher, not to mention innumerable corsage decorations of diamonds and pearls.

Some of these women would still be wearing these dresses Wednesday, standing in bread lines.

Now the lights dimmed slowly on the glittering assembly, and the curtain went up on *Carmen*. The audience was immediately entranced. Physically the fat, dumpy, double-chinned little Enrico Caruso might not be the ideal representation of the dashing Don José, but vocally he was all anyone could ask. From parterre to gallery they succumbed to the glorious golden tenor. People were standing, shouting "Bravo" before the first tiny duet with Micaela was over. In the foyer between acts men discussed the performance excitedly. (Few San Francisco women in 1906 had succumbed to the sophisticated eastern and European custom of strolling to the foyer between acts.) It was Caruso's night. *Carmen* had rechristened itself tonight, they told each other. For the rest of the season at least it would be *Don José*.

The curtain fell on the final act with a veritable hail of "Bravos." Caruso took curtain call after curtain call. It was the last time he would ever sing in San Francisco.

Out of the Opera House they poured then, in holiday spirits, to the mile-long line of hacks that had been jockeying for position at the door, or to private carriages, or to ornate, massive new automobiles, each so unique in those days of few cars that there was never any doubt as to whose automobile—Fred Hotaling's Pope-Toledo, Dr. Cluness' White Steamer, A. M. Rosenstern's new four-cylinder Oldsmobile—was passing.

The celebrating would go on for hours. San Francisco had no closing law, and bars and restaurants stayed open as long as they pleased. Few closed before 3:00 A.M., and most went on all night. From the opera, from the theaters, from the roller skating at Mechanics' Pavilion, light-hearted people would gather to laugh and talk, at Coppa's, the Bohemian gathering place on Montgomery Street, or at the dozens of Italian restaurants in the Latin Quarter, or the "French" restaurants, such as Delmonico's and the Poodle Dog, those schizophrenic establishments whose ground-floor utter respectability diminished floor by floor as the elevator went up—where "on the first floor, Society dines with her husband; on the second, she trifles with her reputation; and the third is not mentioned." (The unmentionable third, fourth, and any further floors contained combination "supper-bedrooms.")

Whatever the bon vivant was looking for was available in San Francisco. If he wanted opium, the *San Francisco Bluebook*, that "fashionable address directory," listed an Opium Den at 614 Jackson. If he wanted girls, and had managed to get past the hundreds of prostitutes hawking their wares at the top of their voices from cribs and cow yards, he could still be sure of finding one at a dive on the Barbary Coast with a friendly sign hanging out front, "Ye Old Whore Shoppe."

Many would go on to the Palace Hotel, still a gathering place for society after thirty years, although there was severe competition now from the Crocker family's St. Francis Hotel, which had opened to much fashionable acclaim in 1904, and there would be more when Tessie Oelrichs' beautiful white marble Fairmont, now nearly finished, opened at the top of Nob Hill. Some of the members of the Metropolitan Opera Company had chosen the St. Francis, but a great many, including Caruso, were at the Palace, which was only a block or so away from the Opera House. The little Italian made his way back to the Palace, the air still seeming to echo with the "Bravos" for his performance, and there he and some other members of the cast toasted the evening before going their separate ways to continue the celebration. Caruso and Scotti were to dine with a small party, and, already late, they downed the last of their drinks and rushed on their way. One of the members of the party, a plump young San Francisco girl named Elsa Maxwell, recalled somewhat later that they had dined at Zinkand's, which she remembered as "an Italian restaurant" where Caruso "dived into heaping platefuls of spaghetti." A trying evening for Zinkand's, which was famous all over the country for its German food, and not made any better by Caruso's drawing caricatures of the guests on the tablecloth between courses, cutting them out and presenting them to the subjects, while Miss Maxwell played operatic arias on the piano.

Some people insisted afterward that a spirit of foreboding had lain under the evening's feverish excitement, a haunting, unvoiced feeling that somehow tonight was San Francisco's last night to celebrate. Firemen claimed that all evening there had been a pervasive tension in the air, fire horses starting unaccountably in their stalls, a feeling that something was going to happen. At one o'clock in the morning a huge fire broke out at the California Cannery Company on Bay Street in the North Beach district, and while firemen fought to subdue the flames leaping over twenty thousand cases of canned fruit in the block-long warehouses, they felt that perhaps this was what they had been expecting.

At 5:13 A.M. Wednesday morning, April 18, 1906, the fire was out at the California Cannery Company. Fire Chief Dennis Sullivan lay asleep by his wife on the third floor of the Bush Street firehouse, next to the California Hotel. The last of the all-night parties was breaking up. John Barrymore, his white tie and tails a little ruffled, put on his top hat to go home—earlier than usual, because he was scheduled to sail for Australia at noon. A weary celebrant peered out from the Poodle Dog's private entrance, then hastened across the sidewalk into a hack. A carriage stood drawn up at the Palace Hotel, waiting for its owner. At the Italian Market the produce growers' wagons had already arrived to unload the morning's deliveries.

Then all along the California coast for a hundred and ninety-two miles, from Point Arena to the Pajaro Valley in Monterey County, disaster struck. A steamer off Point Arena hit something with such force that the captain thought he had run aground, although he was in water twelve fathoms deep. From there vast mountain-making forces, rending the earth along the ancient line of the San Andreas fault, entered the California coast at Alder Creek, just above Point Arena. Along the fault the earth opened up and closed again, and the land on the western side of the rift was now sixteen feet north of where it had been, sixteen feet north of the spot it had once joined on the other side of the rift.

Straight south the rift went, unswerving, through hills and lowlands. When it crossed the side of a hill the land fell away, leaving chasms twenty feet wide. When it crossed level ground the earth closed again, tighter than ever. Under the bridge at Alder Creek, leaving it a shambles of splintered wood. Through villages, heaving the buildings aside. Nothing along the surface deterred the massive force. Buildings were torn off their foundations as the land on the western side of the fault moved north and settled again. Giant redwood trees astride it were ripped in two.

Through Sonoma and Marin counties it went, the earth's displacement gradually lessening, but not the violence of the shock. At Santa Rosa, twenty miles east of the fault, fifty-one people lay dead in the ruins of the buildings. At Marshall the hotel that had sat on the headland above the bay now sat *in* the bay, intact, its boarders unharmed. The waters receded, and farther south, in Tomales Bay, left a fishing boat stranded in the mud and then came back in a rush of ten-foot waves to take it afloat again.

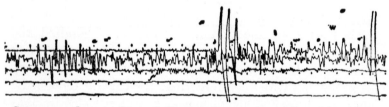

Seismograph recording of the San Francisco earthquake, Tokyo, Japan

At Point Reyes, the 5:15 train for San Francisco was ready to pull out. The conductor had just swung aboard when the train gave a great lurch to the east, then another to the west, and, while the conductor hastily dropped off again, heaved over on its side. Suddenly, in the same moment, Paper Mill Creek, near Point Reyes, was six feet narrower than it had been and its bridge, still clinging to both banks, was humped up in a six-foot arc at one end.

Capriciously it passed the island of Alcatraz in the Golden Gate without dislodging a brick of its grim military prison (Alcatraz had not yet become a Federal prison), and struck with its full force at San Francisco, while lesser tremors rocked Oakland, across the bay. South it ran, still undeviating in its course, through the Baden marshes at San Bruno, toppling the wooden trestles and shearing off the huge iron pipes that carried the city's water supply to San Francisco. Then for six miles the path of the fault ran directly under the conduit to the Pilarcitos reservoir and in that six miles every section was broken, collapsed, telescoped or torn apart—so utterly destroyed that the line would never be used again.

That was all that was necessary. After that the rift passed straight through the three reservoirs themselves, Pilarcitors, San Andreas and Crystal Springs, that supplied most of San Francisco's water, without doing any damage at all, leaving a billion gallons of water intact, beyond reach.

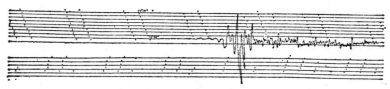

Seismograph recording of the earthquake, Washington, D.C.

Through Stanford University it went, wrecking buildings, killing two men, hurling statues down from its Arch of Triumph to bury them waist-deep in the ground below. In the narrow gorge at Loma Prieta the mountains on either side collapsed, burying the sawmill and its nine workers below, and moving hundred-foot redwoods to stand above the site, as though they had always grown there. Shocks reached out to shake San Jose, destroying hotels and houses and public buildings, killing twenty-one people.

At the State Insane Asylum at Agnews, a patient cried, "I'm going to heaven in a chariot of fire! Don't you hear the rumble of the chariot wheels? It's coming low to get me!"

With a roar louder than chariot wheels the two-block long brick building collapsed with many of the surrounding smaller buildings. The Superintendent and his wife were dead; eleven nurses were dead; eighty-seven patients, out of a thousand and eighty, were dead. Scores lay pinned, still alive, in the wreckage. A giant inmate, in a momentary flash of sanity, lifted a fallen beam off one of the guards, and then ran off into the hills. It was days before workers dug the last body out of the wreckage, before a dozen deputy sheriffs rounded up the last of the madmen.

The fissure tore on across country to the Chittenden Ranch in the Pajaro Valley of Monterey County, tearing off hillsides, destroying the highway at their base, shifting the pier of the railroad bridge eighteen inches northwest. There the open line of destruction came to an end, although the fault continued, underground, for hundreds of miles farther, rattling the windows in Los Angeles and shaking the earth on out into the desert.

There was no wind or fog this Wednesday morning in San Francisco. It was quiet and still, and the air was clear and fragrant with April. Then the earthquake struck, with a sound that began as a low roar and grew in volume until it ended in a crescendo of noise. The city seemed to shake as though it were held in a giant fist: violently, then nearly subsiding, then more violently than ever.

Tugs in the bay set up a shrill clamor. Piers trembled, and the sheds on them collapsed. Pier 3 crashed into the bay. A huge iron girder fell across the steamer *San Pablo,* and the steamer sank. The tower of the Ferry Building at the foot of Market Street whipped back and forth like a poplar in a gale. All along the waterfront, East Street (now called The Embarcadero) heaved and billowed "like a carpet with a wind under it," and great gaping holes opened up in it. On

Market Street, the wide commercial street bisecting the city, "the cobblestones seemed to dance." Streetcar tracks buckled up as though the streets underneath them were suddenly shorter.

Wherever there was "made" ground the damage was worst, and much of San Francisco stood on this improvised footing. Sixty years before, Montgomery Street had been close to the waterfront. Now it was a quarter of a mile inland, and the city had rushed over the intervening space to reach the deep water, hastily filling in the shallows and marshes. Where ships rotted at anchor as their crews abandoned them to head for the gold fields, the land was simply filled in over them, or in some cases, around, making buildings of them. One of these had been used as an early jail, another as a boarding house—less than adequate for either purpose, and soon built over. Much of the area south of Market Street had been swampy ground, and this too had been filled in and covered over as the city grew. Here and there on steep hillsides there was more "made" ground, where fill had been added to support streets.

Along these steep hillsides the retaining walls and streets were suddenly in the giant grip of irresistible pressure. Huge bulges appeared in the walls of steep Vallejo Street (so steep that for four blocks it was merely steps) and stretches of the street sank as much as two feet. North of where it crossed Vallejo, Van Ness Avenue, filled in over a gulch that once led to Washerwoman's Lagoon (before that too was filled in), spread apart in deep crevices. "Houses and fences and back yards" slid ponderously down the hill. Out on Union Street, where it was built on filled land along a hillside, the car track was twisted six feet to one side and the street slid from under it, down into the truck gardens below.

In Golden Gate Park driveways bulged and cracked and along them trees lurched at drunken angles. South of Market, where swampy creeks had once meandered to the bay, the uneasy fill caved and settled. On Mission Street, a block south of Market, the ground sank as much as five feet. Great difficulty had been experienced in finding solid foundations for the new Post Office when it was built at Mission and Seventh Streets. Now the Post Office stood, hardly damaged, but to the east of the building the land had fallen away six feet.

Other buildings in the "South of Market" district were not so soundly founded. It was an area of cheap hotels and boarding houses. They collapsed, taking their varying tolls: the Denver House on lower Third Street; the Royal, on Fourth; the boarding houses at 35 and 39 and 119 Fifth; the Porter House and the five-story, 300-room Brunswick on Sixth. As far out as Valencia and Nineteenth Streets, on the filled land over Willow Creek, the wooden Valencia Street Hotel pitched and twisted and then telescoped all at once. Where there had been four stories, it was now only one story high, and twenty people were dead in the wreckage below. Nearby the land under a new apartment building sank so far that the second floor was now level with the street, and as the shaky earth under the street fell away and left it unsupported, the street too collapsed. Broken water mains shot geysers of water thirty and forty feet in the air.

Everywhere there was the ear-splitting roar of brick falling, steel girders being torn apart, wood collapsing into splinters. Ninety-five per cent of all the chimneys in the city were damaged or destroyed. Where the workmanship was poor and the mortar was made of the loamy sand from San Francisco's beaches, chimneys disintegrated into piles of bricks. Otherwise, the top third simply snapped off intact and as often as not went crashing through the roof of the house. Brick fire walls fell. On Broadway the brick jail was in ruins. The cupola of the California Hotel crashed through the Bush Street firehouse, carrying Fire Chief Sullivan, fatally injured, all the way down to the first floor. At the produce market drivers fought to get away from their wagons as the walls tottered. There was no time to save the horses; two drivers who tried lost their lives with the horses under the falling walls.

If there was a single place where the noise was worse than in any other, it was at the City Hall. The huge columns that fronted the low circular porch hurtled out into the street and behind them poured an absolute deluge of debris as tier after tier of smaller columns peeled off the dome. Underneath the City Hall, in the Receiving Hospital, doctors and patients alike lay pinned by falling walls and ceilings. Old Mrs. Kane, the Matron in the Detention Hospital, and John McLean, the policeman assigned there Tuesday night, managed to run to safety; their wards, six insane patients in locked cells, were left behind.

The City Hall (then located in the triangle formed by Larkin, McAllister, and City Hall Avenue, about two blocks east of where it is now) had cost between six and seven million dollars. The building of it had enriched a generation of corrupt politicians since its construction began in 1871 and continued during the reign of political boss Chris Buckley, "the blind white devil." The work on it had been so slovenly and amateurish that when soldiers and conscripts began to clear away the rubble later, rumors crept out that wheelbarrows were found where they had been accidentally walled up while it was building.

On and on the earthquake seemed to go, with buildings pitching and tossing. Across Market Street from the City Hall, the roof of the Majestic Theatre caved in. Above the City Hall, on Turk and Larkin and Golden Gate Streets, whole walls peeled away from the fronts of apartment buildings, revealing the unwary occupants startled from their sleep or shaving or dressing. Heavy furniture slid across floors, people were thrown out of bed, plaster crumpled and fell. There was a last sickening lurch, like the sudden descent of an elevator, and it was over.

It had lasted forty-seven seconds.

Large sections of San Francisco had actually suffered surprisingly little damage beyond cracked or fallen chimneys; the wooden houses which so many people had built after the earthquake of 1868 had repaid the faith placed in them. The skyscrapers which had sprung up in the last few years, principally along Market Street, and about which there had been much speculation as to their fate in an earthquake, likewise stood nearly intact, triumphs to their builders.

Quite a few people had slept right on through the earthquake. Others, wakened by the noise and motion, told themselves it was "just another earthquake" and turned over and went back to sleep. Some seasoned Californians rushed to brace themselves in doorways, which were thought to be the safest place during an earthquake. Many were calm. One dry report tells of a woman who sat watching the wall of her room pull away from the ceiling and then come back again, like a giant mouth opening and closing. Finally, because "she was a woman easily disgusted by foolishness . . . she arose and went out of there."

But for thousands of others, as chimneys crashed through ceilings, as walls tumbled, as plaster fell, and beds and dressers hurtled across floors, there were reactions from alarm to utter, desperate panic. Hordes of people rushed out of shaking buildings, down hotel stairways—no elevators were operating. A man caught at a woman just as she was about to step through a window at the end of a hotel corridor and yelled, "Where are you going?" "Downstairs," she told him. It was fifty feet down. They poured out into the streets in whatever clothing they had been able to lay their hands on. There were women in nightgowns, men in long underwear—here a man in a top hat, tailcoat and underwear; there another with only a purple striped shirt pulled on over his long johns—some in other oddly matched combinations, some in nothing at all. Nearly everyone was barefooted: blood began to spurt as they ran heedlessly over the broken window glass in the streets.

Chinese swarming out of Chinatown and Italians down out of Telegraph Hill rioted in Portsmouth Square, fighting madly for safety in the open space. There were additional shocks, small ones, at 5:18, 5:20 and 5:25. Men fell on their knees on the sidewalk, some to pray, others "in a maudlin voice, begging to be told how to formulate a prayer." A newspaper delivery boy threw away the rest of his papers when a man told him, "What do I need a paper for? It's the end of the world."

At the Palace Hotel a clerk was telephoning guests to reassure them, but many were not to be reassured. On the fifth floor various members of the Metropolitan Opera Company rushed wildly into the hall. Caruso reached conductor John Herz, and according to Herz, "embraced me hysterically and, crying like a child, repeatedly insisted that we were both doomed." It was not Caruso's finest appearance, but as fellow singer Pol Plançon explained later, "The Latin races are different. They are all excitement in sudden danger and go to pieces." Plançon himself had only an overcoat on over his underwear, and some said that his beard, which he had failed to dye as he usually did each morning, had turned green. Caruso fled on downstairs and there the other singers found him, sitting unhappily on a small valise in the lobby. By this time the other guests milling around the lobby had calmed down enough that it seemed to Plançon's outraged sensibilities that "everyone acted as if the whole thing had been scheduled and they'd been expecting it." Perhaps Caruso felt the same thing; at any rate he is said to have sworn never to return to a city "where disorders like that are permitted," and he never did.

North of Market Street, indeed, and in the Western Addition, where the damage had been small, people calmed quickly and a certain holiday atmosphere began to grow. San Franciscans were always their own best audience: they had a way of sitting back and admiring their city's extravagances. Some sketchily dressed people returned to repair the gaps in their costumes. Neighbors and strangers began to compare notes and tell each other that this was "really a big one!" Marvelous escapes were recounted. Nearly everyone, to hear them tell it, had gotten out of bed the very instant before the chimney crashed down on it, or, even more harrowing, had still been *in* the bed, but the bed had skidded out of the way just as the chimney fell. Droves of people descended on Market Street to see if the tall, slender Call Building was still standing. Few expected it to be. (It was standing, hardly damaged at all, but during the days that followed, rumors swept the city again and again that it had collapsed in the earthquake, or that it listed fifteen degrees to one side, or that it had been blown up because it was unsafe.)

Caruso, who had arrived at Union Square with a towel wrapped around his neck and clutching a framed picture of Theodore Roosevelt, feebly tried his voice, hardly daring to hope that it had survived such a shattering experience. At the St. Francis Hotel, across the street, the chef was preparing coffee and yesterday's rolls for the guests crowding the lobby. Along O'Farrell Street a young woman and her husband, who had left their apartment carrying a suitcase, found it growing heavy and left it in a doorway, intending to come back for it later. (Long before they were able to come back for it, fire had destroyed both suitcase and doorway.) On Ellis Street young Josephine Fratinger cast an admiring glance at the decorations she and her intended had stayed up late the night before to prepare, and began to dress for her wedding.

After all, it was just another earthquake, and San Francisco had had 417 of them in the last "eighty years of reasonably accurate observation."

Well enough for those who had escaped to laugh and talk. For others there was nothing but stark tragedy. A woman caught hysterically at Madame Goerlitz' arm as she went to join the other singers at Union Square, and begged her to help revive the baby in her arms. Madame Goerlitz could not bring herself to tell the distraught mother what she knew at once: the baby was dead, its skull crushed. All over the waterfront, in the wholesale district, in the district south of Market, the screams of wounded horses mingled with those of trapped humans. In the ruins of the rookeries south of Market, people struggled to get out of the wreckage. At the Valencia Street Hotel those still alive stepped out of what had been the fourth floor, onto the street.

Some waited helplessly to drown as broken water mains filled sunken rooms, and others to be burned alive as fires, starting from overturned stoves, broken electric wires, exploding gas mains, damaged chimneys, swept through the buildings. Mrs. Zink, crawling out of her second-floor room onto the roof at 35 Fifth Street (the rest of the boarding house had collapsed, taking the stairway with it) saw a building across the street, and then all at once the whole block, spring up in flames. In a cheap waterfront restaurant run by two old partners named Nelson and Johnson, Nelson, who had done the cooking, lay helpless, beyond reach, under the overturned stove, as flames consumed the building.

At fifty other places it was the same. "Down to the south the sky was a streak of orange," Frederick Bowlen, a fireman at the Howard Street station, wrote later, "with huge flames leaping up into the air."

San Francisco was burning.

TWO

Wednesday, April 18, 1906

▲▲▲

Fire Chief Sullivan lived until Sunday morning, but he never regained consciousness, never knew that a single fire had broken out in San Francisco. Perhaps, as people said, if he had not been injured he would have been able to exert the necessary leadership, devise the necessary plan, make use of the available facilities to cope with the fire. But more than likely he would have been helpless as was stubborn, walrus-mustached Assistant Fire Chief John Dougherty, who had to take his place while San Francisco burned.

For there were scores of fires, almost instantly, all over the city. In some cases people were able to put them out themselves; in other cases, the fire department responded. In half an hour it had answered fifty-two calls, from the Mission district, from the Western Addition, from North Beach, from the waterfront, from south of Market. Before they knew it, the city's 585 firemen were scattered at a hundred locations beyond communication with each other.

At one spot after another they made a terrible discovery: there was no water. The earthquake had done more than destroy the conduits from the city's four major supply reservoirs in San Mateo and Alameda counties. There were still three storage reservoirs, with eighty million gallons of water —nearly two and a half times San Francisco's daily requirements—within the city. But these too were almost entirely useless; the underground water mains that led to them had been wrenched and sheared apart. All that remained was part of an ancient water system that dated back to before water mains had been laid under the streets, a system of cisterns scattered through the older parts of the city at strategic spots and filled with water for fire protection. Originally there had been sixty-three of these. Now there were only twenty-five, with about 850,000 gallons of water. Most of these had not been used in more than fifteen years.

With what water there was, firemen scored some initial victories. At Twenty-second and Mission, drawing on a cistern three blocks away at Shotwell, they were finally able to put out a fire that had swept up in the three-story wooden building of the Lippman Dry Goods Store. In the Western Addition three engines, pumping in tandem from a cistern 3000 feet away, managed to overcome fires at Buchanan and Golden Gate, at Hayes and Laguna, and, after it had burned half a block, at Fulton and Octavia—all these within a few blocks of each other in a closely built wooden residential district.

The major battles were beginning, however, in two areas: in the flimsy buildings south of Market; and above Market, on the waterfront and in the wholesale district between there and Sansome Street. Both these areas were on "made" ground and had suffered heavily from the earthquake. Now fires took hold quickly as firemen hurried desperately from hydrant to hydrant, finding some dry from the first, others with water briefly, which then trickled to a stop. South of Market they watched, grim and helpless, as fire destroyed a

Chinese laundry right across the street from No. 4 Engine House on Howard Street. Flames shot up in every street from the waterfront to Eighth; soon a dozen fires were roaring out of control. North of Market, in more flimsy buildings near the waterfront, a fire was making equally fast progress. Further along the waterfront another fire was raging at the foot of Pacific Street, and still another a few blocks over on Sansome Street, near California, at the edge of the wholesale district.

While the firemen worked and refugees hurried to safety, others were rushing frantically through the streets, looking for missing relatives. Rescue parties were already going in to try to save those injured or trapped in the wreckage. At the City Hall the Detention Hospital Matron, Mrs. Kane, near hysterics, was clutching at Patrolman McLean and pulling him back with her to the ruins they had barely escaped from. He was an old man, but a huge one. Using brute strength he forced his way through the rubble to the cells, guided by the screams of the insane prisoners, and he and Mrs. Kane began to drag them out. They were then marched over the hills to the Presidio and locked up again. Patrolman McLean returned to headquarters and reported for duty. Mrs. Kane went to work at the Presidio Hospital; it was fifty-four hours before she had a chance to stop.

At the Central Emergency Hospital other rescuers were digging patients, nurses and doctors out of the rubble, finding them shaken, frightened, but uninjured. The patients were transferred to Mechanics' Pavilion nearby, which had immediately become an emergency hospital, and then Dr. McGinty, who had just been saved, set out to rescue others. It was dangerous work. Dr. McGinty was injured and trapped again by a falling brick wall as he helped carry a man out of a ruined building, but he insisted on continuing.

Over in the wholesale district a man named Baker was killed as he tried to drag a body from the ruins of a commission house.

Soon ambulances and automobiles carrying the wounded were hurrying to Mechanics' Pavilion, to the Harbor Emergency Hospital, to private sanitariums hastily opened. In the areas already burning, rescuers worked desperately to drag people from the wreckage before the flames got to them. Over and over again—at places like the Phillips Hotel, where a few days later the Red Cross would dig out forty bodies—the flames got there first.

Hundreds of people jammed the Western Union offices on Market Street, but no messages were leaving there. All the Western Union wires were out. Telephones were dead too, all their lines to the outside world broken. At the Postal Telegraph office across Market Street from the Palace Hotel a harried operator was working feverishly. Finally, at ten minutes to six, he was able to get through with the first information anyone outside had received from San Francisco:

THERE WAS AN EARTHQUAKE HIT US AT 5:15 O'CLOCK THIS MORNING, WRECKING SEVERAL BUILDINGS AND WRECKING OUR OFFICES. THEY ARE CARTING DEAD FROM THE FALLEN BUILDINGS. FIRE ALL OVER TOWN. THERE IS NO WATER AND WE LOST OUR POWER. I'M GOING TO GET OUT OF THE OFFICE AS WE HAVE HAD A LITTLE SHAKE EVERY FEW MINUTES AND IT'S ME FOR THE SIMPLE LIFE.

R.

SAN FRANCISCO 5:50 AM

"R" decided to forego the simple life temporarily, however, and stuck by his post, getting through occasional fragmentary messages that recorded the progress of the fire.

By six o'clock, barely forty-five minutes after the earthquake, it was already clear that the entire district south of Market at least as far as Sixth Street—a mile in from the waterfront—was doomed. For that matter, without water there appeared to be no possibility of stopping it even there, nor the three fires heading toward each other in the second major fire area, the wholesale district north of Market. "Everything thin enough to go through the hose" was sprayed into the fire; the watering troughs in front of saloons were emptied, even the sewers were opened and the sewage pumped into the flames. There remained only one last resort, and Acting Fire Chief Dougherty made up his mind to use it now. Hastily he dispatched a messenger to the Presidio, the Army post on the northwestern side of San Francisco—send all the explosives you have, and send a crew to use them.

The messenger was banging on the door of the Presidio's Ordnance Officer, Captain Coleman, at about 6:30. There was no dynamite, but there was plenty of black powder; Captain Coleman hurriedly ordered field battery caissons out and soldiers began to load the bulky, awkward barrels onto the ammunition wagons. The caissons were not suitable for carrying barrels, and Coleman was dubious of using black powder anyway. Finally he decided to send Lieutenant Briggs and the soldiers on with what had already been loaded, forty-eight barrels, and set out himself to dig up regular wagons to carry the rest of the powder, and if possible some dynamite.

Meanwhile, in Market Street and on the hills north of Market, people watched with dazed horror as the smoke rose from the fires to south and east of them. San Francisco had too much of a tradition of destruction by fire for them not to realize what was happening. Businessmen, watching the firemen's futile efforts, began to hurry to their own establishments, not yet endangered, hoping to save part of their goods, or at least records and money. Everywhere downtown there was confusion and disorder, people milling in the streets, dodging racing ambulances, avoiding live electric wires that lay across streets, uncertain where to go or what to do. Transportation was instantly at a premium. Where the day before the rate for a two-horse carriage "for shopping and calling" had been $2.00 an hour, and less for a one-horse gig, hacks began to charge $5.00, then $30.00— anything frightened people would pay.

Out of the disorder grew more disorder. Looting began. Thieves seized the opportunity to rob buildings abandoned by frightened refugees. Wholesale liquor houses were looted and the plunderers were soon drunk. On Jessie Street, near Sixth, a crowd caught a man crawling out through a broken pawn-shop window, carrying a sack crammed with the miscellaneous odds and ends he had stolen. There was angry talk of hanging him, but he was turned over to the police. One of the *Examiner's* foremen, a man named Denkel, came upon a man looting a dead body. The vandal turned and stabbed viciously at him with a keyhole saw, but Denkel was able to overcome him, and he too was turned over to the police. Later on, looters would be shot—and hanged— "without time to say their prayers."

Fortunately, San Francisco had men to call on as chaos approached. One of these was the Commanding General of the Department of California, a cocky, tough, hot-tempered, red-headed little man named Frederick Funston. He was a Medal of Honor winner who hated the sight of blood ("Such spectacles are too much for me," he would say), a tiny dictator whose soldiers worshiped him—they called him "Freddy" and "Little Man of War" behind his back.

Funston was forty years old and he had spent most of his life as an adventurer and soldier of fortune. One newspaper was to say of him that he was "a Renaissance hero, born four hundred years too late," but that overlooked two facts: his

appearance—he was "so small as to appear insignificant"—
hardly fit the romantic conception of a Renaissance hero,
and, in any case, his own era provided him with more than
ample opportunity for adventure.

Before he was thirty he had helped survey Death Valley—"the only man still alive and sane from that expedition," a newspaper claimed. He had blazed a new trail
through Alaska and sailed down the Yukon River alone in an
open boat. He had started and given up a coffee plantation
in Central America, and although "my own artillery experience," he admitted, "consisted in once having seen a salute
fired to President Hayes at a county fair in Kansas," he had
become Chief of Artillery for the Cuban Army during Cuba's
revolt against Spain.

Twenty-three battles later, survivor of capture and a
death sentence by the Spaniards, slowly healing from a bullet that had torn through his lungs, he returned to the
United States. This was early in 1898; the *Maine* had been
blown up and the United States was at war with Spain.
The governor of Kansas sent for Funston to be a Colonel of
the new 20th Kansas Regiment, the 20th was called to duty,
and Funston was in the United States Army.

The Army, ignoring his Cuban experience, ordered him
with his regiment to the Philippines. The war was over before they arrived, but a far worse war was about to begin.
Like the Cubans, the Filipinos had been waging a revolu-
tion of their own against Spain, and were approaching inde-
pendence, only to have Spain surrender the Philippines to
the United States. Angry and disappointed, the Filipinos
soon declared war on the United States, and Funston was
in the thick of it.

The Filipino rebels fell back in battle after battle. Funston
was a "volcano of energy," reckless and daring, apt to be
making a target of himself by riding up and down the lines

in a white shirt on a black horse, swooping off to aim an artillery piece himself, moving ahead in an ancient train on which his soldiers painted the sign, "Freddy's Fast Express." In a major battle at Calumpit he coolly poled his way across the river under heavy enemy fire to establish a beachhead on the opposite bank, practically at point-blank range from the enemy. He was awarded the Medal of Honor and promoted to temporary Brigadier General.

The war deteriorated into deadly guerilla action which kept seventy thousand American soldiers pinned down, unable to prevent scores of furtive bloody massacres. For a year and a half General Aguinaldo, leader of the Philippine resistance, managed to elude expeditions sent to capture him, and the war went on. It remained for Funston, operating with typical audacity, to slip through the wilds of northern Luzon and capture the rebel "Dictator" in his stronghold. It marked the virtual end of Filipino resistance.

Aguinaldo's capture had made Funston a national hero and a permanent Brigadier General in the Regular Army. Instead of being mustered out as the war ended, he had returned to San Francisco to command the Department of California. He had held the job for five long, quiet years since then. Perhaps it was inevitable that his senior officer, dignified, Dundreary-bearded, pince-nezed General Greely, who commanded the Pacific Division, was away. Adventure had caught up with the "Little Man of War" again. As the earthquake dumped him out of bed this Wednesday morning he knew instinctively that there was trouble brewing, and he was to be in it from the start.

Funston's quarters were at 1310 Washington Street, almost the highest point on Nob Hill. He stumbled out of the house barely dressed, without waiting even for a cup of coffee for breakfast, and hurried up the street. From this height he could see smoke rising in straight columns a thousand feet high from the fires below. He glanced at the other people gathered watching; they were calm, but their faces were shocked and white. There were no streetcars running; he hurried on down the hill on foot to Sansome Street.

It was not yet six o'clock when he reached Sansome. Smoke filled the narrow street. Half a dozen fires were going, new ones starting up while he watched. Firemen were chopping away with axes, beating at fires with gunny sacks. Fire engines stood by, steam up ready to pump, with useless, empty hoses strung out idle on the street. Police were keeping back anxious, helpless watchers. He stepped through the crowds and asked a patrolman if there was any way to get in touch with the Mayor or the Chief of Police. The patrolman shook his head. The telephone system was paralyzed. Probably Chief Dinan would go directly to the Hall of Justice on Portsmouth Square; since the City Hall was destroyed, undoubtedly the Mayor would go there too—he could see them there.

The Hall of Justice was hardly six blocks away, but Funston couldn't take time to go there now. He had seen cities burn before, and he knew at once what would happen to San Francisco. Soldiers would be needed for rescue work, for police action. Thirty-five years before, General Sheridan, faced with the same problem as Chicago burned, had come a cropper: he had ordered the Regular Army in, only to have to withdraw the soldiers at the infuriated governor's demand. Nevertheless, Funston's mind was already busy exploring the fastest means to get orders through to his soldiers —too busy to consider the illegality of the Army's taking over the city. That was not something that Funston would ever worry about, although his superiors would. Secretary of War Taft is reported to have said that "it would take an act of Congress to relieve him of the responsibility for the violence the Army did to the Constitution in San Francisco."

("Congress will acquit you, sir," Senator Talliaferro assured him.)

Funston told the patrolman to go and tell the Mayor that all the Army troops available would be called out, and as the policeman departed in one direction he hurried off in the other, toward the Army stable at Pine and Hyde Streets. Several automobiles were dashing back and forth; he hailed one after another without success. Indulging in "a pious hope that they would all get burned out," he set off to make it on foot, three quarters of a mile up the steep slope of Nob Hill, alternately running and walking.

He arrived at the stable gasping for breath and told his carriage driver to mount a horse and ride for Fort Mason with a brief verbal order: Send all troops. As his aides, Lieutenants Davis and Long, arrived, he scrawled a note, hardly thinking what to say, for them to take to Colonel Morris at the Presidio: Turn out the entire garrison and send them to Police Chief Dinan at the Hall of Justice. The couriers were on their way immediately, the two aides one behind the other on the one horse: there hadn't been time to saddle two.

Captain Walker, the commanding officer of Fort Mason, had been awakened by the earthquake, but had gone back to sleep. Roused by the carriage driver, he soon had all his company of Engineers on their way to Funston.

At the Presidio Lieutenants Davis and Long went directly to the home of Colonel Morris and began to knock on the door. There was no answer. They knocked louder and harder. The door was opened finally by a sleepy-eyed Colonel Morris, attired in an old-fashioned nightgown and cap. The two lieutenants watched nervously as he read Funston's message. By the time he had finished, "the old gentleman was beside himself with rage." Quivering with anger, he told the young officers, "You two damned fools go back and tell that newspaperman that he had better look up his Army Regulations and there he will find that nobody but the President of the United States in person can order regular troops into any city!" With that he slammed the door in their faces.

General Funston's aides knew very well that they could not go back to the General with any such message as that. Dawn was just breaking. They looked at each other helplessly, and then at a bugler just passing on his way to blow Reveille. The same idea struck both of them and they rushed out to the bugler.

Grabbing the soldier, Lieutenant Long said, "Look, we've just come out of the Colonel's house."

"Yes, sir, I saw you," the bugler said.

"Well," Lieutenant Long told him, "the Colonel says for you to immediately sound the Call to Arms."

Without questioning the two officers, the bugler began to blow the Call to Arms—an order for everyone to fall out, regardless of condition, and await orders. Almost immediately an unkempt, half-dressed, motley company of about 350 men was lining up. Before anyone could interfere, Lieutenant Long had shouted, "Fours left!" and the soldiers were marching toward town, with Lieutenant Davis ducking in and out of the ranks, weeding out men missing shoes, pants or other vital clothes and sending them back on the double to finish dressing.

General Funston, meanwhile, had made his way on up the hill to his home on Washington Street to drink a hasty cup of coffee and make hurried plans with his wife for packing and moving. She could be depended on to do the rest; later he was relieved to find that even an old war souvenir from the Philippines, an Igorot shield with a bullet hole through it testifying as to how it became available, had been saved. (Eda Funston was, after all, not one to let little things bother her; in the days of the Philippine insurrection she had frequently hired a buggy to drive out and watch the battle.) On his way home he noticed a strange thing: the absolute silence. Although the streets on the hill were crowded with people, there was no talking, and from the city below not a single sound reached him. "The terrific roar of the conflagration, the crash of falling walls, and the dynamite explosions that were to make the next three days hideous had not yet begun."

The other man to whom San Francisco must turn to avert chaos was its Mayor, Eugene Schmitz, a man who had been called "the smallest man mentally and the meanest man morally that ever occupied the Mayor's chair." As the patrolman had told General Funston, Mayor Schmitz was at the Hall of Justice, and with him, briefly, was a ferret-faced little man with cold, calculating eyes, named Abraham Ruef. The two had come a long way together in the five years since Ruef, casting about for an instrument with which to rob San Francisco, had used his political genius to elect Eugene Schmitz mayor.

In 1901 Eugene Schmitz had been a big, handsome young man with a bluff, hearty, easy-going manner, who had at first glance little to recommend him as a candidate for mayor except his appearance. Ruef, a brilliant young lawyer who had made up his mind to be political boss of San Francisco, saw other virtues, however. It was a time when San Francisco was torn by bloody labor strife. A "man of the people" was called for, and Schmitz was that. His father was a German who had come to California with the gold rush of 1849, and his mother was Charlotte Hogan, born in Ireland. His parents were poor, he had not finished high school, he had sold newspapers, worked as a drummer boy at the old Standard Theatre, and finally risen to be conductor of the orchestra at the Columbia Theatre. He was a good labor man, too; he was president of the Musician's Union—a union fortunately not important enough to have engaged in factional disputes with the other unions. And the fact that Schmitz had never shown the slightest interest in politics, nor run for any office, was likewise an advantage. He had made no enemies.

So Ruef ran him for Mayor on the "Union Labor Party" ticket. He made an excellent candidate. As Ruef said, "He had a power of assimilating ideas and a gift of memory, and he developed a marvelous faculty of joining thoughts and sentences from many speeches, prepared for him, into new ones of his own." He was elected, and he and Abe Ruef withdrew to an out-of-town hideaway where Ruef could tutor the new Mayor in city government and practical politics.

They returned and began to investigate the potential financial returns of "practical politics." They were hampered at the outset by the fact that the Union Labor Party had elected only three members of the Board of Supervisors, San Francisco's legislative governing body, in addition to Schmitz, and by the fact that the various commissions were appointive bodies, held over from the previous, honest administration of Mayor James Phelan. Nevertheless, there were numerous opportunities for graft. Various firms, particularly public utilities like the Pacific Telephone and Telegraph Co. and the city's public transportation system, the United Railroads, found it advisable to hire Ruef as their attorney, with vague, unspecified duties, but a handsome monthly salary.

Schmitz failed again to carry his Board of Supervisors when he was re-elected in 1903, but graft and extortion grew, as he was able to appoint his own police and public-works commissioners. Ruef began to draw heavy fees from fight promotors and the owners of the various "French" restaurants, of which there were about a dozen in San Francisco, to arrange their permits and licenses. Schmitz had appointed his brother Herbert to the Board of Public Works and through this handy device was able to have the city tear down an old Chinese opium den on Jackson Street and issue a permit for a new building. Shortly thereafter there rose on the site a three-story house of prostitution, with ninety cubicles for the trade, which came to be known as the "Municipal Crib." Schmitz and Ruef split twenty-five per cent of the take between them.

Ruef was by no means a shadowy, sinister figure in the background during this time. There was no attempt to hide his relationship with Schmitz, nor his position in the city government. Most of Schmitz' official papers were prepared by Ruef at his own office at Kearny and California Streets. There and at the Pup, a French restaurant where he regularly dined, job and political favor seekers waited to speak to "Boss" Ruef. Most of San Francisco ignored the obvious implications. It was no worse than the rest of California, they told themselves; even the state legislature was said to be so crooked that "you couldn't get the Lord's Prayer passed without money."

Criticism was beginning to be heard in San Francisco, however, particularly from the San Francisco *Bulletin*. The *Bulletin* had a long history of fighting editors, and tall, gaunt Fremont Older was a fighter in the great tradition. He began to make serious charges against the administration. Ruef was unconcerned. He held no office, he pointed out; there was no law prohibiting a firm from hiring the attorney of its choice. If the *Bulletin* knew of corruption, let it present proof. For the moment, all Fremont Older had was suspicions; he had no proof.

At the end of 1905 Schmitz was re-elected to a third term, and for the first time carried the entire Union Labor

Party slate of supervisors in with him. This had been considered so unlikely that Ruef had had a hard time getting anyone to run; he had finally chosen some of the candidates almost at random. Even so, he had chosen well: of the eighteen supervisors, seventeen not only were willing to accept graft, they demanded it. As one of them, Dr. Boxton, expressed it a few weeks later to a franchise applicant, "We are not in business for our health . . . How much money is in it for us?"

The time had arrived that Abe Ruef had worked and planned for. With Mayor Schmitz as his willing tool, he controlled the entire city administration of San Francisco. In rapid succession he became attorney for the Parkside Realty Co., which wanted a franchise for a car line through their new Sunset subdivision; the Home Telephone Company, applying for a franchise to operate a new telephone system in competition with Pacific Telephone and Telegraph Co.; and the United Railroads, which wanted the Board's authorization to convert all its lines to the overhead trolley system. The fees were divided as usual: half to the Board of Supervisors, 25 per cent to Schmitz, and 25 per cent to Ruef. There was a certain amount of embarrassment when it turned out that in the case of the telephone franchise, eleven supervisors had already accepted $51,000 from the *other* side, the Pacific Telephone and Telegraph Co., to turn down the Home Telephone Company's application. They were so hungry "they would eat the paint off the walls," Ruef stormed. But then Ruef himself had been on Pacific Telephone's payroll, at $1200 a month, since 1902.

In spite of the obvious success of their operations in the early months of 1906, there was beginning to be cause for worry. The District Attorney, William A. Langdon, whom Ruef had hurriedly chosen, proved to be uncomfortably honest. He began to raid and close the French restaurants which were paying Ruef for the privilege of staying open. The *Bulletin*'s fighting editor, Fremont Older, found two others willing to fight: James Phelan, the able, honest millionaire who had been Schmitz' predecessor as Mayor, and Rudolph Spreckels, another civic-minded millionaire. Together they mapped a campaign. Spreckels would put up $100,000 to finance prosecution of the corrupt officials, with the willing co-operation of District Attorney Langdon. William J. Burns, the famous detective, would be borrowed from President Roosevelt to get the proof that had been so miserably lacking before. And Francis J. Heney, who had triumphed over corruption in public office in the famous Oregon land cases, would be brought in as special prosecutor.

Disaster loomed ahead of Schmitz and Ruef, and only another disaster could save them. It promptly did. San Francisco's catastrophe was an unexpected blessing which could be expected to throw the opposition off the track and keep them busy elsewhere indefinitely.

Ruef and Schmitz eyed each other this morning, in the midst of the crowds hurrying back and forth in the Mayor's temporary office. There was no time for any kind of conference; Schmitz was busier than he had ever been in his life, groping for means of handling the massive problems that were already beginning to mount. His first action had been to order all sources of liquor closed and kept closed, and this alone was a large undertaking. San Francisco had a thousand saloons, more saloons than grocery stores, and the grocery stores sold liquor too. Hurried messages had to be sent, to Governor Pardee, informing him of the disaster, to Mayor Mott of Oakland, asking for any aid that could possibly be spared—firemen, fire engines, dynamite. Word of looting was already reaching the Hall of Justice. When the first soldiers, the detachment of Engineers from Fort Mason, reported at 7:30, Schmitz was ready to give grim orders:

They were to guard the fire lines, and if any looters were discovered, they were to shoot to kill.

Abe Ruef did not stay long. He had a fairly low opinion of the Mayor's intelligence, but even Schmitz wouldn't have to have pointed out to him what golden opportunities for new graft the approaching period of disorder would present. For the moment, Ruef had problems of his own. By now he owned a great deal of real estate in San Francisco, and he was concerned about some of his buildings, particularly the new eight-story A. Ruef Building just being built a few blocks away on Montgomery Avenue (now Columbus Avenue). Keeping his face carefully composed to hide his relief, nodding to Police Chief Dinan and others along the way, he strode on out to Kearny Street.

There was one characteristic in Schmitz' makeup that Ruef had overlooked, although there had been more than one warning of it in the past. Schmitz had been a poor boy who had grown up without education or advantages. Being Mayor had thrown him into entirely new surroundings, where he was in frequent contact with the rich, the cultured and the powerful. It was a new experience for a "common fiddler." He was flattered by their attention and he longed to be accepted as their equal. "Social attention was as nectar to him," Ruef remembered later.

Presumably because he valued the applicants' friendship and respect more than money, Schmitz had seen to it on one or two occasions in the past that franchises were granted properly, without the suggestion of bribery. This had outraged the Board of Supervisors and alarmed Ruef, but rather than wreck a machine which was otherwise working perfectly, they had agreed. One of the applicants so served was the Ocean Shore Railway, constructing an interurban line to Santa Cruz. Thus it was that J. Downey Harvey, an outstanding and wealthy businessman (and son of San Francisco's social empress, Mrs. Eleanor Martin) who was one of the line's major owners, was on good terms with Schmitz, and Schmitz in turn respected and admired Harvey. Harvey was not blind, however, to the cloud of suspicion which lay over the city administration. It was as apparent to him as it had been to Ruef that the disruption which the earthquake and fire were bound to cause would present extraordinary opportunities for graft and extortion to a corrupt Mayor and city council. Early Wednesday morning, therefore, he too was calling on Mayor Schmitz at the Hall of Justice.

Harvey urged the Mayor to call on the city's outstanding men to provide protection for the city and relief for the great numbers who were certain to be homeless. Perhaps neither of them realized the consequences at the moment. Schmitz agreed, and together they began to make out the list. Shortly invitations began to go out to an extraordinary group of men into whose hands, as the Committee of Fifty, under Schmitz' leadership, government of San Francisco was to pass. Not a single member of the Board of Supervisors was included. Abe Ruef was not included. Three of Schmitz' bitterest enemies were invited, however: James Phelan and Rudolph Spreckels, whom he knew to be actively fighting for his overthrow, and Francis Heney, who was to prosecute him.

There would be no opportunities for corruption for the time being. Morally supported by the Committee of Fifty, and free for the moment of Ruef's influence, Schmitz was to bring to San Francisco a brilliant leadership, "a degree of executive ability and a genius for improvisation," that nothing in his previous career had ever indicated he possessed. He frequently said afterwards that his life began the day of the earthquake.

·   ·   ·

None of this could be anticipated by Abe Ruef as he walked confidently down Kearny Street and over to Sansome, greeted respectfully by policemen and firemen, stopping to reassure anxious acquaintances in the crowds. The fire had already crossed over to the west side of Sansome. Only the solid construction of many of the buildings hampered its progress: they began to burn, one at a time. Without water the firemen were helpless; they were counting on dynamite to halt the fire here, before it swept on through the city. It *must* be stopped here, at any cost. Lieutenant Briggs had arrived with the caissons loaded with black powder. The firemen eyed them anxiously, but Briggs had persuaded them that black powder was too dangerous to use if stick dynamite could possibly be obtained. He had learned that there was a supply of stick dynamite at Angel Island. They agreed reluctantly to wait.

Streets in the financial district, just ahead of the fire, were scenes of wild activity as tenants rushed back and forth to save what they could. Harried clerks were securing money and records in bank vaults. Merchants were bringing valuables to the safety of the vaults. Soldiers and police were fighting to keep back crowds who wanted to withdraw money from the banks. A banker loaded half a million dollars in gold and silver coins into a carriage and set off down Montgomery Street, but there was no place else to take them; he finally stored them in another bank vault a few blocks away.

At the building known as the Montgomery Block, at the corner of Montgomery and Merchant, officials of the Sutro Library drove their helpers to load the fabulous Sutro library into wagons to be carried away. Adolph Sutro, whose millions came from the Sutro tunnel that drained the Comstock gold mines, had spent years assembling the 200,000 volumes of the finest private library in the western hemis-

phere, a collection notable for Shakespeare folios, Gutenberg
Bibles, priceless volumes from the earliest days of printing.
Now, driven by the flames, the library officials were hurrying to transfer the volumes to safety at Mechanics' Pavilion,
more than a mile away, blindly hastening to a kind of appointment in Samarra: the Montgomery Block was to come
through the fire unscathed, but Mechanics' Pavilion would
be a heap of ashes by noon.

In the other major fire area, south of Market Street,
speechless, staring refugees were pouring out of the district,
bringing with them whatever they had been able to snatch
ahead of the fire, using whatever transportation they could
improvise—pushing sofas or baby carriages or tables on
casters, loaded with possessions; dragging trunks, with a
sound that became as integral a part of the next few days
as the sound of dynamite exploding: the rasping sound of a
trunk dragged over cobblestones. Horses were running
loose, set free to escape the fire. Dead bodies were being
carried down the streets in garbage wagons. Funeral parlors
were opened as emergency morgues. At 8:14 there was another earthquake, the strongest since the first one, toppling
already shaky walls, bringing a new spasm of fear. Thousands of people crowded the Ferry Building, at the foot of
Market Street, hoping to escape the city. "At the iron gates
they clawed with their hands as so many maniacs. They
sought to break the bars, and failing in that turned upon
each other . . . When the ferry drew up to the slip and the
gates were thrown open the rush to safety was tremendous.
The people flowed through the passageway like a mountain
torrent that, meeting rocks in its path, dashes over them.
Those who fell saved themselves as best they could."

The scores of individual fires south of Market were merging into one giant conflagration. Only at the waterfront was
there any hope of fighting it back. Tugs had been hosing

down the Ferry Building in a desperate effort to save it. One of the Mayor's messages had been to the Naval station at Mare Island, "EARTHQUAKE. TOWN ON FIRE. SEND MARINES AND TUGS." Now two Navy fireboats, the *Active* and the *Leslie,* joined the tugs; Marines landed and went to work with the firemen. Stretching out hundreds of yards of hose, racing back and forth to Goat Island for water for the boilers, they were able to keep the fire from crossing East Street into the Ferry Building and the piers below it, and even to beat the fire back on the other side of East Street for a few blocks below Howard Street. But except for that the "ship chandleries, 'cheap John' clothing stores, sailors' hotels, restaurants, little corner groceries, all burned like paper," and as these fires swept up into billows of flame, the factory buildings beyond began to catch. Flames shot up in sheets two hundred feet high, heat so intense that a hundred thousand gallons of water from the cistern at First and Folsom had absolutely no effect; streams of water directed into the fire simply evaporated into steam.

Flames swept up into the south side of Mission Street and old wooden buildings served to ignite more solid buildings —the Crocker Estate Building, the Army Medical Supply Depot, Tessie Oelrichs' newly acquired Rialto Building. At the same time the fire began to reach into Market Street, first in Smith's Cash Store, then in the other buildings in the half dozen dingy blocks between First Street and East Street on the waterfront. North of Market the three fire centers had also grown into one and the fire was reaching down toward Market itself. Just before nine o'clock the block between Sansome and Battery on the north side of Market burst into flame, and then the two giant fires joined into one across Market Street all the way from Sansome to the waterfront.

Driven back by the soldiers and cut off from the ferry by

the flames on both sides of the lower end of Market, hundreds hoping to escape from the city were heading for the Southern Pacific depot at Third and Townsend. The direct route there was cut off too by the South of Market fire. They made their way back along Market as far as the City Hall, then down Eighth, dodging fires there, crossing toward the depot along Townsend Street, only to find that approach cut off ahead by fire. They turned to retreat and there was fire behind them; the way they had come was cut off. Only by plunging south and making a wide detour around could they return to Market Street.

Market Street was crowded with tens of thousands of people. Soldiers, re-forming fire lines, herded them back, struggling to keep them at least two blocks away from the fire. More soldiers, ordered in by General Funston, were on their way. Funston had spent only a few minutes at home giving hasty instructions and then hurried to his Department of California headquarters in the Phelan Building on Market, there to begin a steady stream of orders. The first soldiers, one of the two companies of Engineers from Fort Mason who had reported to Mayor Schmitz, reached Market Street at 7:45. With their full cartridge belts and fixed bayonets they presented a stern appearance, but a reassuring one; there were cheers from the crowds as they took up their posts, two to a block, along Market. At 8:00 the soldiers from the Presidio began to arrive, reporting directly to Funston. Some were sent to guard the Mint and the Post Office, on Mission Street; others to reinforce the fire lines and keep people from breaking into stores and saloons.

The soldiers were to fill a vital function—the turbulent crowds would surely have grown out of hand—but they were seldom gentle. Harsh orders were backed up with bayonets. Few people questioned their authority. They simply assumed, as did most of the soldiers themselves, that martial law had been declared. It had not; there was no legal way in which it could be, and both the Army and Mayor Schmitz insisted afterwards that the Army had acted only with the consent and under the final authority of the civil authorities. It was a fine distinction. The soldiers took orders only from their own officers. As the day wore on the Army gradually clamped down with an iron hand on San Francisco, and General Funston assumed virtual dictatorship of the city.

The soldiers from the Presidio and Fort Mason would not be nearly enough for the job. Soldiers were needed everywhere. Humming with impatience at the lack of communication facilities, his face growing as red as his hair, the little general snapped out orders for more troops to be sent. The Army tug *Slocum* was dispatched to Angel Island with orders to bring back the battalion of the 22nd Infantry stationed there. Captain Wildman, the Chief Signal Officer, was ordered to get in touch with the commanding officer at Fort Miley, at the farthest northwestern tip of San Francisco, and order his troops in. Wildman left immediately by automobile for the Presidio. The telephone line from the Presidio to Miley was still working and two coast artillery companies set off from there. There were soldiers at the Presidio of Monterey, south of San Francisco, too, and Funston wanted them, but there was no communication of any kind left to the south.

It was nine o'clock and the two major fires had already joined into one across Market Street before the dynamite arrived from Angel Island. Firemen sped across the city to begin dynamiting at Eighth Street, at one end of the fire, while Lieutenant Briggs made hurried preparations to begin at the other. Abe Ruef was at Sansome Street with Battalion Fire Chief Murphy and a fire commissioner; Briggs

left it up to them to decide where to begin. At the corner of
Clay Street the eight-story Zellerbach paper warehouse was
burning furiously; the heat from it had already ignited the
buildings across Sansome Street to the west. In an effort to
head off the fire, demolition began just ahead of these buildings, in the block between Sansome and Montgomery. It was
work already begun by the earthquake: Clay Street was
full of debris; three men and two horses still lay where falling walls of the Bailey and LaCoste Building had killed
them at 5:13 A.M. Civilians were ordered to remove the
bodies to the City Morgue behind the Hall of Justice and
the destruction of the remaining buildings began, soldiers
ordering tenants out, placing charges, lighting fuses, rushing back before the buildings exploded.

Briggs insisted that their plan of attack was wrong, that
dynamiting this close to the fire merely provided more rubble and kindling for the fire to feed on. The three men making the decisions were determined to proceed cautiously,
however. It was a terrifying responsibility, destroying property; they would not give up the hope that the fire could be
stopped by dynamiting buildings that were almost certain
to burn anyway. Unconvinced, but bowing to their authority, Briggs continued. Soldiers impressed civilians at gun
point to assist, and, crossing Commercial Street, they began
to work down both sides of narrow little Leidesdorff Street
which runs between Sansome and Montgomery. Many of the
produce houses, printing shops and other dingy establishments on Leidesdorff were already in ruins from the earthquake; dynamite soon leveled the rest. Firemen running
hoses from two cisterns in Montgomery Street kept right behind the soldiers, fighting to keep the fire back from the
shattered buildings.

The demolition teams moved on into the next block, laying charges in the What Cheer House, at the corner of

Leidesdorff and Sacramento. The What Cheer House had been one of San Francisco's better hotels in its early days, but that had been when Leidesdorff was one of the city's better streets. They had deteriorated together; the What Cheer House was now occupied by such people as "Kanaka Pete," who two or three years before had figured in one of San Francisco's more notorious triangles when he shot up another man at the Eyewink Dance Hall on the Barbary Coast for the love of a Madam known as Iodoform Kate. The What Cheer House was quickly razed and soldiers moved on to another building. The fire was all along the west side of Sansome Street now. The crackle of the flames on Sansome made a constant background to the roar of dynamite explosions. As they looked back the flames were in Leidesdorff Street too, springing up in the ruins they were leaving behind.

South of Market firemen were dynamiting the west side of Eighth Street, working down from Market, leaving heaps of shattered wood. Behind them the conflagration, growing steadily larger, was reaching into Market Street at one vulnerable spot after another. Fire spread from the power station and the Winchester Hotel, just behind the Call Building at Third, into a stationery store on Market between Third and Fourth. Suddenly there were fires in the next three blocks too, between Fourth and Fifth, Fifth and Sixth, Sixth and Seventh. There were no cisterns in Market Street; no water remained now in any of the ruined mains. Unretarded, the various fires grew and spread into stronger buildings.

Soldiers continued to drive the crowds back ahead of the fires and they retreated farther up Market Street or into the cross streets. Grim stories spread through the crowds, passed on eagerly from one person to another. Three men, they said, had been caught looting in the Palace Hotel. Their bodies, the story went on, were still hanging in one of the arches there. A young man, they said—a nice looking, well-dressed young fellow—had been picked up in the street overcome by the heat. When they took him in to revive him and opened his coat and vest, three women's fingers fell out, rings still on them. The man had been revived, the story concluded, and then taken out and shot. Soldiers figured heavily in the stories, administering prompt, ruthless justice. No one knew what was true and what was not.

It was true at least that now, at ten o'clock Wednesday morning, there were seventeen hundred soldiers on duty in the city, busy at every kind of job: burying a heap of dead bodies in a sand lot on Bay Street, dynamiting buildings, holding fire lines, helping out firemen, policing the city. Like his soldiers, General Funston was everywhere, keeping office in the streets, hurrying from spot to spot. Soldiers grinned and worked harder than ever as his red head appeared—Funston was not above giving a man a good boot in the backside if he caught him lagging.

Lieutenant Briggs had demolished the buildings on Leidesdorff Street as far south as California and was getting ready to start in the next block, a stretch of Leidesdorff known as Pauper Alley—the home of the San Francisco stock market's bucket-shop operators, catering to poor people who, caught in the get-rich-quick spell of San Francisco's turbulent market, came to plunge, and lose, whatever money they could get hold of. Before they could begin here there was an urgent call from the firemen. All the water had been used up and the fire was out of control at Commercial Street, close to where they had started earlier. They would have to start all over again.

Mayor Schmitz, who, like Funston, was to keep office just ahead of the fire for the next four days, was with the other officials when Briggs came up. He had reluctantly agreed for dynamiting to begin on Montgomery Street. This was still just ahead of the fire and the young lieutenant was bitterly opposed to it. The only way to use dynamite successfully, he insisted, would be to start at a point far enough ahead that a whole strip could be razed, leaving a bare area which the fire could not cross. Schmitz shook his head. Lieutenant Briggs would not have to face the consequences of such a step if buildings were razed and it later transpired that there had been no need to destroy them because the fire could be stopped before it reached that point; Mayor Schmitz would.

Briggs appealed to General Funston when he appeared briefly, and Funston tried to convince Schmitz. Soldiers watched, delighted, as they argued: the huge, burly mayor, who was six feet one and weighed 205 pounds, towering over the cocky little general, who was five feet four. ("Altitude is not one of my charms," was a saying of Funston's.) In spite of his lack of height, Funston could hold his own in an argument. He had a voice that, while not the equal of his father's—fellow congressmen had called his father "Foghorn" Funston—could still be heard "from one end of the regiment to the other." No amount of arguing could convince Mayor Schmitz, however. For the rest of that day and most of the next, the Army was allowed to use explosives only on buildings "in immediate contact with others already ablaze."

General Funston left and the soldiers proceeded to demolish the building at the corner of Montgomery and Commercial Street. But before they could lay a charge in the adjoining building, a fire had sprung up in the cellar of a store on Commercial Street toward Kearny, still farther west of where they were working. This was next to the Subtreasury Building, a primary responsibility of Federal troops to protect, but soldiers and firemen together were helpless to put out the fire—there was no water. What concerned the city officials even more was that it was only two narrow blocks from the Hall of Justice—police headquarters, and since early that morning, Mayor Schmitz' own headquarters. The fire must not be allowed to reach the Hall of Justice. As the fire grew bigger the soldiers moved hastily to block it off by destroying a building ahead of it, between the fire and Kearny Street.

With that charge they used the last of the stick dynamite. There was nothing but granular powder now; if the work was to continue, it would have to be used. Reports differ on who decided to use it. Briggs said he didn't want to, that he knew granular's combustion was a matter of flame, but that the officials insisted. In any case, they proceeded with granular to destroy the buildings at the corner of Kearny and Clay, and a cheap boarding house next to it. Both caught fire, and flaming bits of bedding and curtains thrown across Kearny Street set still another block on fire. And this block, running up the hill by the side of Portsmouth Square, led into the densely packed streets and alleys of Chinatown.

All this time the other end of the fire had been inexorably encroaching on Market Street. The major buildings there resisted the fires beating about them from smaller, more pervious buildings, but one by one they began to burn. Between Fourth and Fifth the huge Emporium, the largest department store west of Chicago (and on the top floor of the same building, the chambers of the State Supreme Court) caught fire, and then the others: Hale's fine new department store, the Grant Building, the Bancroft History Building. By ten o'clock Wednesday morning only the Call

Building on the western corner of Third Street, and the block between Third and Second—the Examiner Building, the unfinished Monadnock Building, the massive brick Palace Hotel and its annex, the Grand Hotel—still held out. Every other building on the south side of Market Street from the waterfront to Seventh Street was on fire or already reduced to ashes.

Behind Market Street the fire raged back down on the buildings remaining on Mission Street. At the Post Office, at Seventh and Mission, soldiers laid dynamite charges to the light wooden buildings adjacent to it and demolished them. They burned rapidly and left the Post Office surrounded by a bare zone of protection. Down the street at the Mint, whose granite walls and iron shutters had withstood the first onslaught of the flames from across Mission Street, a new desperate defense was beginning against flames rolling in this time from Market Street, behind it, and Fifth and Sixth Streets on either side. Old St. Patrick's Church, its steeple toppled over in the street by the earthquake, was burning, and beyond it the Opera House, with eight carloads of the Opera Company's costumes and equipment. The Crossley Building began to burn, and behind it, on New Montgomery, the Army Clothing Depot. Together they made a fire so intense that, deep within the "fireproof" vaults in the Crossley Building, rolls of silver dollars were melting into solid ingots.

The last of the Army supplies were going. The Army Medical Supply Depot on the south side of Mission and the Army Clothing Depot on New Montgomery were burning and there was no hope of saving them. The Army Commissary on Market near the waterfront was already gone. With the entire wholesale district north of Market rapidly being destroyed, the city would face dangerous shortages, shortages which the Army now could not even begin to fill. More soldiers would be needed, General Funston realized. The city would need food, thousands would need shelter.

It did not occur to him to leave the city's problems to the city's officials, or to wait to be asked for aid (as did the Navy). A soldier was summoned and while he waited to take the message across the bay to Oakland to be filed from there, Funston scribbled a terse dispatch to the War Department. "WE ARE DOING ALL POSSIBLE TO AID RESIDENTS OF SAN FRANCISCO IN PRESENT TERRIBLE CALAMITY. MANY THOUSANDS HOMELESS," he began. Then, as though suddenly conscious of the fact that he had committed the Army to the fight without any authority to do so, he served defiant notice that he intended to continue: "I SHALL DO EVERYTHING IN MY POWER TO RENDER ASSISTANCE AND TRUST TO WAR DEPARTMENT TO AUTHORIZE ANY ACTION I MAY HAVE TO TAKE." ("OF COURSE, DO EVERYTHING POSSIBLE," Secretary of War Taft replied when the message finally reached him.) He ended with his first request for supplies, "WE NEED TENTS AND RATIONS FOR 20,000 PEOPLE." Long before this message reached Washington—it was not delivered until 2:50 the following morning—he had amended his request, first to supplies for 100,000, then simply to "all available supplies."

At eleven o'clock the Winchester Hotel, behind the Call Building, crumpled into incandescent ruins and almost at the same time the Call began to burn. Flames reared up first in the fourth floor and, in the next instant, using the center elevator shaft of the tall slender building as a flue, shot out of the round windows in the dome, eleven stories above. Once it began to burn the destruction was furiously fast. In two hours the city's tallest building, its most famous skyscraper, was a burned-out shell.

Now only the buildings between Third and Second remained. Firemen decided to dynamite the Monadnock

Building, between the Examiner and the Palace, in an effort to save the other two, although the Monadnock was a fireproof building, still unfinished; standing it was the best safeguard the other two buildings could have. The firemen went ahead and set off their charge. There was so little inflammable in the building that even though they were using granular powder, the explosion did not start a fire—nor was the building destroyed. The Army had the same experience elsewhere; their report later noted rather irritably that "steel and concrete buildings were found to be practically impervious to anything except enormous charges."

Nothing could save the Examiner Building; its going was merely a matter of time, no matter how sturdily it resisted. Only the Palace Hotel had any real possibility of being saved, a possibility owed its flamboyant builder, William C. Ralston. Ralston had spent five million dollars in his determination to make the Palace the biggest and finest hotel in the United States. (Briefly, until overtaken by the United States Hotel in Saratoga, N.Y., it had had more rooms than any other American hotel; it was so big that it was a quarter of a century before it could be operated profitably.)

In the building of it, Ralston had provided it with two major protection factors. It had been built to be earthquake-proof (construction began shortly after the great earthquake of 1868) and it was. Although built of brick, its heavily reinforced walls and its massive foundations twelve feet thick had withstood the shock this morning with little damage. Cut off by narrow streets—Annie, Jessie and New Montgomery—from the rest of the block, it had also been built to be fireproof, as much in anticipation of danger from within as from without, since every one of the eight hundred rooms had an open fireplace (there was no central heating) and conflagrations in the rooms were all too frequent. Heroic precautions had been taken: three artesian wells, with a capacity of 28,000 gallons of water per hour, were drilled; a storage reservoir holding 630,000 gallons had been dug under the building; seven tanks, with 130,000 gallons more, on the roof. There were 350 outlets, 20,000 feet of hose, and an elaborate alarm system in place. The Palace Hotel seemed to have more water on tap this Wednesday morning than the entire city of San Francisco.

All over the hotel now, from subbasement to roof, hotel employees and firemen were busy wetting down the seven floors, soaking the walls, determined to keep the fire at bay. But all their efforts, and all of William C. Ralston's extravagant precautions, would not save the hotel; in a few hours the water, drained off by firemen in futile attempts to rescue other buildings, would run out, and the Palace too would be destroyed.

While firemen and soldiers fought unavailingly at the fires working steadily up from South of Market and westward from the wholesale district, danger had sprung up almost unobserved on a new front. At ten o'clock, across the city in the Hayes Valley, a woman had grown tired of watching and gossiping with the neighbors and went back into her house at Gough and Hayes Streets and built a fire to start breakfast. She was cooking ham and eggs—or so the story had it—but before they were done fire blazed up in the earthquake-damaged chimney and swept through the house. This was only two blocks away from where firemen had successfully overcome a fire early in the morning, but this time the fire was beyond control almost as soon as it began. It reared into the surrounding blocks in Oak, Hayes, Grove, Fulton and McAllister Streets, through rows of closely packed wooden houses. Although firemen fought it all day, the "Ham and Eggs" fire alone destroyed thirty blocks.

At eleven o'clock Wednesday morning a strong wind

sprang up from the west, the wind the fire fighters on the other side of the city had hoped for all morning. Now it served to drive the Hayes Valley fire east at furious speed, moving so fast that there was no chance to save anything. Ahead of it, on Van Ness Avenue, stood the many-spired St. Ignatius Church with its magnificent organ and murals, said to be the grandest Jesuit church in the world. The fire had a diabolical frenzy of its own; while it was still blocks away the spires of St. Ignatius began to burn in the super-charged atmosphere. As they became flaming torches, the fire leaped a whole block to reach the church below. Immediately the entire building, with its treasured paintings and works of art, was in flames and the fire raced on toward the City Hall and Mechanics' Pavilion.

Mechanics' Pavilion, a huge barn of a place covering an entire block between Larkin and Polk Streets just west of the City Hall, had been called into service as an emergency hospital. It was a new use—and the last—for the vast wooden building whose high-vaulted ceiling had looked down on almost every other kind of activity. In years past it had been crowded time and again for fairs, conventions, horse shows and the first flickering silent movies. Pretty girls and dignified old gentlemen alike had displayed their skill on ice skates. Grand society had attended such gala social events as the annual Mardi Gras Ball, a high point in San Francisco's social season. Fight fans had crowded it a few nights back to see "Philadelphia Jack" O'Brien beat Bob Fitzsimmons in the thirteenth round, and only the night before it had witnessed a "grand march on roller skates."

This Wednesday morning, though, Mechanics' Pavilion was a scene of horror and wild activity, part hospital, part morgue. Injured had been pouring in since before six o'clock. They lay on the floor until the city's sprinkling wagons—now all too useless for their original purpose—could bring cots and mattresses. Operating tables were set up and were in constant use. There were hundreds of patients, and teams of rescue workers were constantly bringing more. Doctors—Doctor Miller, Chief Surgeon of the Central Emergency Hospital, and fifty or more volunteers—worked unceasingly at maimed and burned children, at a paralytic who had dragged himself over burning embers, at the broken and protruding bones of men and women rescued, terribly mangled, from under fallen buildings. Amid the din and clatter Catholic sisters, Salvation Army women, and Navy nurses rushed in from Mare Island worked side by side attending the patients.

Everywhere there was mad confusion, the Sutro officials bringing in loads of books to store in one corner, dead bodies being hauled in to be stacked in another corner and joined by those who died on the operating tables, thousands of people searching frantically among the rows of patients for missing relatives. Suddenly the Hayes Valley fire was upon them, sweeping in from the west at incredible speed. There was a stampede to evacuate the crowded buildings, patients and dead bodies hauled out into the streets, wagons and automobiles commandeered to carry them away from the path of the onrushing fire. As the last patient was hurried out—or were there some left?—flames touched the building. In fifteen minutes it was completely destroyed.

The flames rushed on into the ruins of City Hall, which caught from the blazing sparks of Mechanics' Pavilion, spreading on to destroy the 85,000 books in the Public Library on the second floor, feeding on the documents of the County Clerk's office, the Recorder's office, the Assessor's. The fire in the City Hall was to burn and smolder for three days. Some of the city's records—notably the tax-assessment rolls—would be saved, stored either in the vaults of the City

Hall itself or carted out to the receiving vault at the Masonic Cemetery. Many more, records of suits filed, deeds, titles, would be destroyed.

Only soldiers and firemen remained in Market Street now. As the Hayes Valley fire bore down on Market the people who still crowded the street, compressed into an ever smaller area by the fire's advance, had been forced to move out. They went in a flood finally, driven by soldiers on horseback, herded into the side streets to join the other refugees ahead of them. They jammed Union Square, thousands of them, clutching their rescued belongings—bird cages, phonographs, trunks. They retreated from there while others took their places. They made their way north to watch the fire from Nob Hill or Telegraph Hill, or hoping to come south again along the waterfront on the other side of the fire and thus reach the ferry. They straggled out toward the Western Addition, heading for Golden Gate Park or, dazed and incoherent, simply wandering along the streets.

Only occasionally were there individuals headed in the other direction. A wildly honking automobile, carrying dynamite. A minister, with a card on his lapel reading, "A servant of God. Let me help." Miss Elsa Maxwell, fighting her way against the crowd to keep, so she thought, a luncheon date with Enrico Caruso. There were to be no more operatic arias and cut-out caricatures, however; Caruso had stood Elsa up. He and Scotti had departed quite a while before in a carriage which Scotti had paid $300 to hire, for the outer reaches of the city.

More than ever rumor swept the milling crowds headed away from the fire. Actual events had a way of reshaping themselves into a dozen frightening variations. A woman, ordered not to start a fire in her stove, a story went, had started one anyway. The authorities—soldiers, policemen, special officers, who knew?—made her put it out. In defiance of their orders she had started another fire, and when that was put out, still a third. At that point she had been taken out and shot. The story of the young man with the women's fingers appeared again and again, changing, growing. There were a dozen fingers. The women had still been alive when their fingers were cut off. One man after another claimed to have seen it happen. One nervous little man, suddenly bold as he told the story, said he had seen a soldier shoot a thug as he bent over an unconscious woman, wrenching a ring from her finger. Then he insisted he had seen, only a few blocks away, another thug wresting food from a pitiful old woman and a little girl, and he himself had brained the thug with the butt of his pistol. Still another man said he had been standing by his wife and the thief had grabbed the ring right off her finger—only to be shot, as always, by a soldier. Listeners nodded indifferently. Violence no longer had any meaning.

Wilder and wilder they grew. The ferries and the ferry slip had burned. The Call Building had been destroyed by dynamite . . . or fire . . . or earthquake. All the prisoners in the jail had been killed. (They were very much alive and under guard, as a matter of fact, and the authorities were wondering what to do with them.) All the patients at Mechanics' Pavilion had been burned alive. Still more stories— every city on the Coast had been destroyed. Chicago had slid into Lake Michigan. A tidal wave had submerged New York. It seemed likely enough that they were true.

Behind the fleeing refugees there was a ring of fire halfway around the city now, the fire in the wholesale district on the east extending down across Market and joining the huge South of Market fire, stretching all the way across that district, leaping over the lower part of Eighth Street where firemen were fighting with dynamite to keep it back, heading on up toward where the Hayes Valley fire was sweeping down from the north to meet it. From Eighth Street back to the waterfront, on the south side of Market Street itself, there was still the one brief gap in the line: the block between Second and Third Streets. But at noon the annex behind the Examiner Building at Third caught fire; at 12:30 its rear wall fell. Minutes later there were flames on the seventh floor of the Examiner Building. Only the Palace and the Grand, and the indestructible Monadnock remained, now, on this side. On the other side of Market the fire had reached the street only in the few blocks from Sansome east to the waterfront, but how long would that last?

Only at the northeastern end, so close to the Hall of Justice and Chinatown, had the fire slowed its onward march. Firemen and soldiers and the crowds in Portsmouth Square had watched, breathless, for it to sweep into the tindery, crowded warrens of Chinatown, but that was not to be until later, and through another avenue of entry. As the flames grew larger in the block along Portsmouth Square between Kearny and Dupont, Captain Coleman had finally arrived, with three hundred pounds of dynamite secured from civilian employees of the Army Engineers. With it he quickly shattered two flimsy houses just beyond the fire. The firemen, belatedly discovering a cistern in Dupont Street (many firemen had never known cisterns to be used in all their time with the department), had been able to keep the fire under control when it spread into the dynamited rubble. And the west wind had sprung up. While it drove the Hayes Valley fire ahead with such intensity, it had had just the opposite effect on this end of the fire.

Water and wind could not be counted on for long, however, and three hundred pounds of dynamite would not go far. Now that Captain Coleman was here, Lieutenant Briggs took the opportunity to go and see about getting a boat to go to the du Pont works, across the bay in Contra Costa County, for more dynamite. Boats, he found when he reached the waterfront, were not to be had merely for the asking. Many a tug owner was getting rich carrying refugees at high prices and had no intention of halting such a lucrative business to go for dynamite. But where orders from civilian authorities might have been ignored with impunity, "people soon learned that defiance of an Army order was likely to land a man among the unidentified dead." Briggs and his soldiers got two boats on their way to bring back loads of dynamite from the California Powder Works across the bay, and others followed. The explosions began again, all over town. John Bermingham, Jr., the powder works superintendent, came back with one of the boatloads and began dynamiting along Montgomery Street. Army teams spread throughout the city with dynamite. Firemen laid down empty hoses and turned to dynamite.

How much dynamite was used? Nobody knows, but enough, General Funston said later, that sometimes the explosions were so constant that they reminded him of a bombardment. By noon a young lieutenant had blown himself up, running into a building to see why a charge had not gone off; a few hours later a wagonload of black powder blew up, scattering wagon, driver and horses in small pieces. Still the dynamiting went on, and still it was just ahead of the fire, having only temporary effect, or none at all.

Shortly after one o'clock, with the city burning on three fronts, a number of prominent men were making their various ways to the Hall of Justice in response to the Mayor's invitation. A few of the men invited had refused to come, unwilling to serve with the Mayor. Others, their hands full with their own problems, had been unable to come. Twenty-five arrived, however. (Although it was called the Committee of Fifty, there were never exactly that many members; eventually more than eighty men served on the Committee of Fifty for Relief, and the Committee of Forty for Reconstruction which succeeded it.) There were men like M. H. de Young, publisher of the *Chronicle* (but not R. A. Crothers and his editor, Fremont Older, of the hated *Bulletin*); Garrett McEnerney, the brilliant lawyer; and the city attorney of Mayor Phelan's administration, Franklin K. Lane. There were Hartland and Herbert Law, who owned vast amounts of real estate—it was Herbert Law's Monadnock Building the firemen were trying unsuccessfully to blow up, next to the Examiner Building on Market Street; and it was the Law brothers who now owned the Fairmont Hotel Tessie Oelrichs had built on Nob Hill, having recently traded for it the Rialto and Crossley Buildings on Mission Street. The Rialto and Crossley Buildings—they had already burned this morning, but the Fairmont still stood beautiful and unapproachable on top of Nob Hill. Tessie Oelrichs was reported to be in a state of collapse at the news.

There were the brothers Magee, also large real-estate owners; F. B. Stratton, the Collector of the Port; Judge Slack; J. Downey Harvey, the meeting's instigator, and several others, including two whom no one had expected to see: Rudolph Spreckels and former Mayor James D. Phelan, who had made no secret of the fact that they were attempting to bring Mayor Schmitz to trial for extortion and bribery.

The air was tense as Schmitz looked across the candlelit basement of the Hall of Justice at the men who had set out to ruin him: heavy-set, stolid Rudolph Spreckels, withdrawn and indifferent looking (and concerned at the moment with his own problems—his wife was expecting a baby at any time) and short, stocky, sandy-haired James Phelan, with his lively eyes and his finely proportioned features—a head that, Gertrude Atherton said, "might have come, via Ireland, from ancient Rome." There was to be no evidence of any political animosity today, however. While Phelan and Spreckels were furious at the delay their plans to prosecute Schmitz would now inevitably encounter, there were more important problems to face for the time being, and they were willing to do anything they could to aid their city. Day after day the Committee would meet in an atmosphere of cordiality—"earthquake love," Phelan called it, his eyes twinkling with mild cynicism.

Schmitz took immediate charge of the meeting this Wednesday afternoon, as he was to do throughout the crisis. It was fortunate that he did; few of the men present would have been able to. "It was a revelation," said one observer, "to see men who were masters of business and captains of industry utterly at a loss and incapable of any initiative in such a terrible emergency." Belying all his years of weak acceptance of Ruef's orders, Schmitz had become a leader himself; he "ran the Committee of Fifty as he would a hurry rehearsal . . . He swung his baton and played his new band with as much aplomb as if he had been conducting it for years."

Almost his first words to the meeting concerned his determination to prevent looting. "Let it be given out," he said sternly, "that three men have already been shot down without mercy for looting. Let it also be understood that the orders have been given to all soldiers and policemen to do likewise without hesitation." There was a swift murmur of agreement from the group. Other suggestions were made, other dangers considered. The folly of lighting fires in homes—with the "Ham and Eggs" fire in the Hayes Valley an all too present warning—was denounced. A proclamation was quickly drafted:

PROCLAMATION BY THE MAYOR

The Federal Troops, the members of the Regular Police Force and all Special Police Officers have been authorized by me to KILL any and all persons found engaged in Looting or in the Commission of Any Other Crime.

I have directed all the Gas and Electric Lighting Co.'s not to turn on Gas or Electricity until I order them to do so. You may therefore expect the city to remain in darkness for an indefinite time.

I request all citizens to remain at home from darkness until daylight until order is restored.

I WARN all Citizens of the danger of fire from Damaged or Destroyed Chimneys, Broken or Leaking Gas Pipes or Fixtures, or any like cause.

E. E. SCHMITZ, Mayor

Dated, April 18, 1906.

No time was wasted considering the legality of the proclamation. Neither the Mayor nor the Committee, of course, had the right to order soldiers to kill civilians, or even to tell people to stay home at night. But if there were doubts, if Garrett McEnerney, the lawyer, or Franklin Lane, the former City Attorney, or Police Chief Dinan or Judge Slack had reservations, they did not press them.

It was essential that the proclamation be before the public as soon as possible. It was sent out to be printed at once in a printing shop at Mission and Twenty-second, well beyond the fire. There was no electric power to run the presses; soldiers ordered passing civilians in to turn the heavy wheels by hand. Five thousand copies were run off, to be posted throughout the unburned parts of the city.

The Committee proceeded quickly to the matter of giving aid to the thousands of homeless refugees. Mayor Schmitz' own efforts had already obtained twenty-four hundred tents to be set up in parks, and arrangements had been made to

PROCLAMATION
BY THE MAYOR

The Federal Troops, the members of the Regular Police Force and all Special Police Officers have been authorized by me to KILL any and all persons found engaged in Looting or in the Commission of Any Other Crime.

I have directed all the Gas and Electric Lighting Co.'s not to turn on Gas or Electricity until I order them to do so. You may therefore expect the city to remain in darkness for an indefinite time.

I request all citizens to remain at home from darkness until daylight every night until order is restored.

I WARN all Citizens of the danger of fire from Damaged or Destroyed Chimneys, Broken or Leaking Gas Pipes or Fixtures, or any like cause.

E. E. SCHMITZ, Mayor

Dated, April 18, 1906.

ALTVATER PRINT, ◁▷ MISSION AND 22D STS.

California Historical Society, San Francisco

care for a few hundred in Oakland; but these were pitiful
beginnings in a crisis where a quarter of a million people
were soon to be homeless. A member of the Committee
moved that the Mayor be authorized to draw checks for any
amount for relief and aid, with those present pledging to
make the checks good. There was general approval, but a
curious element of hesitation: more than one member
thought it would be just as well to keep the Mayor's hands
off the money. Schmitz tactfully presented no objection to
the appointment of James Phelan as chairman of a Relief
Finance Committee to handle the money, with authority to
select its members himself.

There were so many problems. All morning wagon and
automobile owners had profiteered on people's misfortune,
charging ever-increasing sums to carry belongings even a
few blocks. There were angry denunciations of these extortionists in the Committee, and stern measures were
promptly authorized to deal with them. The Mayor instructed Police Chief Dinan to seize the conveyances and
use them for the public good. Whatever payment the owners were to receive could be worried about later.

All during the meeting the dynamiting had been coming
closer and closer. On Montgomery Street at the corner of
Sacramento, John Bermingham's demolition team was making desperate efforts to save the Pacific Mutual Building, a
slender eight-story building, San Francisco's first "sky-
scraper." But while they dynamited the buildings adjoining
it, the fire was creeping in from the What Cheer House on
Leidesdorff to the Italian-American Bank across the street
from the Pacific Mutual; from there it was but a step, and
an inevitable one, into the old insurance building.

Other teams were busy on Clay Street, on Kearny Street,
back to Montgomery, leapfrogging from one location to another as the fire pushed ahead into more buildings. Cavalry-

men galloped through streets running with smoke, driving people out; soldiers unloaded dynamite; flames crackled and roared. While the Committee of Fifty continued to discuss means of meeting the crisis, raising their voices now and then to be heard over the crash of explosions, the fire was moving steadily closer to the Hall of Justice, and the fire fighters moved closer with it, working feverishly to head it off.

Soldiers had reached the Montgomery Block now, only a short distance east of the Hall of Justice. The Sutro officials had taken what books they could and gone, leaving the rest to be destroyed. Oliver Stidger, the building's manager, pleaded helplessly with the soldiers, pointing out that its sturdy fire wall—the Montgomery Block had been completed in 1853, when memory of the city's six disastrous fires was still fresh—was more likely to hinder the fire standing than as a heap of rubble. The soldiers continued to unload dynamite, preparing to blow it up.

Then a different obstacle arose, one which the soldiers were helpless to resist. As the Block's historian, Idwal Jones, recounted it later, there suddenly appeared in a window above them "the eccentric and religious Elder Treadwell . . . He leaned out of the large window, arms raised heavenward, prophesying woe upon all who laid impious hands upon the Ark. With his long white beard and black cap, the role of the prophet sat grandly upon the elder. His voice smote down upon them: 'Their visage is blacker than a coal; they are not known in the streets. Their skin cleaveth to their bones; it is withered, it is become as a stick.'" Horrified soldiers scattered pell-mell at the appearance of the mad figure through the pall of smoke. The Montgomery Block escaped dynamiting and, protected by its fire wall and water from four cisterns (all of them closer to the Hall of Justice and to Chinatown than to the Block) and later by strenuous hand efforts, suffered little damage from the fire. It was fifty-three years old then; it was to last another fifty-three years, until it was torn down in 1959 and a parking garage built on the site.

There was no going back to the Montgomery Block. The soldiers moved across the street to begin dynamiting in the block of shabby buildings just behind the Hall of Justice, where the Committee was still meeting. Committee members jumped out of the way as windows in the Hall of Justice crashed and cornices came hurtling down at the violence of the nearby explosion. It was too dangerous to stay inside any longer; there was a hasty motion to adjourn to a safer location.

Everyone was pouring out of the building. The Police Department had already set up temporary headquarters in Portsmouth Square, across the street from the Hall of Justice, leaving behind nearly sixty years' accumulation of records and documents, and the evidence and transcripts in all the criminal cases pending in San Francisco—all to be destroyed before the day was over. From behind the building, on Dunbar Alley, nurses and soldiers were hurrying out with patients and corpses from the Morgue, which had been converted into an emergency hospital while still serving its original purpose. They commandeered wagons to take them to the Presidio, frantically loading the wounded, piling the corpses in, in one of the nightmare tasks of the fire, the constant carting off of dead bodies ahead of the flames. The wagons were loaded finally and they set off, only to have some of the soldiers themselves wounded by exploding dynamite a few blocks away, and added to the wagonloads of victims.

Tons of dynamite and barrels of granular powder had been piled up in Portsmouth Square. The Committee of Fifty adjourned to the steep little plaza and wound up its meeting quickly, shooting a nervous glance now and then at the grim piles of explosives. The Police Department was getting ready to move again, this time to the Fairmont Hotel, and the Committee decided to make the Fairmont its meeting place too. A motion was made to meet there at ten the next morning, Thursday, and the meeting broke up.

Captain Coleman was waiting for Mayor Schmitz. The ordnance officer had made up his mind to dispose of the barrels of granular powder, partly because it was dangerous to leave it this close to the fire, partly to remove the temptation of using it in misguided efforts to halt the fire. The safest thing to do, he felt, would be to put it on a boat and get it out of the city, but the firemen and police insisted on keeping it; they wanted it stored at the Fairmont Hotel, to be used "as a last resort." The Mayor listened to their arguments, finally told the angry Captain briefly, "Let them have it." Coleman insisted on a receipt from Mayor Schmitz. When the Mayor had impatiently signed for the explosives, the police began to move them up the hill to the Fairmont.

The Committee members departed in their separate directions; some, like James Phelan and Tom Magee, to use their cars for carting dynamite to places where it was needed, or, like Rudolph Spreckels, to duties as special policemen. They were a discouraged group. Although for the moment dynamite and the solid nature of most of the buildings here were holding the fire back, a short distance away the flaming tower of the Pacific Mutual Building was an ominous reminder of how temporary the restraint might be. But Phelan, looking ahead, stopped long enough to tell a reporter, "We shall have a great modern city here. It may take some time to do it, but it will be done." Before he had a chance to say any more, a bedraggled woman with two children and a bundle stepped up to his car and asked him how to get to Jefferson Square. "Help the lady into the car," the richest

man in San Francisco told his chauffeur, and they set off
to reunite her with the rest of her family at Jefferson Square.

While the members of the Committee of Fifty were meeting at the Hall of Justice, with the fire kept barely at bay
along Montgomery Street, the long struggle for the last of
the buildings holding out on the south side of Market Street
had failed. The Call Building, which had begun to burn at
eleven, was completely gutted by one o'clock Wednesday
afternoon and flames were in the upper floors of the Examiner, across Third Street. On the other side of the Examiner
firemen set off another charge of explosives in the Monadnock Building, but like the morning's charge it did relatively
little damage to the Monadnock Building, and no good at
all to the Palace Hotel, just beyond it across Annie Street.
For the fire was approaching the Palace from the rear, and
the last of the hotel's great reservoirs was running dry.

At two o'clock the Palace began to burn. The upper floors
on the back side caught first, and then the flames swept on
through the building, lighting a last fire in the ornate hotel's
eight hundred fireplaces. At 2:20 the Chief Operator at the
Postal Telegraph office across the street was sending out the
last message to leave San Francisco:

THE CITY PRACTICALLY RUINED BY FIRE. IT'S WITHIN HALF A BLOCK
OF US IN THE SAME BLOCK. THE CALL BUILDING IS BURNED OUT EN-
TIRELY, THE EXAMINER BUILDING JUST FELL IN A HEAP. FIRE ALL
AROUND US IN EVERY DIRECTION . . . LOTS OF NEW BUILDINGS JUST
RECENTLY FINISHED ARE COMPLETELY DESTROYED. THEY ARE BLOW-
ING STANDING BUILDINGS THAT ARE IN THE PATH OF FLAMES UP WITH
DYNAMITE. ITS AWFUL. THERE IS NO COMMUNICATION ANYWHERE
AND ENTIRE PHONE SYSTEM IS BUSTED. I WANT TO GET OUT OF HERE
OR BE BLOWN UP.

Then the Postal wire went dead.

At four o'clock, at the other end of Market Street near Van Ness Avenue, the Daily News Building, on Ninth Street a short distance below Market, began to burn. Here dynamite had been effective for a while in keeping the flames back, and the paper's staff had used the time to hurry together two extras which they distributed free on the streets. Without power the newspaper's own presses had been unusable; the one-page editions were printed on colored circular paper at a job press two blocks away, with the presses run by hand. Now the brief respite had expired. The dynamiters had long since abandoned their stand at Eighth Street, and flames leaped across Eighth, Ninth and Tenth along Market, and at the same time were reaching out below into the Mission district.

The battle was over—lost—in the South of Market district. Lost, that is, except for the Post Office and the Mint. Saving the granite Post Office, set well in from the streets and surrounded only by small buildings which were quickly demolished, had been a relatively easy matter. The fight for the Mint had been altogether different, a long desperate struggle that had lasted all day and was only now finished. The building's own monolithic construction, its granite and sandstone blocks, its iron shutters on the lower floors, had been enough to protect it as the fire made its first attack, sweeping up the opposite side of Mission Street, in the morning. There was an artesian well in the basement, although it had been of no use then. Its pump was broken and workmen were still trying frantically to repair it. They were just getting it fixed when the attack began from the rear, swirling down from the inferno of the Emporium on Market, sweeping in from the Metropolitan Hall and the Lincoln School as the flames surged up Fifth Street on one side, and, driven by the wind, from the wooden buildings between Sixth Street and narrow little Mint Street on the other. One of the buildings already burning just behind the Mint was the No. 17 Engine Company firehouse.

One of the Mint employees had formerly been the Fire Chief of Oakland. Under his direction soldiers and Mint employees were everywhere, sloshing vitriol out of the storage tanks in the courtyard until the floors ran ankle deep with it, ripping out everything inflammable in the upper floors, tearing out huge timbers and the tank staves from the refinery and throwing them into the courtyard below. On the tar roof, the building's most vulnerable spot, another group worked, amid smoke and flying firebrands, to keep the blaze from catching hold, keeping the refinery roof wetted down with buckets of water (the pump was working now, but there was only seventy-five feet of hose, too short to reach the roof), ignoring the two huge brick chimneys that tottered above them, threatening brick towers that a new shock might bring crashing down on them.

Sheets of flame roared in from the candy factory and the other wooden buildings across Mint Street. The men on the roof had to retreat inside. There they went to work again, playing the thin stream of water from the hose on the blazing window sills. Outside, the flames swept across the building, shattering the face of the granite and sandstone blocks, melting the windows, spitting tongues of fire inside, forcing the fighters to retreat another floor. There was a momentary lull and they hurried back, to extinguish the blazing woodwork, shoot a stream of water onto the roof, then clamber onto the roof itself to rip out sections of burning tar and throw them over into the streets and the courtyard. At four o'clock the Mint was out of danger.

At four o'clock the Call Building, where the flames had apparently completed their work three hours before, suddenly began to burn again with eerie intensity. The ruins of the Examiner blazed up once more, and the fire in the Palace

Hotel roared with new fury. But by five o'clock Wednesday afternoon it was all over. The south side of Market, from the waterfront all the way west to Eleventh Street, was destroyed.

The fire was far below Market now, burning in the factories and oil works, flaming across the far side of Rincon Hill, quickly leveling the shabby boarding houses around once elegant South Park. (South Park had once been so elegant, in fact, that George Gordon, the real-estate promoter who developed the area, had imported English sparrows to remind the frontier aristocracy of better things.)

The fire had reached the Southern Pacific depot at Third and Townsend. No trains were leaving there, no passengers were waiting. There were only a few men at the lonely station, and they were busy! With one thin line of hose from three blocks farther south, where a fire engine was pumping from the channel, they were dashing back and forth, trying to cover all sides of the rambling building—catching a blaze as it started up in the freight sheds along Townsend Street, running back as danger loomed on Third Street, climbing up on the roof with wet sacks to stamp out blazes catching hold there. The fight would go on until four o'clock in the morning, flames reaching so close that "the paint was literally stewed from the walls," but the Southern Pacific depot would be saved.

Between this line and Market Street the South of Market district was a smoking ruin of streets piled high with debris, hollow shells of buildings, and here and there a stark chimney standing alone. Only two buildings remained intact—the Post Office and the Mint.

By now the Hayes Valley fire was about out. All day long street after street had witnessed the familiar sequence: a fireman with megaphone lifted to his mouth, shouting, "Leave the area! These buildings will be dynamited!"; the hammering on doors and rude eviction of occasional people unwilling to go—unwilling to go, with the fire a block away; the dynamite wagon with its red flag, the houses exploding three at a time, and then the fire sweeping on. Clutching hastily snatched possessions (how many people would wish they had let the bird cage go and brought some blankets instead), dragging hurriedly packed trunks, the people evacuated to Jefferson Square, left their belongings there and came back to watch the fire. Late Wednesday afternoon, with the help of dynamite and a small stream of water, the western side of the Hayes Valley fire was finally halted at Octavia Street. On the other side it had reached Market Street in the triangle formed by McAllister and Market, but everything across Market was already burned; there was no place else for it to go and it was burning out.

As darkness fell Wednesday evening, the flames appeared to die down a little on all three fronts and it seemed for a moment that the conflagration might be brought under control.

It was a momentary breathing spell for General Funston. He had been dashing back and forth on his horse, attending to one problem after another, conferring hastily with Mayor Schmitz, directing fire fighters and dynamiters in person at a dozen spots. His face was black under his red hair, and his clothes were soaked from the spray of fire hoses. No word had arrived from Washington. The War Department had not even received his first telegram, and although they had sent a flurry of inquiries as the news of the disaster filtered back, none of them reached San Francisco until the next day. Funston was used to being ahead of the battle line and out of communication with his superiors; there was no choice but to go ahead and do whatever he thought best, on his own.

San Francisco was in a state of indescribable confusion. Strong measures were necessary to bring about even a semblance of order. Contributing to the disorder were the hundreds of people who had begun to flood into the city: families looking for relatives, thieves come to loot, dazed refugees who got to towns across the bay and then wandered back to San Francisco. Crowds of idle visitors were arriving to watch the spectacle of San Francisco burning, and the Army had all it could handle without tourists.

Funston made a swift decision. The city was closed completely; whoever left—and the ferries, tugs, barges, fishing boats and even Chinese junks were carrying thousands away —had left for good. Passengers coming from Oakland and Alameda on the ferry were forced to return. A last train, carrying among others Mrs. Robert Louis Stevenson, returning from Mexico, and members of the State Supreme Court, was allowed to enter from the south, and thereafter trains were to be turned back at the county line. No one could enter the city. (Later it would still be necessary to telegraph police chiefs of surrounding towns, begging them to keep curiosity seekers at home.)

Soldiers guarding the piers made no distinction in applying the rule; their orders were that *no one* came in. Outraged newspapermen telegraphed Washington that Funston was interfering with their dispatches. The Western Union, which had retreated to its office at the Oakland Ferry, sent pleas to Funston to issue "passports" for its employees to come back to San Francisco, and at the same time telegraphed the War Department (in a message which reached Washington well before Funston's urgent messages for supplies) sputtering that "MARTIAL LAW HAS SO FAR MADE IT IMPOSSIBLE FOR ANYONE TO GO FROM OAKLAND TO SAN FRANCISCO."

The stormy little general had a fairly low opinion of newsmen (although he had once been a reporter himself, briefly) and little patience with critics in general. If you cut their heads open "you wouldn't even find sweetbreads inside," was his way of putting it. The passports were not arranged until the following day.

For the moment there were more important problems. Policing the city was an enormous job. The police force—six hundred men—was badly disorganized; they had experienced their own personal disasters, homes destroyed by earthquake or in danger of destruction by fire, possessions lost, families separated. The National Guard, which had begun to assemble at Governor Pardee's order, was in much the same condition, and young and inexperienced besides. The responsibility fell in large measure to General Funston's 1700 soldiers, in a job where, as a newspaper said later, "60,000 would not be enough." (The entire U. S. Army in April 1906, as a matter of fact, consisted of 60,385 men.)

Extortion was running wild over the city. Harried refugees, who in the confusion and disorder had in many cases had nothing to eat all day, were desperate for food. Those who had money (many had rushed out without bringing any; no money could be had from banks, which had been closed all day; and checks were no good, since for all anyone knew the banks might never reopen) found that even a soda cracker was now five cents. A loaf of bread, normally five cents, was now a dollar; a dozen eggs, five dollars. Water was twenty-five cents a glass.

Soldiers had their own rough but effective way of dealing with cases that came to their attention. A soldier walked into a profiteering baker's shop, slammed the butt of his rifle down on the counter, announced that the price of bread was back to five cents whether the baker liked it or not, and stood guard as the people made their purchases. At a grocery store out at Baker and Jackson a grocer defiantly told a lieutenant, "I'll sell my goods as I please." The lieutenant looked around at the crowds, then at the soldiers with him, finally back at the grocer. "You won't charge anything for your groceries," he told the grocer. "You'll *give* them to these people just as fast as you can hand them out or you'll soon be dangling from the nearest telegraph pole."

Often the situation was reversed, however. Soldiers stood guard to protect grocery stores stormed by hungry refugees all too ready to grab and run. They made sure of orderly distribution for grocers who, realizing their stores were bound to go, were giving their stocks away. There were never enough soldiers to go around. One dealer, with no other protection available, nailed slats at four-inch intervals across his windows; the crowds were allowed to have whatever they could reach through the slats.

Much more hideous to people's minds was the thought of looting, and, underneath the frightened, exaggerated rumors, looting *was* going on. Soldiers pursued a gang of thieves from shattered houses on Mason Street; robbers were caught breaking open a safe and running off with a hatful of gold coins; a man emerging from a ruined store with his arms full of stolen goods was marched up the street and shot. Pickpockets were busy in the crowds. Refugees who left their belongings for a moment came back to find them stolen. There were millions of dollars in the vaults of the burned-out Subtreasury that had to be guarded. Now that the Mint was out of danger from fire, soldiers stood braced for attack from looters; there was nearly $200 million in gold and silver in the Mint.

To soldiers, too, fell the brunt of carrying out the Mayor's order to close saloons and keep them closed. There was no time for courtesy; they simply smashed the stocks of any found still open. Then, somehow, the order came to be understood to mean that even the stocks in closed saloons should be destroyed. In vigorous application of preventive medicine they opened saloons and rolled barrels of whisky and kegs of beer out to be emptied in the gutter. Now and then it seemed a pity to see good whisky go to waste; many a weary soldier was soon sampling the stock.

Perhaps that had something to do with the way the Delmonico fire started. At any rate, Wednesday evening, as the fire seemed at last within reach of control, a group of worn-out soldiers set up camp in the ruined Delmonico restaurant, one of the famous French restaurants, on O'Farrel Street, just a block below Union Square. They built a camp-fire in the restaurant; before very long the whole building was burning. From there it spread into the Alcazar Theatre on one side and a three-story boarding house on the other, spurted across the street into Fisher's Music Hall, and was out of control in every direction. There was no fire-fighting equipment, no water, no dynamite. Before long it was reaching down toward Market Street, and up into the buildings behind the Delmonico on Union Square—first the Cordes store, then Breuner's, both six-story furniture stores.

A few blocks away the Hayes Valley fire, halted in the west and at the ruins along Market Street on the south, began to burn more intensely than ever in a new direction, north, leaping into new blocks along Golden Gate Avenue, eating its way toward the raging Delmonico fire. In the east, where the fire from the wholesale district had seemed to be burning itself out, it suddenly burst out of its boundaries and sent a new line of fire racing down Montgomery Street toward Market and up in the other direction into the ruined buildings behind the Hall of Justice. At seven o'clock Wednesday evening the entire region behind the Hall of Justice was on fire; an hour later the Hall of Justice itself was burning.

Below, flames leaped across Montgomery at one point after another. At eight-thirty the huge Merchants' Exchange Building, between Montgomery and Kearny on California Street, began to burn; at nine o'clock the Crocker Building in the gore between Montgomery and Kearny at Market was on fire and flames were heading across Kearny into the retail district and into Morton Street, sending the tarts fleeing into Union Square. (Morton Street is now called Maiden Lane, though not, one is assured, in memory of the hundreds of prostitutes who lined its two-block length in 1906, leaning from their cribs naked from the waist up so that passers-by might conveniently fondle their breasts—ten cents each, two for fifteen cents.)

At the same time the fire was going back to take care of some unfinished business. It had seemed to skip one block between Sansome and Montgomery earlier in the day. Tenants of the Brooklyn Hotel, bringing their belongings and congratulating themselves, were already moving back in. But at nine o'clock the Brooklyn Hotel, and then all the other buildings in the block—the Mills Building, the Stock Exchange, the Telephone Building—began to burn.

On Market Street the fire had not yet reached as far as the *Chronicle;* the last of the three great newspapers in the triangle with the *Call* and the *Examiner* across the street was still holding out. But above Market it moved steadily westward, reaching another block ahead now along Pine Street into Dupont (now Grant Avenue), sending Japanese and poor whites scuttling out of the tenements there, men and women dragging frightened children, pulling at trunks, packing household furniture on their backs, one Japanese hurrying up the steep hill with a huge portrait of the Emperor on his back. And now that the fire had reached Dupont Street, it swept on, unopposed, into Chinatown.

Almost anyone in San Francisco in 1906 would say that

Chinatown should have been burned long ago, although in a way they were secretly proud of it, just as they were of the city's other excesses. The Chinese were among the city's oldest inhabitants, but they remained aliens; they formed almost a separate city, self-governing, settling their own differences in their own inscrutable way. Within the confines of Chinatown buildings were transformed with balconies and curving eaves; cobblestoned streets and winding alleys lost their everyday names and became "Avenue of Virtue and Harmony," or "Alley of the Consort of Heaven." They remained dark, narrow and ill smelling, and unbelievably crowded; nearly twenty-five thousand Chinese lived in the twelve blocks of Chinatown.

Most Chinese pursued respectable enough occupations as souvenir-shop proprietors, as sweat-shop laborers, or as laundrymen and servants; Chinese servants drew considerably higher wages than their white counterparts. But at the same time Chinatown was a vice center of extraordinary proportions. Opium dens flourished side by side with goldsmiths and purveyors of dried toads and pulverized shark's eggs. Gambling—fan tan, pie gow, chuck-a-luck—was everywhere.

Prostitution had been a major business since the first famous Chinese prostitute, Madame Ah Toy, arrived in 1851 and began permitting a look at her undraped figure for a pinch of gold dust. Unscrupulous characters had ruined Madame Ah Toy's business by slipping in pinches of brass filings, but prostitution had flourished ever since. Now there were probably a thousand prostitutes in Chinatown and the price had come down considerably: their standard cry was "Two-bittee lookee, flo-bittee feelee, six-bittee doee."

With all of the vice at hand, it had been necessary to create imitation vice. The opium dens were real enough, but most of them existed for people, Chinese and white, who could pay for privacy. The ones shuddering tourists were taken through were usually make-believe dens, set up by resourceful Chinese tour guides, who knew what the public wanted to see.

The Chinese Guides Association was responsible for another common belief in San Francisco: that there was a system of subterranean passages under Chinatown by which the Chinese could go from one end of the settlement to the other, underground. Although when the area was later mapped and surveyed there proved to be no such passages, the belief was so persistent that people swore after the fire that they had seen tunnels a hundred feet deep in the ruins. Here again the wily Chinese had simply been providing atmosphere, leading tourists into cellars which seemed to have dark, dangerous passageways going off in every direction, with villainous looking Chinese (in the pay of the guides) flitting through the shadows, armed with knives and hatchets. The real thing was nothing so romantic or exciting: just huge, dark airless cellars like the one the fire would be rushing over before long, a place sometimes sardonically called the "Palace Hotel," where nearly five hundred people lived in crowded squalor; or like another cellar, almost as crowded, contemptuously known as the Dog Kennel.

Now flames leaped over the opium dens and souvenir shops, over St. Mary's Church, mocking the injunction under the clock in its steeple, "Son, observe the time and fly from evil." Thousands of Chinese fled in every direction, to Union Square, up the steep streets over Nob Hill and Russian Hill, down to the waterfront. Stolid men, their hair in queues down their backs, women in baggy pants stumbling on tiny bound feet, loaded with their bundles of possessions, dragging their trunks. To observers watching from the hilltops, Chinatown was soon "a whirlpool of flame."

While Chinatown burned, the flames rushed on across the city, up Pine, Bush, Sutter, and there were more thousands of refugees. People in the apartment buildings and houses along these streets had been confident that the fire would not reach this far. At the last minute they abandoned one block after another, just ahead of the fire. "Quickly filled trunks grated up the hills. Wagons, most of them pulled by men, rattled over the rough cobblestones. Baby carriages and toy express wagons rolled along packed full with the 'things' people had snatched up in their flight. Pianos were bumped along the sidewalks—some went to pieces in the process. Sewing machines slipped along on their rollers with stacks of bedding and the like lashed to them. Women hid their valuables on their person, or carried trinkets Gipsywise in handkerchiefs. Men wore columns of hats five-high. Some carried only a book. Parrots jabbered and scolded from many cages. Some people had blankets. Girls usually had bandboxes. Boys stretched poles between them and carried, suspended there, bundles of clothing and provisions. Once it was only a ham."

Making his way through the refugee-choked streets, galloping on horseback along the perimeter of the fire as it grew with such awesome speed, General Funston knew that his original request, sent at 10:15 in the morning, for tents and rations for 20,000 people, was now totally inadequate. Reigning up his horse abruptly, and without dismounting, he dictated another telegram to be taken by cavalryman-courier to the pier and thence across the bay by Army launch to be filed in Oakland:

WE NEED THOUANDS OF TENTS AND ALL RATIONS THAT CAN BE SENT. BUSINESS PORTION OF CITY DESTROYED AND ABOUT 100,000 HOME-LESS. FIRE STILL RAGING. TROOPS ALL ON DUTY ASSISTING POLICE. LOSS

OF LIFE PROBABLY 1000. BEST PART OF RESIDENT DISTRICT NOT YET
BURNED.

The troops were assisting the police, in their own independent way. By Wednesday evening there were five separate bodies, all armed, attempting to police the city: the
Army, the Police, the special police whom Mayor Schmitz
had appointed, the National Guard, which Governor Pardee
had called to active duty, and a group of Marines from
Mare Island. There was already beginning to be friction
among the various groups, challenges of authority, fist fights,
and prospects of more.

Funston was willing to take command of the Marines.
They were "regular troops" and as such worthy of being
welcomed into the family by the Regular Army; they came
under his command the following morning, as did the men
who came ashore when the Navy's Pacific Squadron arrived.
But he had no intention of policing the police, or of taking
any responsibility for the National Guard. Consequently, at
a last conference with Mayor Schmitz, the city had been
divided into sections, and the Army alone made responsible for the entire area west of Van Ness Avenue. This included a major portion—primarily the "Western Addition"
—of the remaining residential part of the city, as well as
Golden Gate Park and the Army posts. With refugees pouring into the streets and small parks of the Western Addition
and out to the Presidio and Golden Gate Park, the area
was soon to contain almost the entire population of the city.

The Army sector was placed under the command of Colonel Morris, who had reluctantly reconciled himself to the use
of troops in the emergency. Funston himself continued to
exercise a great deal of control over the entire city, and the
soldiers were by no means limited to the area west of Van
Ness. The lines of the Army area—to be revised several times

—in effect kept conflicting authority out, but did not keep the soldiers in. Part of the troops on duty continued guarding, fire fighting, policing in other areas too; "assisting" the police, ignoring the National Guard.

In the flame-shot darkness of this Wednesday evening— it never grew darker than a weird red twilight—the streets of the Western Addition were thick with people. Even those who lived in this section, which had suffered little damage from the earthquake, were in many cases leaving their houses. Some, convinced that fire would destroy the entire city, were making their way to Golden Gate Park or to the Presidio. Others, frightened by the frequent earthquake shocks that had continued all day (there were seventeen distinct shocks Wednesday) refused to stay inside and were camping out in yards where no chimneys threatened to fall. "The streets, walks and lawns were wiggling with little parties, one or two families in each." All night long in the eerie red streets ghostlike hordes of refugees from the burned areas trudged through with their possessions, or, too weary to go any farther, dropped along the way.

Soldiers patrolled the streets, guiding refugees to the parks, keeping stern watch for looters, making sure that those who remained in their homes lighted neither lights nor fires. The rare person who defied the Mayor's orders by having a light inside—there was little need to, since "at night the fire was so bright one could read in any part of the house without light"—would soon hear a loud banging on the door, or a bayonet rapping against the window, and a peremptory order to extinguish the light.

West of Van Ness Avenue the Hayes Valley fire had reached down across Market and, joining the South of Market fire, was sweeping on into the Mission district. The other end of the Hayes Valley fire was rushing to join the fire that had started at the Delmonico, and together in one roaring front they beat down on Market Street. From the east, burning in a solid line all the way from Chinatown to Market, the fire was advancing block after block. It surged along Market Street, still skipping for the moment the Chronicle Building, and met with the fire from the west at the Phelan Building, where General Funston's California Department had had its headquarters. The Phelan Building began to burn. By midnight all of the north side of Market from East Street on the waterfront, to Gough, beyond Van Ness Avenue, was burning or already destroyed, except for two buildings: the Chronicle Building and its sixteen-story annex, and, just beyond where the Phelan Building was burning, the massive granite Flood Building.

In Union Square, two blocks above Market, thousands of refugees watched as the fires inexorably began to surround their sanctuary. Flames leaped through to the front of Cordes Furniture Store and Breuner's on the south side of the square. At the eastern end of the square they stole into the rear of the City of Paris store; smoke seeped through cracks and crevices the earthquake had left in front and billowed out the top. Flames followed, streaming all at once out of the top-floor windows, and then all over the building. Above Union Square the fire, moving steadily westward, reached the old Temple Emanu-El on Sutter Street. From its copper minarets "tiny green, coppery flames next began to shoot forth. They grew quickly larger, and as the heat increased in intensity there shone from the two great bulbs of metal sheathing an irridescence that blinded like a sight into a blast furnace. With a roar the minarets exploded almost simultaneously" and as the showering sparks fell on the Union League and Pacific Union Clubs on the north side of Union Square, they began to burn too.

The crowds watched in silent horror. Suddenly a man began to scream, "The Lord sent it—the Lord sent it!" Soldiers shut him up ruthlessly as they ordered the people out of the square. They went in mad flight, dragging their trunks and household goods, women loaded with bedding, men struggling with furniture, or they abandoned in their haste what they had desperately held onto until now. They grew frantic at the thought of losing their last possessions and besieged wagons carrying goods from the stores on Kearny and Post Streets. Some were able to bribe the drivers to add their things to the already top-heavy loads. Others left everything behind. As they left, the remaining buildings were beginning to burn, one after another, making a solid ring of flames around the three sides, lighting with vivid red intensity the empty square, the Victory monument, the piles of belongings left behind.

The fourth side of Union Square was different. The sturdy St. Francis Hotel, on Powell at the western end of the square, had not begun to burn. Exhausted, smoke-blackened firemen began to estimate the possibility of stopping the fire at Powell Street. The St. Francis would stand, they were sure. That and Union Square would be the southern barrier. Beginning from there on the west side of Powell, half a block up there was an empty lot for a new building at Powell and Sutter. Two blocks farther up the hill, between Pine and California, was the Stanford house, set in a huge yard, nearly two hundred feet from the nearest buildings. Beyond the Stanford house all of the next block was occupied by the wide terrace of the Fairmont Hotel. Surely with all these gaps where there was no chance of the fire taking hold, the line could be held at Powell.

The line had two weak links, the two blocks between Sutter and Pine, but there was a little water available and fire engines concentrated here, braced to keep the fire from crossing Powell. The fire reached Powell Street at about one o'clock in the morning. The spire of the Baptist Church at the corner of Bush Street caught fire from flying embers; it spread, indifferent to the streams of water the firemen were directing into it, into a row of flats just below it. While firemen turned their hoses onto a corner grocery and laundry to keep that from catching, the fire from the blazing church reached across over their heads to the western side of Powell Street, setting fire to the cornices of a tall apartment building. Another stand had failed. Beyond Powell Street to the west the streets led through block after block of densely packed wooden residences, stretching all the way to Van Ness Avenue and across into the Western Addition.

Below Union Square the Delmonico fire reached across Powell unhindered. Soon Moe Gunst's store, a three-story wooden building on Geary, just across from the St. Francis, began to burn. The St. Francis, like all the other seemingly unassailable buildings the fire had consumed, had its vulnerable points. Flying sparks from the burning wooden building across the street ignited its window sills, the windows broke, the curtains caught fire; at 2:30 A.M. the St. Francis was burning.

And on Market Street, the Chronicle Building had finally surrendered. Flames caught first in its tar roof, making an inferno on the eighth floor, eating at the foundations of the nineteen heavy linotype machines there until they gave way and their dead weight went crashing down through floor after floor all the way to the basement. Only the Flood Building remained now. It was a new building, hardly more than a year old; it occupied the triangular block between Powell, Ellis and Market where the Baldwin Hotel, once the city's only real competitor in elegance to the Palace, had stood. "Lucky" Baldwin's fine hotel had been no match for fire—it burned to the ground in 1898—but the new Flood Building was another story. It stood, solid and impregnable, a monolithic stone building, twelve stories high, while everything else on Market burned. The fury of the Emporium fire across Market Street from it in the morning had had no effect. It had held out as the Phelan Building, east of it on Market, burned and the flames went rushing up behind it, across Ellis Street. Now every building in the block across Powell on the third side of the triangle (including the Columbia Theatre, where Mayor Schmitz had once conducted the orchestra) was burning too. Hundreds of feet high the flames were leaping, the face of the Flood Building's granite blocks disintegrating in the heat, and still the flames found no foothold. But there was no such thing as a fireproof building in the path of this fire. At 4:30 A.M. the Flood Building began to burn, catching first on the eighth floor, then spreading through the building. It was the last building on "downtown" Market Street. The destruction was complete.

Most of the hundreds of refugees congregated on the top of Nob Hill were asleep, but those who still watched could see below them the line of fire from Chinatown on the north, southwest around the hill, reaching out to Valencia Street on the west. Here and there they could pick out specific buildings burning: old St. Mary's Church in Chinatown, the Grace Cathedral at California and Stockton, the St. Francis Hotel, the row of skyscrapers on Market. Otherwise it was a solid line, moving steadily, though slowly, up the hill. One man, watching, tried to estimate the value of property being destroyed. About a million dollars an hour, he thought—but he was not even close; for the seventy-four hours of the fire the rate was nearly six million dollars an hour.

San Francisco seemed cut off from the world. With all lines of communication broken, no one knew whether anyone outside was even aware of the disaster. But the news was getting through: messages, sometimes garbled and disconnected, over the Postal wire; newspaper accounts filed from Oakland; messages from fleeing refugees as they reached points with telegraph or telephone facilities. Help was on the way. At eight o'clock Wednesday morning the *Chicago*, flagship of the Navy's Pacific Squadron, cruising twenty miles off San Diego, had received a strange, unsigned message:

EARTHQUAKE AT 5:24 AM SAN FRANCISCO NEARLY DEMOLISHED THE CITY. CALL BUILDING IS DOWN AND PALACE HOTEL BOTH TELEGRAPH OFFICES WELLS FARGO BUILDING. ALL WATER PIPES BURST CITY FIRE DEPARTMENT HELPLESS CITY IS IN FLAMES.

Like much of the news leaving San Francisco it was exaggerated, but there was no way of knowing that and it was just as well; reality would fast overtake exaggeration. Admiral Goodrich had headed immediately for San Francisco at top speed.

At Los Angeles preparations were being made to send a special relief train with doctors and nurses to San Francisco. In cities across the country where anxious people crowded around telegraph offices waiting for news, supplies were already being gathered for the shattered city. Chicago's Mayor Dunne had wired Mayor Schmitz asking what form of relief would be most acceptable, and appointed a five-hundred-man committee to take general charge. Chicago's Chief of Police Collins, taking it for granted that disorder breeds crime, had dispatched ten of his "shrewdest thief-catchers." (San Francisco did not appreciate the gesture at all. The shrewd thief-catchers arrived Tuesday morning and were sent back to Chicago Tuesday afternoon.) In twenty minutes, $85,000 had been pledged on the floor of the New York Stock Exchange.

General Greely, Commanding General of the Pacific Department, who was in Chicago on his way to Washington for his daughter Adola's wedding, telephoned the War Department that he was starting back to San Francisco. E. H. Harriman, putting his vast railroad system at the disposal of relief supplies, was on his way to San Francisco. Governor Pardee had moved his office to Oakland—his home—to organize relief supplies for San Francisco. Late in the afternoon he had issued a proclamation declaring Thursday a legal holiday throughout the state, to prevent runs on banks and to postpone legal deadlines falling on that day.

As the news reached Washington, the War Department had swung into action. Secretary of War Taft had conferred with President Roosevelt and prepared a message to Congress recommending an appropriation of $500,000 for relief, and authorization for the Army to use any available supplies to aid the people of San Francisco. The House of Representatives had passed the bill in ten minutes, without discussion, and sent it on to the Senate.

It was an anxious day as it passed without any word from Funston. It was soon apparent that all the Army communications facilities had been destroyed. A Signal Corps Company was ordered to San Franciso from Fort Leavenworth to restore communications. It left Wednesday afternoon, commanded by a young captain named Billy Mitchell (a Signal Corps officer who had not yet flown a plane, but who would one day lead the fight for air power).

All day long Taft waited, increasingly apprehensive, while no word came from San Francisco. He was doubly responsible, as Secretary of War and President of the American National Red Cross. The Red Cross secretary, Charles Magee, had telegraphed Judge Morrow, the president of the California branch, "HAVE JUST BEEN ADVISED OF DISASTER. CAN RED CROSS BE OF ASSISTANCE?" and again, "NATIONAL RED CROSS READY TO AID SAN FRANCISCO. PLEASE CONFER WITH MAYOR AS TO BEST MEANS OF ASSISTANCE. REPLY CARE OF WAR DEPARTMENT." Neither of these messages reached San

Francisco until Saturday. Meanwhile, Judge Morrow, who lived in San Rafael, had come to San Francisco Wednesday morning, but when he arrived the fire was raging in the buildings facing the waterfront and on both sides of Market, and the authorities advised him it would be dangerous to try to get around it to enter the city. He returned to San Rafael.

Mrs. Merrill, the head of the San Francisco Red Cross Society, had put out the Red Cross banner at her home at the corner of Van Ness Avenue and Washington Street and was feeding as many of the passing refugees as the house would hold. Neither she nor Judge Morrow made any effort to get in touch with the National Red Cross Wednesday. Not until late Thursday afternoon did Judge Morrow send a telegram to Charles Magee in Washington, "EARTHQUAKE YESTERDAY . . . RED CROSS RELIEF WILL BE GRATEFULLY RECEIVED."

At 11:40 Wednesday evening Secretary Taft received the first word from General Funston (the second telegram he had sent), "WE NEED THOUSANDS OF TENTS AND ALL RATIONS THAT CAN BE SENT . . . ABOUT 100,000 PEOPLE HOMELESS." General Bell, the Chief of Staff, was immediately summoned to conference. Quartermaster General Humphrey and Commissary General Sharpe were routed out of bed and told to meet at the telegraph office in the War Department. An order went out immediately to General Williams at Vancouver Barracks to ship 200,000 rations (the component parts of one day's meals for one person, value 23 cents) and all available tents, "BY QUICKEST POSSIBLE ROUTE, EITHER BY WATER OR RAIL. ALL RAILROAD AND TELEGRAPH FACILITIES SURROUNDING SAN FRANCISCO REPORTED BADLY DAMAGED AND DEMORALIZED HAVE AN OFFICER (ACCOMPANY . . . ACKNOWLEDGE RECEIPT AND REPORT ACTION."

Then at 2:50 Thursday morning Taft received a second

message from Funston (the one Funston had sent at 10:15 Wednesday morning), "I SHALL DO EVERYTHING IN MY POWER TO RENDER ASSISTANCE AND TRUST TO THE WAR DEPARTMENT TO AUTHORIZE ANY ACTION I MAY HAVE TO TAKE . . . WE NEED TENTS AND RATIONS FOR 20,000 PEOPLE." Taft read it thoughtfully, weighing it against the reports of high-handed activity and martial law that had filtered in during the day, feeling a sudden anxiety as he remembered the little general's bold, impetuous ways, bracing himself instinctively against the "constitutional cranks" who were bound to make trouble if the Army stepped over the legal limits of its authority. It was no time for half-hearted measures, however. At four o'clock Thursday morning Taft's answer was in the War Department telegraph room to go out to Funston:

YOUR DISPATCH RE 20,000 RECEIVED. HAVE DIRECTED SENDING 200,000 RATIONS FROM VANCOUVER BARRACKS, NEAREST AVAILABLE POINT. DO YOU NEED MORE TROOPS? OF COURSE DO EVERYTHING POSSIBLE TO ASSIST IN KEEPING ORDER IN SAVING LIFE AND PROPERTY AND IN RELIEVING HUNGER BY USE OF TROOPS MATERIAL AND SUPPLIES UNDER YOUR ORDER. HOUSE PASSED ENABLING RESOLUTION TODAY, SENATE WILL TOMORROW.

TAFT

It was all very well for Taft to give Funston *carte blanche* in his handling of the situation. But General Bell, the Chief of Staff, studying Funston's telegram with the antagonism Funston usually aroused in his superiors, found it extremely unsatisfactory. "I SHALL DO EVERYTHING IN MY POWER," Funston had said, but what did that mean? If he had declared martial law, why hadn't he said so? Why was he holding up newspaper men, preventing them from entering the city? What was going on in San Francisco? As Taft's message went out, General Bell was filing messages of his own, to find out. "WIRE DETAILS AS COMPREHENSIVELY AS POSSIBLE," Funston was instructed.

While Taft and General Bell considered the aspects of General Funston's telegram that most concerned them, General Humphrey, the Quartermaster General, was busy complying with the telegram's basic request for tents for 20,000 people. No one in the War Department realized that this was Funston's first telegram. By being delivered after the second telegram, which called for "THOUSANDS OF TENTS AND ALL RATIONS THAT CAN BE SENT" and advised that 100,000 were homeless, it had effectively superseded it. This was less disastrous than might have been expected, since Humphrey had been a little vague about the "thousands of tents." (There were, after all, 3000 tents at the Presidio of San Francisco, where supplies for the Philippines were stored; why didn't Funston use *them?* He sent a telegram to find out.) He had ordered all those available at Vancouver Barracks; that amounted to 477 tents.

With the arrival of the second telegram, General Humphrey knew that tents for at least 20,000 were required; those ordered from Vancouver would not be enough. Tents for 20,000 . . . Humphrey gave instructions for orders to be sent to all the departments to send tents, and as the dawn began to break in Washington the telegrams were going out: COMMANDING GENERAL DEPARTMENT OF DAKOTA, SHIP BY EXPRESS TO DEPOT QUARTERMASTER SAN FRANCISCO ALL WALL, CONICAL AND HOSPITAL TENTS NOW AT FORT SNELLING . . . COMMANDING GENERAL DEPARTMENT OF LAKES, SHIP ALL WALL, CONICAL AND HOSPITAL TENTS NOW AT FORT SHERIDAN . . . COMMANDING GENERAL DEPARTMENT OF MISSOURI . . . COMMANDING GENERAL DEPARTMENT OF COLORADO . . . DEPARTMENT OF TEXAS . . .

General Humphrey's instructions had been to send the orders to *all* the departments, and to all they went, including one to General Funston, the Commanding General of the Department of California, who was directed to "SHIP BY EXPRESS TO DEPOT QUARTERMASTER SAN FRANCISCO ALL WALL, CONICAL AND HOSPITAL TENTS . . ."

General Sharpe, the Commissary General, had already gone home to sleep. He had ordered 200,000 rations from Vancouver and that was enough to feed Funston's 20,000 people for ten days. There was nothing more for him to do.

THREE

Thursday, April 19, 1906

▲▲▲

Dawn came Thursday morning to San Francisco almost
unheeded by the thousands of fire fighters or by the refugees. There were nearly 200,000 homeless now, exhausted
from a night of sleep caught on the ground in the parks and
plazas or in the streets. It was a beautiful day, but there was
no sign of it in San Francisco; such a heavy cloud of smoke
hung over the city that it seemed dull and overcast. Only
those on the hills, looking down at the bay where the water
sparkled in the sunshine, could tell what kind of a day it
was.

Behind the fire line, hundreds of acres now lay in ruins
from Octavia Street, west of Van Ness Avenue, to the waterfront. The entire business district of San Francisco had been
destroyed. The huge bonfires the buildings on the north side
of Market had made during the night were over except for
an occasional fire like the one still raging in the basement of
the Hobart Building, under what had been the Postal Telegraph office. Jutting empty shells loomed along both sides of
the street. The wholesale district was a shambles of leaning
and fallen walls and streets piled with rubble. South of Mar-

ket was "like a smoking Arizona desert," where for vast areas
it was not even possible to tell where the streets had been.
There were occasional walls, chimneys, and what were pre-
sumed to be the ruins of the Post Office and the Mint. Communications, even within the city, had reached such a state
that the authorities did not know these buildings had escaped. Far to the south an immense conflagration was roaring into the Mission district; how far, no one in the rest of
the city knew.

North of Market the fire was spreading like a huge, irregular black stain: one arm creeping toward Telegraph Hill;
another, having swept Chinatown to destruction, now making its way along the eastern slope of Russian Hill, through
the residential district there. Both these fronts were moving
very slowly, against the wind, about one block every two
hours. Two broad walls of fire from the east and south were
advancing on Nob Hill, and here the pace was much more
rapid. By seven o'clock Thursday morning it was clear that
the homes of the "Nabobs"—Nob, for short—who had given
the hill its name were doomed.

A great many very wealthy people lived on this "hill of
palaces," as Stevenson called it. California Street, as it
passed over the crest of the hill, had been taken by the railroad kings and the silver kings, who first gave the peak its
importance as they began to erect their mansions here in the
seventies. The Southern Pacific's president, Leland Stanford, had built a mammoth wooden dwelling set in a two-
acre lot at Powell and California. Then Stanford's partner,
thin-lipped, penny-pinching Mark Hopkins, had amazed
the city by giving way to his wife's long-denied ambitions
and erecting, side by side with the Stanford mansion, a hideous wooden jumble of turrets, towers and steeples. All this
was set on massive foundations; to counteract Nob Hill's
steepness the stone foundations on the Pine Street side

were as high as a three-story house. San Franciscans, who subscribed heartily to the principle of conspicuous consumption, found it very satisfying. Much finer, they thought, than the Huntington mansion on the other side of California Street, a severe Georgian structure with hardly any ornament at all. The million-and-a-quarter-dollar wooden mansion—"the delirium of a woodcarver"—of the fourth railroad king, Charles Crocker, beyond the Huntington house, was more suitable. What did it matter if rough-hewn, portly old Charles Crocker, buying paintings from the Gallery of the Medicis, insisted on speaking to Mr. Medici himself, or if he did not know whether his Gobelin tapestries "should be hung on the walls as paintings or on the floor as mats?"

The railroad kings were joined by the silver kings, or by James Flood, at least. Using the new brownstone just becoming popular back east, he built a forty-two-room residence at California and Mason and surrounded it with a $60,000 hand-wrought bronze fence which required one man's full time to keep polished. Across the street his partner, James Fair, made plans to build a house that would dwarf all the others, until a bitter divorce changed his mind. It was here that the five-million-dollar Fairmont stood, built by his daughter Tessie and now almost completed.

The railroad kings and the silver kings were gone long ago. Most of their houses were closed or devoted to public institutions. (They were, the *Overland Monthly* observed, "unsuited to California, where domestic servants are hard to get, incompetent and expensive.") Mark Hopkins had never even lived in the turreted wooden nightmare. His widow had married the young decorator who was responsible, perhaps, for the ebony-walled bedrooms inlaid with ivory and jewels. When she died he gave the house to the University of California and it was now the Hopkins Art Institute. Charles Crocker no longer surveyed the city from the 76-foot tower of his house; the "brass rail" fence no longer reminded Flood, as San Francisco claimed, of the days when he had tended bar at the Auction Lunch Saloon; Mrs. Stanford had died the year before, amid dark suspicions of poison.

Mayor Schmitz and the Police Department had headquartered on Nob Hill overnight, but they were gone too: the police down the hill to the North End Police Station on Washington Street near Van Ness; Mayor Schmitz for the moment holding office at a small table in the middle of the street at Sutter and Van Ness.

EXTRA Oakland Tribune. EXTRA

VOL. LXV   OAKLAND, CALIFORNIA, THURSDAY EVENING, APRIL 19, 1906   NO. 50

CITIZENS ARE FORCED TO FIGHT FLAMES AT POINT OF REVOLVER

Three hundred thousand persons will be left homeless in San Francisco by tonight. Help is needed at once.

This morning a young lieutenant named McMillan, with a group of sailors off the revenue cutter *Bear* who had reported to General Funston for duty, was in command of Nob Hill, and he was a man, so the *Oakland Tribune* reported later, with "a cool eye and a wicked looking pistol." While sailors and soldiers and firemen fought the approaching fire, drawing on the Hopkins Institute's 20,000-gallon cistern, Lieutenant McMillan was impressing helpers at gunpoint from the crowds in California Street in an effort to save the paintings and statues in the Institute. "Here, you fellows," he barked at a group of onlookers. "Hurry in there and get those paintings out." There was no reply. The lieutenant's long pistol came up. "Now you get over there, all of you, and hustle those paintings out. And I mean business."

"Are—are you swearing in deputies?" one man asked nervously.

"I don't have to swear 'em in when I need them," McMillan snapped. "I swear at them. Now git!"

Ordering one man after another into the building, he came to a fat man who protested, "But I'm a member of the Humane Society. See, here's my badge."

"This is humane work," McMillan told him shortly. "Get on in there and get busy."

The fat man joined the others, carrying out paintings and statuary and depositing them in the yard of the Flood mansion across the street. The fire was getting closer and closer; it was obvious that there was not enough time. At 8:00 Thursday morning flames bridged the vast open yard surrounding the Stanford house and it began to burn. At 8:20 they were sweeping up the fortresslike foundations of the Hopkins house, leaping into the wooden turrets, and it began to burn too.

They had not gotten nearly all the paintings out. Lieutenant McMillan went back out to get more men. Some responded willingly; some had no intention of being ordered around by anyone. One burly type snarled, "What business have you got to order us around?"

"You see this gun?" Lieutenant McMillan asked him. "Well, I think it's aimed right at your eye. Now come here, I want to have a little talk with you."

No talk was necessary; the gun carried its own message. "All right, boss," the man said quickly, and hurried on into the house.

"This is martial law," McMillan told the crowd. "I don't like it, you may not like it, but it goes."

As they continued getting paintings out and leaving them in the Flood yard, the fire, skirting the impregnable bastions of the Fairmont on the south and east, raced past it up Sacramento Street. From there the wind swept the flames back into the hotel and in a moment it was burning. Briefly the gleaming marble building "poured up volumes of smoke from the top alone, while the hundreds of windows were like plates of brass"; then it was engulfed in flame. Firemen had emptied the Hopkins cistern. Artillery officers with dynamite fell back to establish a "deadline street" at Clay and Mason. All the way over the crest and down the north side of Nob Hill residents were routed out of their houses.

The Flood mansion, surrounded by fire on three sides, was bound to go soon. The paintings, in their huge ornate frames, and the marble statuary from the Hopkins Institute still lay in the yard. There was no place to take them, no possibility of getting transportation to move them. One of the volunteers, Professor Edmond O'Neill, began to cut the canvases from their frames and roll them up. Without the frames he was able to get them away to safekeeping at the University of California in Berkeley. There was nothing to do about the statues; they remained in the yard as the flames swept over them into the Flood house.

All over San Francisco the dynamiting had continued through the night; it still continued in the murky light of the early morning. Families in block after block watched and knew that the time had come as an Army officer arrived, exchanged salutes with the sentry in the block, gave his brief instructions and hurried on. The sentry would turn and, making a megaphone of his hands, yell, "This street is going to be dynamited!" There would be only a few minutes to get away. The flames were moving west with ravenous intensity across the south face of Nob Hill, a sheet of fire that blotted out streets; through the flames it was impossible to see a hundred feet down Geary or Post Streets. A wall of heat preceded the fire itself; in the face of it papers lying in the streets half a block ahead burst spontaneously into flame. Gases formed and could not burn under flames so intense all the oxygen in the air was consumed; they rolled on up the street and mysteriously burst into flame, convincing people that arsonists were at work spreading the fire.

Streets where the fire was still blocks away were turbulent with crowds. On Larkin Street some of the neighborhood groceries had thrown open their doors. Crowds of people were stripping the shelves, returning to the street with whatever they had grabbed, sometimes realizing suddenly that there was no limit to what they could take and returning for more. Hunger was no respecter of station; doxies from the Uptown Tenderloin elbowed stately dowagers from fine mansions.

Not all of the grocery stores were open. At some, even nearer the fire, guards still patrolled to prevent looting. At one a crowd had gathered and there were yells of "You can't save the place; let us in!" and "Break down the door!" Someone was pushed against a glass window and it broke; while the guard's attention was diverted the doors gave way and people poured in. "The stuff would have burned anyhow," the guard shrugged. "It's better to let them have it."

In spite of the Mayor's prohibition rule, "a number of men were under the influence of liquor, some hopelessly so." (Among other misfortunes, the Keely-Cure had burned during the night.) Some of the area's prostitutes, not so concerned with food, were serving champagne—the Uptown Tenderloin had a better-class whore than those on the Barbary Coast, who by and large drank beer and sometimes wore diapers so they wouldn't have to leave the floor and miss any business. On Ellis Street a crowd had broken into a saloon looking for stronger stuff. They came out loaded, only to meet an Army lieutenant, who proceeded to break up the party. "Throw that booze into the street," he ordered, and went through the entire crowd smashing bottles. If he happened to smash one in a man's pocket, the *Examiner* reported, so much the better.

Broad Van Ness Avenue was streaming with refugees. Hundreds had taken refuge in the huge brick St. Mary's Cathedral (not the same as St. Mary's in Chinatown); others had left their trunks and belongings in its basement and gone back by way of East Street to the ferry. Autos piled high with bedding and hastily saved possessions honked constantly amid the crowds. In one curious means of transportation two men and three women had their goods loaded on a long ladder. One woman ran ahead and put rollers under the front and the others pushed the ladder along; it was good for fifteen feet each time. Drays loaded with furniture and swarming all over with men, women and children crowded express wagons, buggies and carts; but most people were on foot, their loads on their backs.

The crowds met and fought their way down the choking length of Bay Street to the waterfront. They flowed down East Street, joined by groups of Italians, the women with baskets on their heads, men with huge bundles. Horses fell, trying to avoid the rifts in the street. Auto tires burst and the drivers continued on the rims. All along the way people had dropped out and lay on the sidewalk or in doorways, some resting, some sleeping, some drunk. A great camp ground had sprung up under Telegraph Hill, swarming with broken-down outfits. The rest continued on their way, past the gaping crevices, partially boarded over, in front of Pier 22, past the topsy-turvy walls remaining from the burned-out district near the ferry, the twisted tracks of the belt railway, past ominous groups of tramps and toughs with soldiers watching them warily.

The waiting rooms of the Ferry Building were packed with people and so were the streets outside; some waited for hours for a chance to get aboard. All day long they went; the Southern Pacific estimated that on Thursday its ferries carried people out of the city at the rate of seventy a minute.

Elbowing his way through the crowds at one point early Thursday morning was Enrico Caruso, still clutching his picture of Theodore Roosevelt, trying to get through to where Scotti and some of the other singers were already in a launch, ready to leave for Oakland. Policemen guarding the gates failed to recognize the great tenor; fierce arguments had no effect; the President's picture, autographed, was produced, and the policemen, suitably impressed, allowed Caruso to pass. The opera company set off, with Caruso, it is said, turning to shake his fist at San Francisco.

Here and there in the burned districts behind the fleeing refugees various scattered groups were beginning inevitable tasks. Workers were beginning the search for bodies in the ruins. While Papa Coppa (his restaurant in the Montgomery Block was unharmed, but he could not, of course, light a fire in it) boiled a sheep's head in one corner of Portsmouth Square, making soup for the refugees, soldiers dug a shallow grave in another corner for a perfunctory burial of twenty-three bodies gathered from the ruins. Bodies lay, under makeshift coverings, on Market Street, waiting to be taken off. Along the blackened skeleton walls of Montgomery Street seventy cavalrymen stood guard against looters and bankers alike. The superheated vaults could not be opened for days yet; in those that were, papers burst into flame as the air rushed in.

The imperturbable Judge Morrow, President of the California Red Cross, had arrived once more from his home in San Rafael, but he was not concerned with Red Cross duties. He was a judge of the U.S. Circuit Court of Appeals, and he was on his way to open court. He made his way gingerly through the hot, smoldering ruins, noting with disapproval the buckled streetcar tracks, the gaping hole in Seventh Street, the fire-stained walls around the Post Office where refugees' trunks and possessions, left there for safety, had burned. It was worse as he went on into the Post Office Building to his office. The Court's library was a mess, bookcases fallen over, books strewn all over the floor. Judge de Haven's library (actually the only spot at which the fire had entered the building at all) was destroyed. Court opened, but was immediately postponed until May 7.

It occurred to Judge Morrow to try to get in touch with Mrs. Merrill, vice-president of the California Red Cross and head of the San Francisco chapter. Perhaps, although he did not mention it in his later account of his activities, he wondered what had become of the committees he had appointed, at a Red Cross meeting held in his courtroom the day before the earthquake, to be prepared for any future emergencies. In any case, he sent a messenger through the fire lines with a letter to Mrs. Merrill, but the messenger could not locate her or any of the Red Cross officers. Judge Morrow did not pursue the matter any farther.

Mrs. Merrill was at her home on Van Ness Avenue, feeding as many of the passing refugees as her imposing mansion would accommodate. Early in the morning she had gotten in touch with Dr. Girard, the San Francisco chapter's medical director, and together they had rounded up as many doctors and nurses as they could find and advised Mayor Schmitz that they were available. They were desperately needed: there were nearly seven hundred patients at the Presidio hospital alone. There, in a tent hospital that had sprung up overnight, doctors had worked the clock around without sleep. Soldiers looked after patients, brought food, stood guard. They had been on duty so long that when they were relieved they fell asleep on the ground where they dropped.

Beyond the tented hospital, thousands of refugees were spread over the Presidio grounds, tens of thousands more south of the Presidio in Golden Gate Park, still more thousands—an estimated five thousand in Jefferson Square alone —in the small parks and plazas. More thousands were arriving all the time. They began to make the first feeble efforts at providing shelter, and of necessity they were feeble indeed—an improvised tent of sheets or blankets, once only a tablecloth, suspended on four candlesticks. Reluctant indications of permanence appeared: small signs bearing name and former address hung over heaps of belongings, reserving that camp site for all the indefinite future.

They had spirit, though, in spite of all the inconveniences and discomforts. In a gesture that became habit throughout the refugee camps in the days to come, they began to hang up signs, wry or humorous or defiant, but hardly ever bitter, signs like "All Shook Up," or "Hotel Astor, Rooms for Rent," or "No Help Wanted—Do Not Inquire." Only rarely did someone hang out a sign like "Hard Luck Camp" or even "Home Was Never Like This." Not that they minimized their hardships; they savored them, another larger-than-life scene in the spectacle of San Francisco, at which they were both players and audience. One "well-known young lady of social position," when asked where she had spent the night, replied with some pride, "On a grave." An old lady testified with relish that her husband's sufferings at the battle of Vicksburg were nothing to hers now, but "I'm very comfortable, thank you," she added spryly. Rumors still went the rounds, but they were greeted with increasing skepticism. The story of the young man who cut off dead women's fingers for their rings drowned in a sea of exaggeration; he came to be known cheerfully as "Jay Ghoul & Co."

To be sure, one man committed suicide, but that was merely one of the more or less usual "Things To Do Today" in San Francisco, which, then as now, had one of the highest suicide rates in the country. Most people never looked back. This Thursday morning, and in the days to come, there were more important things to do. A couple applied for a marriage license, the first of seventy to be issued in San Francisco in the week after the earthquake. All the forms in the County Clerk's office had been burned; the licenses were painstakingly handwritten until a supply of forms could be borrowed from Oakland, "Alameda County" to be crossed out and "San Francisco County" substituted.

Confusion and disorder remained and grew worse through the day—the city's considerable population of criminals had as much spirit as anyone else—but morale in the parks stayed amazingly high. Let the panic-stricken abandon San Francisco, let the insurance companies fail (it was already taken for granted that at least twenty insurance companies would go out of business), their attitude was expressed by a sign one man tacked up in front of the odds and ends he had been able to save: "San Francisco Still In It."

There was only one thing that reviving spirits and good morale could not make vanish: real, aching hunger. By Thursday morning, hunger was acute. The grocery stores that had been thrown open and stripped fed only a fraction of the people who needed food. Others went from place to place seeking whatever they could find, pawing through the burned-out ruins of the California Cannery Company at

North Beach, perhaps, for a can of peaches. A good pro-
vider was one who brought back a couple of cans of sar-
dines and a box of crackers to his refugee family. In spite
of the stern treatment they could expect to receive from soldiers if caught, black marketing of food continued to flour-
ish; eggs—they had been thirty cents a dozen—might be
forty or fifty cents or even a dollar *each* this morning.

By nine o'clock a newspaper with the unfamiliar mast-
head *Call-Chronicle-Examiner* was being distributed
through the streets and in the parks; price ten cents to those
who had it, otherwise free. The stark headlines "SAN FRAN-
CISCO IN RUINS" and "ENTIRE CITY OF SAN FRANCISCO IN DANGER
OF BEING ANNIHILATED" were hardly news. Whether they were
sticking it out to the very last in their homes, or setting up
camp in the parks, or fleeing from the city, it was already a
deep-seated conviction with most people that the city would
be destroyed. They read it avidly, though; it was a vivid re-
counting of their own experiences on the first day of the disaster.

The newspapers in San Francisco had been faced with a
newspaperman's nightmare: the greatest natural catastrophe
that has ever happened in the United States and, by the end
of the day, not a single newspaper's presses left to print the
story. The three morning papers—they had faced each other
in a triangle on Market Street, the *Call* and the *Examiner* on
opposite corners of Third, the *Chronicle* across the street in
the Kearny-Post-Market triangle—had met in the *Bulletin*
office a few blocks up Kearny Street to discuss getting a paper out, though not on the *Bulletin*'s presses, since there was
no power to run them. Fire closed in on them and they had
to give up their temporary headquarters in the Bulletin
Building. They fell back to Oakland, made a deal with the
afternoon *Oakland Tribune,* and as reporters straggled
in from San Francisco with breathless accounts of the hor-

rors they had seen, began to piece together a four-page "Extra," a joint issue of the *Call-Chronicle-Examiner*.

It was a joint issue, but it gave a curious effect of three papers separately edited, each slightly disagreeing with the other. Three separate stories gave three different times for the earthquake's occurrence. Two articles disagreed even on the height of the Call Building: one called it fifteen stories, the other eighteen. (It was eighteen stories high, or nineteen if one counted the last unfinished floor in the dome.) It took many a liberty with the day's events, too: it reported, for example, that martial law had been declared, that President Roosevelt had done so in a telegram sent to Mayor Schmitz at nine o'clock Wednesday morning. Actually, the President had had little idea of what was going on in San Francisco, and none of what General Funston was doing; he had sent a telegram expressing his sympathy to Schmitz, which had not been delivered, and another to Governor Pardee, "HEAR RUMORS OF GREAT DISASTER THROUGH AN EARTHQUAKE AT SAN FRANCISCO, BUT KNOW NOTHING OF THE REAL FACTS. CALL UPON ME FOR ANY ASSISTANCE I CAN SEND."

But for all its discrepancies, its tendency to report as facts events which the reporters felt must have occurred, but actually had not—a tendency that grew much worse in the days that followed—it was a remarkable paper, put out in haste against unprecedented obstacles. More than half a century later it still comes alive with the shock of the day's events. They published only one joint issue; after that the papers went their separate ways.

Newspapermen were finding access to San Francisco considerably easier this morning. General Funston had (thanks to a little nudging from the War Department) relaxed his rule preventing anyone from entering the city. The Western Union workers had been allowed to return, too, and Captain

Wildman was busy issuing Signal Corps equipment from the vast stores Pacific Division Commander General Greely had piled up (it was typical of General Greely that once, as Chief of the Signal Corps during the Spanish-American War, when the Signal Officer in Manila requisitioned 100 miles of telegraph wire, Greely sent him 1000 miles) to them as well as to Postal Telegraph and Commercial Pacific Cable Co. With Signal Corps operators, instruments and material, Western Union was open for business again at noon Friday, Postal Telegraph on Saturday, and Commercial Pacific on Monday. Thursday, however, San Francisco depended on a single line, the line which at 8:30 Thursday morning the Southern Pacific was able to get operating from the Ferry Building.

The Phelan Building, where the California Department headquarters had been, had burned during the night. Most of the records had been moved to the Presidio; for his own headquarters Funston took over the commanding officer's quarters at Fort Mason, at the foot of Van Ness Avenue. Fort Mason became immediately the busiest place in San Francisco. "There was an awe-inspiring dignity about the place," one visitor reported, "with its many guards, military ensemble and the business-like movements of officers and men," but it is safe to say that tempestuous little General Funston did not share the "awe-inspiring dignity" of Fort Mason. He had been up all night, making his headquarters in the streets, close to the fire lines. When he appeared, hollow-eyed and rumpled, at Mason, it was to leaf hastily through the messages that had arrived from the War Department, fume angrily over some of them, make quick decisions. To Governor Pardee went a telegram:

BY DIRECTION OF THE SECRETARY OF WAR I HAVE NOTIFIED THE MAYOR OF OAKLAND TO HAVE ASSOCIATED PRESSMEN APPLY TO YOU

FOR PASSES TO VISIT SAN FRANCISCO. PLEASE ISSUE THEM UNDER MY DIRECTION, WHICH HAS BEEN SENT TO YOU THIS DATE.

The Governor of California began issuing passes permitting reporters and others to enter San Francisco "by authority of General Funston." Then, determined to prove his co-operation with the press, Funston went a step further, had facilities set up for the newsmen at Fort Mason, and ordered regular transportation made available to them between the Army docks at Mason and the Oakland pier.

The need for more soldiers was a constant problem. The ever-widening line of the fire, the ruins that must now be guarded, the large areas which the Army had undertaken to police, called for an army; most of the soldiers already in the city had been on duty twenty-four hours with little food and less sleep. Funston began to order soldiers in from every available spot: two infantry companies from Alcatraz, three Coast Artillery companies from Fort Baker, the recruits and casuals from the Angel Island Depot. New attempts were made to telegraph the Presidio of Monterey; it could not be reached.

There was no water in the pipes at Fort Mason, and Funston, constantly on the go throughout the city, knew how desperate the need was everywhere. He had managed to locate Hermann Schussler, superintendent of the city's water system, but Schussler had little encouragement to offer: some of the lines to the city's reservoirs in San Mateo County were so badly damaged that they would take two weeks to fix even if all the materials were available. With emergency repairs and a rerouted flow of water he had already managed to start bringing water from Lake Merced into the Western Addition, but there it was disappearing through broken mains and wrenched and disconnected household connections. The mains would have to be repaired, and all the Crystal Springs Water Company's maps had been destroyed; only Schussler himself knew where the mains were.

Restoring the water system in other sections, where every house that burned left another connection opened, would be even more of a problem. It was up to Funston to make whatever arrangements he could. A message went to Admiral McCalla asking if he could send fresh water from Mare Island. Orders were given to start an investigation of the available sources of water within the city: the lakes in Golden Gate Park, Lobos Creek in the southwest corner of the Presidio, any others to tide the city over until enough mains were repaired to put the city's water system back into at least limited operation.

At 9:11 Thursday morning General Funston's first telegram to the War Department was going out over the wire Captain Wildman had strung up to connect with the Southern Pacific wire at the ferry:

YOUR FOUR DISPATCHES RECEIVED. HAVE ALREADY FILED SEVERAL FOR YOU. IMPOSSIBLE NOW TO INFORM YOU AS TO FULL EXTENT OF DISASTER. CITY PRACTICALLY DESTROYED. TROOPS HAVE BEEN AIDING POLICE AND MAINTAINING ORDER. MARTIAL LAW HAS NOT BEEN DECLARED. WORKING IN CONJUNCTION WITH CIVIL AUTHORITIES. HAVE NOT INTERFERED WITH SENDING OF ANY DISPATCHES. YOU CANNOT SEND TOO MANY TENTS OR RATIONS. ABOUT 200,000 PEOPLE HOMELESS. FOOD VERY SCARCE. PROVISION HOUSES ALL DESTROYED. ALL GOVERNMENT BUILDINGS IN CITY GONE.

At ten o'clock, with the Fairmont, where they were to have met, on fire and the fire line stretching from there southwest across the face of Nob Hill and moving relentlessly toward Van Ness Avenue, the members of the Committee of Fifty were gathering at the North End Police Station on Washington Street, half a block from Van Ness. The narrow, cramped little station was crowded with people. Each member as he entered was given a policeman's star and a pass to cross Police and Army lines, and then joined the others waiting to talk to the Mayor. There was noise and confusion, people coming and going, refugees asking for water, dynamite-laden cars stopping for gasoline, policemen coming in for a meager breakfast of crackers.

The Committee members were gloomy and pessimistic; they faced all the responsibilities that the refugees fleeing through the streets to the parks and to the Ferry were leaving behind: how to provide food, shelter, order in a disintegrating city; how to stop the fire, which manifestly could not be stopped. One of the members, an insurance man, recalled that more than a year ago the National Board of Fire Underwriters had pointed out San Francisco's vulnerability to fire. "San Francisco has violated all underwriting tradition and precedent by not burning up," the Board had said. "That it has not done so is largely due to the vigilance of the Fire Department, which cannot be relied on indefinitely to stave off the inevitable." As he talked the gloom deepened. The Board's prediction, which insurance men had heeded no more than anyone else, had come to pass. The time had run out, the inevitable was upon them.

Mayor Schmitz was in the center of the steamy, crowded room, surrounded by men waiting to be told what to do. He was no longer the suave, handsome man who had learned to dress so well (while keeping such studied man-of-the-people touches as wearing a soft felt hat at top-hat affairs). He was haggard and drawn, his shirt was wilted, his suit wrecked. He had been up all night, but he was still going. He had a musician's temperament: he was too keyed up to stop. He was tough, demanding, impatient. He drove the Committee members in a manner he would never before have thought of using to the city's tycoons.

The immediate problems were food and shelter. A "Committee to Feed the Hungry" was appointed and told to get busy gathering food and distributing it. The Department of Public Works had wagons available, he pointed out. It would be a start if they were sent to San Mateo County for meat. Arrangements must be made immediately for whatever bakeries were left to start baking as much bread as they possibly could. The obstacles were formidable: flour must be obtained, probably from across the bay; earthquake-damaged equipment must be repaired, some means found to operate it without electricity. The Mayor would listen to no objections. Another group was directed to start work on bedding: to obtain fifty thousand cots of the simplest type, at least (a goal that was never reached).

By 11:30 Thursday morning a start had been made on a great many problems, a great many committees appointed, but no move had been made against the most immediate problem of all. No "Committee to Stop the Fire" had been appointed. While the Committee had been meeting the fire had circled around the top of Nob Hill. The roar of the flames, the hail of cinders, the thunder of dynamite all announced its approach. There was fire now at Jones Street, five blocks up the hill from refugee-choked Van Ness Avenue and the Committee's meeting place at the North End Police Station. Farther south it was closer to Van Ness: at Sutter Street it was only four blocks away, and from there it ate its way in an irregular line, closer and closer to Van Ness, until it reached Van Ness itself at Golden Gate, halted there by the burned-out ruins that remained from the Hayes Valley fire.

A few blocks away reporters were badgering John Dougherty, the acting Fire Chief, for a statement on the progress of the fire. He was weary and defeated, his Fire Department falling to pieces beyond his control. "More than two-thirds of the area of the city of San Francisco has been destroyed," he told them grimly, "and there is no prospect of saving the balance of the city."

It was a foregone conclusion that the city would be destroyed. Now there was nothing to lose by following the Army's advice to dynamite a broad strip ahead of the fire which, when the fire reached it, could not be crossed. For thirty hours Mayor Schmitz had insisted that dynamiting be limited to buildings immediately adjacent to those already burning; now he had made up his mind to take the desperate step. Just west of where they were meeting stretched Van Ness Avenue, one hundred and twenty-five feet wide, the widest street in the city. In a desperate gamble he was willing to give up everything that lay east of Van Ness—all of it sure to go anyway—to save the remaining major residential district of San Francisco, the homes of 150,000 people in the Western Addition. Now, he told the men standing around him, he intended to authorize the Army to dynamite the entire eastern side of Van Ness Avenue from Golden Gate Avenue to the bay, which with the width of Van Ness itself would create a barrier so wide that the fire could not cross it, so long that it could not go around.

Immediately there was loud opposition to the plan from men who the moment before had taken it for granted that the fire would destroy the entire city, east and west of Van Ness. But Van Ness Avenue contained the finest residences in the city, great apartment houses, churches, they insisted. Several of the Committee members lived on Van Ness. Blowing up the twenty-five-block stretch would be destroying the equivalent of a rich city in itself. Look at the Merrill mansion on the corner, crammed with treasures brought back from travels throughout the world. Would he allow that to be blown up? The very building they were in now would be destroyed if his plan were carried out. And what

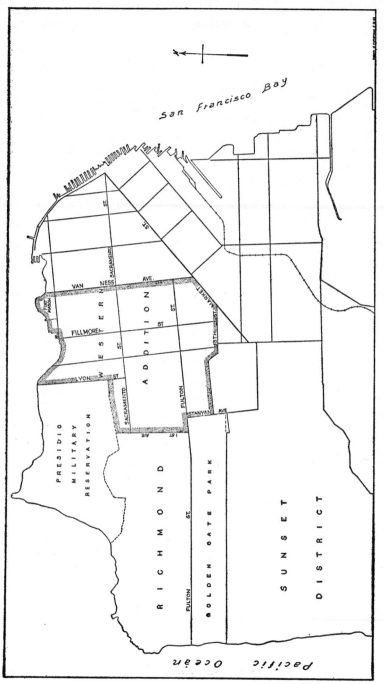

The last major residential area of San Francisco:
the Western Addition, home of about 150,000 people

had dynamiting accomplished up to now? The Army had done more harm than good, the firemen didn't know how to handle dynamite. . . . The Mayor could answer all these questions with a brief question of his own: What else was there to do?

The meeting broke up with the Committee members' uneasy agreement to the Mayor's plan. There was sufficient optimism to schedule another meeting at 4:30 Thursday afternoon, but not at the North End Police Station; by 4:30 that would have been destroyed. Driven, like everything else, still farther ahead of the fire, they agreed to meet in Franklin Hall, a little dance hall seven blocks west of Van Ness— provided that was still standing at 4:30.

Mayor Schmitz wasted scant time in dismissing the group. While they were still straggling out he was sending for Colonel Morris, whom General Funston had placed in command of the Army forces deployed against the fire. It might have been better to consult with General Funston himself, but Schmitz was already finding—as a great many people had found before him—that Funston was not the easiest man in the world to give orders to. The Army forces were nominally under control of the civil authorities, and Colonel Morris was in command of these forces; for the moment, although it was a plan which General Funston had long advocated, Schmitz chose to deal with Morris to put it into effect.

At noon Thursday the scattered fires on Jones Street, five blocks above the North End Police Station, had grown into solid blocks of fire as far as California. At California they had leaped a block farther west to Leavenworth, then closer and closer to Van Ness farther south. At Ellis they had reached Polk Street, only a block from Van Ness. Hurriedly Schmitz told Colonel Morris what he wanted to accomplish, and Morris quickly agreed. From now on every effort would be directed toward halting the fire at Van Ness.

What dynamite there was in the city was scattered in a dozen different locations. The haphazard, disorganized dynamiting was ordered stopped. The Mayor issued orders for launches to go immediately to Contra Costa County for new stocks, sufficient to handle the vast job of demolishing a fire barrier at Van Ness. John Dougherty was ordered to assemble such firemen as he could muster, to be ready at Van Ness. Soldiers fanned out into the intervening streets, into Polk, Larkin, and Hyde, to order people out of houses and apartments, out of the stores along Polk Street—leaving the stocks behind to burn, as many a hungry refugee would remember later. More soldiers began to go through the Western Addition, warning residents to open their windows so that they would not be broken by the shock of the forthcoming dynamite blasts.

In all the furious preparations for the stand at Van Ness there was a sense of waiting for a supreme test that was yet to come. Below Market, though, where the fires had swept west and south into the Mission district, there was no such waiting. Against a conflagration more intense than that which threatened the Western Addition soldiers, firemen, volunteers, isolated from the rest of the city, were fighting to save a district already written off as hopeless. There was no time to stop and estimate the hopelessness of the situation. They could only fight furiously, frantically, with every means available: dynamite, water from private water tanks, water saved in bathtubs, sacks of flour, mud, bare hands. Make a stand, fall back, make another stand. At twelve noon Thursday, while preparations were being made to dynamite Van Ness Avenue, they were dynamiting at Fourteenth and Mission to stave off the fire from the Southern Pacific Hospital, the St. Francis Hospital and the College of Physicians and Surgeons. The fire raced on past and these buildings were saved—but it would be back to destroy them later.

The fire spread in every direction. On the east, a desperate stand at Howard Street, where a pool of water had collected from a broken main, kept it from crossing there, only to have it spread west and south in the still, windless afternoon. It moved so quickly, spurted so unpredictably, that it took people unaware. Firemen coming up to a house on Guerrero Street to order the occupants out found a note pinned under the doorbell to "May," telling her that at 2:00 Ethel had gone to Bessie's in Capp Street, three blocks away. At 2:30 Capp Street was burning.

On Van Ness Avenue, the minutes dragged slowly on as they waited for the dynamite to arrive. Circumstances, second thoughts, brought changes. The northern half of Van Ness, and the part of the city lying east of it—Russian Hill with its scattered houses in huge yards, Telegraph Hill spread over in happy confusion with the shanties of Mexicans, Spaniards, Irish and Italians; and North Beach with its warehouses—were actually not in danger. The Nob Hill fire had not gone beyond Clay Street. East of Nob Hill it had reached as far as Vallejo, but there some soldiers and firemen had fought it to a standstill, using 50,000 gallons of water from cisterns in the street, and elsewhere it was moving so slowly that it seemed likely it could be contained. Consequently it was decided not to dynamite north of Washington Street, a little more than halfway up Van Ness.

That left a strip a mile long from Golden Gate to Washington on which the fire was bearing down with terrifying intensity. At 12:30 it was a block closer to Van Ness, stretching diagonally from Leavenworth and Clay down to Larkin and Sutter. At 1:30 it had advanced still another block: it had reached Hyde on the north; on Sutter it was at Polk, a block from Van Ness; from O'Farrell south it had reached Van Ness. Still the dynamite had not come, and everything stood still as more and more of Van Ness Avenue fell under the onslaught of the fire. The flood of refugees had come to a halt; the streets of the Western Addition, which had teemed all morning with hurrying crowds, were empty. In Van Ness Avenue the fire engines were drawn up, steam burning low, waiting; the firemen lay asleep in the street.

Gradually the Mayor's plan, which had had all the brilliant simplicity and plausibility of a campaign slogan—"Blow Up Van Ness and Save the Western Addition"—was falling apart. To the worried officials watching the fire race down the side of Nob Hill, Mayor Schmitz, Colonel Morris, acting Fire Chief Dougherty, and Captain Coleman, the Army's ordnance officer in charge of dynamiting, it seemed that if the dynamite did not come soon, it would be too late.

Once again it was up to the ever-resourceful Lieutenant Briggs, Captain Coleman's assistant, to go to the waterfront to see what had happened to the dynamite. The answer, as far as Lieutenant Briggs could learn, was that in spite of Mayor Schmitz' order, no boat had left for dynamite. He went immediately to General Funston at Fort Mason; together the red-headed little general and the lanky lieutenant raced to the Army dock, fighting their way through the milling crowds on the pier. The *Slocum*, with three hundred refugees aboard, was about to pull out for Oakland. At General Funston's order the passengers were dumped ashore, the *Slocum* dispatched to Pinole for dynamite.

Briggs started back to where the authorities were waiting, but by now all hope of co-ordinated action was disappearing in the face of the leaping flames and fantastic confusion, the noise and the smoke. The defense of Van Ness Avenue was deteriorating into a series of major and minor skirmishes, individual actions which held the fire back at some points and, by clinging with appalling blindness to the original plan, advanced it in others.

Individuals who would never have dreamed of such action before set out to take matters into their own hands. One of these, Franklin K. Lane (later, as Secretary of the Interior, he would be known as "the great conservationist") was standing on the slope of Russian Hill, talking to a contractor named Anderson, and watching the fire approach Van Ness. To Franklin Lane, absent from the morning's meeting at the North End Police Station, and completely unaware of how anxiously the Army and the civil authorities were waiting for dynamite, stopping the fire seemed perfectly simple. Why didn't they just dynamite a strip that the fire couldn't cross?

"It could be stopped right here . . . I'd take the chance myself if we could get any explosives," he told Anderson.

"Well, there's a launch full of dynamite from Contra Costa County lying right now at Meiggs Wharf," Anderson replied. At that point Tom Magee and his wife arrived, driving their car on its wheel rims. Lane sent them off to Meiggs Wharf, at the foot of Powell Street, for the dynamite while he and Anderson found an electric battery and cut some loose wires from a telephone pole. The Magees returned with a car full of dynamite, Mrs. Magee carrying the detonators in her lap.

They laid the dynamite and strung the wires. "How do you want the house to fall?" asked Anderson. "Send her straight up," chortled Lane. Up it went, intact, twenty feet in the air. It was all "like a scene in a fairy book" to Lane, and he and his cohorts went gleefully "down the line, blowing up houses, churches, schools."

Meanwhile Lieutenant Briggs had arrived to tell Mayor Schmitz and Captain Coleman that the dynamite was on its way—the *Slocum,* which General Funston had dispatched from Mason, not the boat which had arrived unknown to them at Meiggs Wharf and was being briskly unloaded by the Magees. Soldiers began to order the last evacuees out of the fine houses and apartments on the east side of Van Ness in preparation for the dynamiting.

Tradition has it that they went with their heads up, these stubborn millionaires who had waited until the last to leave their mansions, and it is true that many of them, when the orders came, were proud, gallant figures who left their assembled treasures without a backward glance or a murmur of complaint. There were people like Mrs. Merrill, the Red Cross vice-president, who, when soldiers came to tell her that she had half an hour to save what she could before her house was blown up, gestured to the refugees who crowded the house and replied quietly, "All right, but thirty minutes will give me time to feed them." There were just as many, however, who, even now, refused to face the fact that if the dynamite didn't get them, the fire would. They begged, they argued; the Army was "time and again outflanked and importuned by property-owners looking after their own interests," and when they went they went no farther than Franklin Street, a block west.

It was three o'clock Thursday afternoon. Everything was ready for dynamiting, but there was still no dynamite. In desperation, unable to wait any longer, still determined to raze a strip which the fire could not cross, it was decided to set fire to the houses. Soldiers set to work; as one man watching from across the street recorded it, "a soldier would, with a vessel like a fruit dish in his hand, containing some inflammable stuff, enter the house, climb to the second floor, open the front window, pull down the shade and curtain, and set fire to the contents of his dish." If the fire started slowly, soldiers would throw bricks and stones up to break windows and start a draft. Usually it took about twenty minutes for a building to get well on fire; by 3:30 nearly all the houses from Bush to Washington were on fire. Quite a few of the soldiers were in a "hilarious condition," too; indignant observers insisted that all too many of them had stopped in the wine cellars on their way through the houses.

4:30   THE OAKLAND HERALD   LAST
EDITION

FOURTH YEAR VOL. VII. NO. 17.   THE OAKLAND HERALD; THURSDAY EVENING, APRIL 19, 1906.   PRICE FIVE CENTS.

RAGING FLAMES STILL SPREAD; ALL SAN FRANCISCO SEEMS DOOMED

Great City Is Laid Waste by one of Worst Conflagrations in the History of Country

Spectators Appalled by Scenes of Terror Now Being Enacted in the Metropolis of the West

As the houses began to blaze on Van Ness the fire that had been roaring down Nob Hill spread out along Polk Street, one block east of Van Ness. There was still a chance that fire fighters could keep the Van Ness fire under control, have it out by the time the fire approached from behind it, and thus create the unbridgeable gap, as anticipated. But now, for incomprehensible reasons, the Fire Department chose to use the twenty kegs of black powder which still remained from the previous morning, carted up one side of Nob Hill from Portsmouth Square to the Fairmont Hotel and then down the other side to the North End Police Station. While flames took one side of Polk Street firemen used black powder to blow up the other and, as the houses blew up, they burst into flames.

The entire side of Nob Hill was now a solid mass of flames. Van Ness Avenue, both sides of Polk Street, all the streets above them to the top of the hill were on fire. Smoke and flame rose in towering masses that could be seen a hundred miles at sea. Corrugated iron buildings went up in a flash. The cable cars, which had been run out of the carhouse at Pine and California, were overtaken; the cars burned, the tracks melted, the fire struck through the asphalt paving of the streets and shattered the stone foundations underneath. Above the flames pigeons flew frantically, looking for safety.

The fire swept back over the top of Nob Hill to destroy what remained from the morning, hurrying through the Sherwood house, the Whittell house, consuming the furniture laboriously carried out of the houses and then left behind in the streets. It engulfed the Crocker mansion, destroying priceless art treasures: the servants had saved Millet's "The Man with the Hoe," but they had left behind Rubens' "The Holy Family" and many another magnificent painting, and Lieutenant McMillan, who had made such explosive efforts to save the relatively valueless paintings in the Hopkins Art Institute, had made no attempt to save them. It was not his job to save private property. One by one the others fell. The Fairmont Hotel and the Flood house were the only buildings on the top of the hill not made of wood. Their shells remained; otherwise Nob Hill was swept clean.

Down the hill, as the flames rose in ever-increasing intensity, it was but a matter of minutes before the fire would cross Van Ness. It *was* across briefly: flames started up in the steeple of St. Mary's Cathedral, beyond the reach of the feeble stream of water from the fire engine. Volunteers were called for to climb up in the steeple; no one came forth. As the fire leaped up about the cross at the pinnacle of the steeple, two priests, Father Ramm and Father O'Ryan, made their way up the steep steps, armed with axes. Old Archbishop Montgomery followed them up as far as the last landing. From there the priests crawled up the ladder, past the menace of the huge copper bell whose moorings might burn away at any moment and send it crashing down on them, on up to hack at the burning patches in the roof, chopping away until the fire was gone and then staying there to guard against any new danger.

While the priests worked to save St. Mary's, at O'Farrell Street, the line had been breached at California. "FIRE CROSSED VAN NESS AVENUE TO THE WEST," General Funston telegraphed Washington. "ALMOST CERTAIN NOW ENTIRE CITY WILL BE DESTROYED."

Finally the dynamite arrived. Army teams, pulling wagonloads of dynamite from across the bay, appeared, making their way cautiously over the seamed stretches of Van Ness Avenue from Fort Mason. It was too late: too late to stop the fire at Van Ness, too late to save the rest of San Francisco. Most of the firemen had disappeared. There remained only citizen volunteers and the Army, and they, like the firemen, had fought the fire for more than thirty hours; they were reeling with fatigue. But "the real test of morale of troops," to quote General Funston, "is the ability to bring them again and again to face the music, to face almost inevitable defeat." They prepared to face the music again here, this time on Franklin Street, a block west of Van Ness, and defeat was almost inevitable. Unlike 125-foot-wide Van Ness, Franklin was a narrow street, lined with wooden buildings. (But then, when the fire finally ended, its eleven-mile perimeter was almost entirely along narrow streets, and 96 per cent of the buildings it faced were of wood.)

Working with furious haste against the imminent onslaught of the fire, soldiers drove the remaining occupants out of the houses for seven blocks along Franklin, from Clay to Sutter. The dynamiting began again. In spite of the confusion and disorder, and the need for speed, this time it moved deliberately, as though they knew they were having their last chance: the wind and the encroachment of the fire were considered, the houses whose demolition would check the fire were selected.

While the dynamiting went on, fire fighters worked desperately with everything available to keep the fire from leaping into the debris from the dynamiting in Franklin Street, to keep it back where it had not already crossed Van Ness. Isolated little groups fought along Van Ness, swarming all over buildings to protect them, falling back against the intense heat from the fire across the street, giving up in one location, beginning again in another. Franklin K. Lane, having deferred to the Army in the dynamiting of San Francisco, was directing a small band of volunteers on the lower stretch of Van Ness, using the little water that remained in cisterns there to soak blankets, stretching the wet blankets over roofs and eaves against the showers of sparks. Even so, the fire was taking hold. The water mains were empty here, or supposedly so, but Lane "had a hunch, just a hunch, that there was water somewhere in the pipes." Even if there was, it would stay there unless firemen and fire engines could be gotten. Lane had heard that there was a fire company asleep somewhere on a haystack in the Western Addition. He set out to locate them. They were sound asleep when he found them; "they lay like dead men." Undaunted, he kicked the soles of one fireman, got only a grunt, kicked another fireman's soles, finally managed to wake one up and talk him into coming back to the fight.

The fireman got a wrench, and he and Lane went from one hydrant to another in the streets of the Western Addition, turning on the cocks. Nothing happened. The mains were empty. They had tried five or six without results; the fireman was getting cranky and ready to leave. Lane insisted. They tried another one, and out spurted a full head of water. "No one knows to this day where that water came from, but it was there." (Quite a few people did know, of course. Hermann Schussler's repairs on the water mains, carried on unceasingly all Wednesday night and all day Thursday—and spurred on, perhaps, by the fact that his home, at 1905 Van Ness, was in the path of the fire—were beginning to show results. Water was reaching a few of the hydrants, and Lane had happened to hit one of them.)

"It will take three engines to pump it to that blaze," said the fireman. Lane and Anderson, his fellow dynamiter, set off to get the engines. Twenty minutes later, when Lane returned with an engine and company, two other companies were already there, but their hoses were still not connected; they were having an argument over which company, under the rules of the department, should have the position of honor next to the fire hydrant. After a stormy session both companies coupled up the hose; with it they were able to hold one link in the line, keep the fire back until the danger across the street died down.

This was a help and a desperately needed one, although it did not, as Franklin Lane thereafter took credit for doing, singlehandedly save the Western Addition. In a dozen spots other groups were fighting. It was part of the wild unreality of this cataclysmic afternoon that no one knew what anyone else was doing. They acted as impulse drove them, isolated individuals or in little groups. Only the Army remained as a united, cohesive force, hurrying through the murky darkness (under the pall of smoke night had seemed to begin in the middle of the afternoon) to demolish one house after another along Franklin and on the cross streets between Franklin and Van Ness. At five o'clock Thursday afternoon the dynamiters were moving to Clay Street to close off the northern end of the fire gap by destroying the houses on Clay in the block between Franklin and Van Ness

—leaving, of course, Claus Spreckels' huge stone house on the corner of Clay and Van Ness, since it was fireproof.

Not everyone had left the houses on these streets. Again there were the soldiers banging on the doors, the harsh orders, "Get out of that house," arguments, entreaties, refusals. One testy old man named James Stetson (the head of the California Street cable-car system) told a soldier, "But this is my house and I have a right to stay here if I choose."

"Get out damned quick and make no talk about it, either," the soldier told Stetson, and marched him up to Gough Street with a bayonet at his back. Once they reached Gough Street it was easy enough for Stetson to escape from the guard among the throngs of people. Very much ruffled and indignant he slipped away and returned to his house, a large wooden mansion on the north side of Clay Street at Van Ness. There he watched while the earth shook at the explosions across the street. (He meticulously noted that the jar from the blasts had destroyed twelve plates and fifty-four windows in his house).

It was 5:40 P.M. when Stetson returned to his house. As far as he could see down Van Ness the street was deserted; the heat was too intense for anyone to stay. Across the street the steeple of the Presbyterian Church had fallen in; three blocks farther down the Marie Antoinette Apartments were a massive column of fire. In the streets west of Van Ness conditions were chaotic, refugees, fire fighters, hurrying demolition teams, the sprawling bodies of wounded soldiers—half a dozen soldiers were injured as one house exploded; a Dr. Edwards ran up to treat them and another explosion went off and put out his eye. General Funston, on his horse, pausing long enough to read with astonishment one of the telegrams from Washington a courier had brought him, asking the whereabouts and welfare of various people, wondering how anyone in this mad confusion could be expected to know what was happening to this personal friend or that personal friend of someone in Washington, or what had become of the sons of President Diaz and Vice President Corral of Mexico, who were presumably somewhere in San Francisco; then with rare self-control dictating a reply, "ACCOUNT CONFUSION IT HAS BEEN IMPOSSIBLE TO LOCATE INDIVIDUALS INQUIRED FOR BUT ATTENTION WILL BE GIVEN TO THE MATTER AS SOON AS POSSIBLE."

South, in the Mission district, conditions were equally chaotic. By now the Southern Pacific Hospital at Fourteenth and Mission, which fire fighters and dynamiters had worked so hard to save and which at noon had been considered out of danger, was burning. It had been abandoned long ago and its patients (including Fire Chief Sullivan, unconscious, dying, still unaware of what was happening to San Francisco) had been taken to the Presidio. The hundreds of boys, "friendless boys looking for jobs," who lived in the Youth's Directory which the priests maintained on Nineteenth Street had been led out into the hills. Fifty thousand people had left their homes and were huddling in steep Mission Park, beyond Dolores Street between Eighteenth and Twentieth, or trudging on to the hills at Buena Vista Park, or Mount Parnassus or the slopes of Twin Peaks. Behind them they could see the flames reaching out along Seventeenth Street, then Fifteenth, then Sixteenth, toward Dolores.

In the Western Addition, new hordes, frightened by the breaching of Van Ness, apprehensive that the fire in the Mission would sweep up on them (although there were the thirty burned blocks from the Hayes Valley fire between them), were leaving their houses, heading for the parks or abandoning the city altogether. A hundred thousand people had crowded into the 1013 acres of Golden Gate Park. Thousands more refugees piled into the sand lots above Fort Mason. Floods of them descended on the Fort itself until the post was "swamped" with them. General Funston had sent out orders to scour the bay for every available boat; they left in an endless stream, alternately to the Ferry Building and directly across the bay.

At Fort Mason General Funston was busy with a hundred importuning problems: refugees, food, more soldiers, communications. Tents to be issued from Army stores until the sand lots and little Lobos Square (one day to be known as Funston Playground) became a tented city. More to be issued at the Presidio: 3000 tents, 1000 blankets, all the stores accumulated to supply the troops in the Philippines. But these would not even begin to shelter the refugees. Soldiers' barracks were turned over to the refugees, tents issued on strict priority, first to the ill, then to nursing mothers (of which there were an increasing number, eight babies being born at Fort Mason alone Thursday night).

At place after place in the stricken city order was stretching close to the breaking point. Theft, extortion, looting were going on. In the stress of the afternoon minds had snapped. A policeman clearing an area suddenly went berserk and began to fire shots in every direction. Twenty-seven people had been taken to Oakland to be committed as insane. Shots rang out again and again, but none of the authorities knew what was going on; not a single policeman had made a regular report all day. Everywhere there was a heavy film of ashes. People sat in ashes, slept in ashes, covered their eyes against the showers of sparks and cinders that descended on them. They were desperate for food; it was Thursday night, two whole days since people had had any normal sources of food.

That problem had outweighed all others when the handful of Committee members met at 4:30 this Thursday afternoon at Franklin Hall. Rabbi Voorsanger, the head of the Subcommittee to Feed the Hungry, speaking excitedly in his thick Dutch accent, had to admit that none of the plans formulated at the morning's meeting had as yet borne fruit. No one knew what to do. Most of the Committee members themselves were hungry. Thousands of people were standing in line at bakeries not yet operating, which even when they resumed baking could not supply a tenth of them. Hundreds of thousands of Army rations were on their way from Vancouver; they would arrive Friday. An Army Commissary officer had left for Los Angeles to buy two hundred thousand rations, which would arrive, eventually. Governor Pardee was sending frantic telegrams to other California towns, "FOR GOD'S SAKE SEND COOKED FOOD TO SAN FRANCISCO," which would result in an avalanche of food—but not tonight.

EXTRA San Francisco Examiner **EXTRA**

SAN FRANCISCO, FRIDAY, APRIL 20, 1906.

300,000 ARE HOMELESS, HUNGRY AND HELPLESS

THE SPIRIT OF SAN FRANCISCO

Reluctantly Mayor Schmitz made another decision, agreed to still another violation of private property for the general welfare. His standing instructions to the Army had been to prevent looting of stores in the unburned areas of the city and with varying degrees of success they had done so, frequently standing guard long after the owners had abandoned their stores and left the city. Now, at the Mayor's instructions, teams set out, two soldiers and a policeman to each, to commandeer whatever remained in the stores, to tear open those that were locked, assemble the goods and distribute it to the refugees. There was little enough left:

men fought over a sack of walnuts, stood in line to be doled out pickles from a pickle barrel, or a jar of olives, and were glad to get them.

These supplies were distributed from the YMHA, at Page and Stanyon Streets, near the entrance to Golden Gate Park, which Rabbi Voorsanger, his long coattails flapping and his black beard bristling with activity, made his headquarters. On the other side of the city three soldiers were taking relief matters into their own hands with much the same results. Privates McGinty and Ziegler had been cut off by the fire from the rest of their company; joined later by Private Johnson, they found themselves at North Beach among crowds of refugees, mostly Italians and a few Chinese and Japanese. There was no force to guard the few stores in this area; they were being looted by some of the refugees while thousands of others went hungry. As they sized up the situation the soldiers, three privates among three thousand refugees, took charge of the situation, commandeered the stocks in all the stores, drafted help at gun point to carry the goods to the corner of Bay and Jones Street where they established their own relief station and began the orderly distribution of what food there was available. They were endlessly resourceful: before the Army found them they had organized their camp, established a bakery, distributed food, and improvised shelter for hundreds.

Soldiers were spread all over the city now, fighting the fire, dynamiting, handling refugees, policing the streets of the Western Addition. General Funston had already ordered troops all the way from Vancouver Barracks to proceed to San Francisco. He made still another effort to reach the Presidio of Monterey, unsuccessful; sent a telegram to Washington, "MY TELEGRAM TO MONTEREY NOT DELIVERED. CAN YOU NOT COMMUNICATE WITH THEM FROM WASHINGTON

AND ORDER TO REPORT AS SOON AS POSSIBLE. ALL THE CAVALRY
WANTED AND TWO BATTALIONS INFANTRY WITH ALL AVAILABLE
RATIONS."

The need for more soldiers was not a matter on which
everyone agreed. Just as Mayor Schmitz was nursing a growing resentment against General Funston's independent,
highhanded methods, feelings were beginning to rise among
the people of San Francisco against the soldiers, and even
more so against the less disciplined National Guard. The
soldiers were necessarily harsh in their efforts to maintain
order. There were rigid restrictions against moving about in
the city. Occasionally soldiers lapsed into drunkenness and
brutality, National Guardsmen went off into wild shooting
sprees—generally at nothing—which frightened the surrounding neighborhood. Their actions wore increasingly uncomfortably on those who came in contact with them. On
the other hand, illogically enough, many people felt there
should be more soldiers, as protection against the growing
lawlessness in the city.

With the city on the verge of destruction, with authority
being exercised by many who, people could tell themselves,
had no right to it, it was easy to rationalize taking the law
into one's own hands. Out in the Western Addition an adventurer named Donald Gedge, who claimed to have fought
with the French Army, the U.S. Navy and in the Chinese
rebellion, had organized 130 men into a "Vigilante Committee" with the announced purpose of challenging U.S. troops
and preventing lawlessness. They had already arrested one
soldier, accused of patrolling while drunk, disarmed and
handcuffed him, and turned him over to the Army.

Gedge's was the first of a number of such groups. Some
were effective in their efforts to maintain order. Others were
hotheaded, reckless gangs resented fully as much as the
Army or the National Guard. They were supposed to protect

the people; within a few days people would be requesting protection from the Army against their would-be protectors.

The problem had not reached serious proportions Thursday night, but General Funston was already aware of it. All he could do was to deal severely with erring soldiers, maintain a strict hands-off policy regarding the National Guard, and keep up his efforts to get more troops to take the pressure off those already on duty. Small reinforcements continued to arrive, sailors as well as soldiers. At seven o'clock Thursday evening the *Chicago*, flagship of the Pacific Squadron, arrived after a two-day journey at top speed from San Diego. A party was landed as soon as the ship docked at Fort Mason, to offer the Navy's services; they were instructed to come ashore at dawn Friday morning, the 60 Marines to report to Colonel Karmany (whose Marine detachment from Mare Island was already under Army command) and the 262 sailors to report to General Funston at Mason. The Navy became immediately useful in speeding communications. A Signal party came ashore and sailors began to wigwag messages down from Mason to the *Chicago*, to be transmitted by wireless from the *Chicago* to Mare Island and thence to their destination—a cumbersome system but necessary to relieve the overloaded and undependable line from the Ferry.

Even by this means Monterey could not be reached. At General Funston's request, Admiral Goodrich sent the destroyer *Preble* hurrying south in a five-hour trip to deliver the message to Monterey to start marching for San Francisco. (For obscure reasons, the *Preble* brought no soldiers back; it left them to make the hundred-mile trip as best they could by land.)

Meanwhile the fight against the fire continued unabated. In an effort to keep it from going any farther north the Merrill house, at Washington and Van Ness, had been dynamited again and thoroughly demolished this time. Behind it the Wenban residence, facing on Jackson, had also been dynamited. Both houses burned furiously, but the fire was not getting across Jackson Street; when the Wenban house caved in at 6:55, it appeared that the dynamite had effectively stopped the northward progress of the fire along Van Ness.

But the major effort was to defend the Western Addition, and there was never a moment's relief; turned back in one spot, the fire burst its bounds in another. A few minutes later the Spreckels stable on Sacramento Street began to burn; flames spurted through the hay-filled building and at 7:30 spread from there to the dynamited ruins on Clay Street between Franklin and Van Ness. Faced by the blazing buildings on two sides (although the Spreckels house on the opposite corner was not burning) cranky, stubborn old James Stetson kept solitary vigil in his big wooden house at Clay and Van Ness, hot-footing it back and forth from the front windows to the side windows to watch the progress of the fire, glancing at the buckets of water he had lined up and ready in the front and rear rooms (his son had thoughtfully brought the water from Golden Gate Park before he left for cooler climates), an improvised swab in hand ready to pounce on any little fire that started up. The walls grew too hot to touch; outside the paint melted until it hung festooned across the windows like draperies, but Stetson had no intention of leaving.

Up until now they had managed to hold the fire at Franklin Street. They continued dynamiting, choosing buildings one by one as a new danger point arose, fighting to keep fire from catching them, fighting to keep it under control when, inevitably, it did; dynamiting the cross streets between Franklin and Van Ness to complete the fire barrier. Captain Coleman was everywhere, driving property owners out of the way, driving the soldiers, driving himself. He was contemptuous of the firemen—"the Fire Department at this place and time was utterly helpless and unable to meet the situation."

The engines were lined up a long way back pumping, one to another, from a main in the Western Addition. The fire was reaching its peak here. Coleman realized suddenly that there was no water coming from the engines at the fire line. Dropping his other duties he descended wrathfully to find the firemen abandoning their engines. While everything else was burning they had nothing left to burn; they had run out of fuel for their engines without making any attempt to get more, and no longer had any steam up to pump water. They were not going to have a chance to sleep if Coleman had anything to do with it, however. He ordered them to stay where they were, stormed back to the dynamite wagons, had the dynamite dumped and sent the wagons hurrying for more fuel.

It was nine o'clock Thursday night. For some time now there would be no water at all from the fire engines; the fire fighters would be deprived of even this meagre assistance while the flames rose higher and higher in the blocks between Van Ness and Franklin. Fortunately the wind remained on the side of the fire fighters: it was blowing from the northwest, gently—not strong enough to be decisive, but at least not hastening the progress of the fire. But that was not enough. There was not a moment to lose. Efforts must be redoubled with what limited, improvised facilities remained, more help demanded from the crowds in nearby streets, at gun point if they proved unwilling. The dynamiting continued incessantly, massive blasts that demolished building after building. Finally the fire engines started up again.

At ten o'clock the fire had begun to die down a little on

the Clay Street end of the fire barrier. Fire fighters, now certain that it would not cross Clay to the north, nor encroach any farther up Van Ness beyond the ruins of the Wenban home at the southeast corner of Jackson, had moved on to join the others as new portions of the fire gap blazed. But if they had learned anything about this fire, it should have been that it was dangerous to turn one's back on it. Old Mr. Stetson, still clinging to his stronghold on the north side of Clay at Van Ness, suddenly noticed a little flame, "about the size of two hands," starting up in the roof of the Schwabacher house next door. He ran out and offered ten dollars to anyone who would go up and put it out. There was hardly anyone in the street, but finally three volunteers, two civilians and a soldier, entered the house with a can of water, went upstairs and opened a window and in a few minutes had the fire out. When they came back down none of them would accept any reward; the next day the soldier, having thought it over, came back and got his ten dollars.

Now it was Mr. Stetson's turn to take credit for saving the Western Addition: "Had Mrs. Schwabacher's house gone, all in the block would have gone; the fire would have crossed to the north, up Pacific, Broadway and Vallejo, and probably over to Fillmore, when very little would have been left of the residence portion of the city."

Belle Schwabacher's house was, unfortunately, by no means the only point at which the Western Addition was threatened. High above Van Ness the fire had crept unnoticed over the crest of Nob Hill, stealing north across Washington, Jackson, roaring down deserted streets, Jones, Leavenworth, Hyde—these streets had been evacuated early in the morning. At ten o'clock, while the volunteers were putting out the blaze "as big as two hands" in Mrs. Schwabacher's roof, there was a fire four blocks wide, all the way from Jones to Polk, between Jackson and Pacific Streets. At eleven o'clock it was at Van Ness again; the Bothin house between Jackson and Pacific, the block beyond where the dynamiting had halted earlier, was on fire.

Firemen, realizing belatedly that they had been out-flanked, sent an urgent call for Captain Coleman and his demolition teams. Coleman had his hands full on Franklin Street; he sent Lieutenant Briggs, and the soldiers began to blow up the fine residences along the east side of Van Ness at Pacific Street, at Broadway, and beyond. This Thursday morning the Law brothers had watched their Fairmont Hotel, at the top of Nob Hill, burn; now their own homes, Hartland's at the corner of Pacific and Van Ness, Herbert's at Vallejo, were being destroyed, along with those of their neighbors. The Mayor's plan to "blow up Van Ness and save the Western Addition" had been forgotten, but the destruction, through piecemeal, block-at-a-time action, would be the same.

While fire fighters bent every effort to hold it back here, another point was giving way behind their backs. At midnight smoke was welling up inside the Claus Spreckels mansion on the west side of Van Ness at Clay, and this anchor corner in the defense of the Western Addition was finally beginning to burn. As they realized what was happening fire fighters wept, tears etching channels down their blackened faces—not for the loss of the Spreckels mansion's rosewood paneling, its Algerian marbles, its gold-plated faucets and its sterling silver slop jars, but because the building was *fireproof*. It was built of stone, with an iron frame and hollow tile partitions. They had taken it for granted that it would not burn. (Old Mr. Stetson, watching grimly from across the street, harrumphed that if anybody had been paying attention to the place they could have put it out when it started with one bucket of water.) It *couldn't* burn, and it was; and if this massive stone building could burn, what chance was there of saving the rest of San Francisco that stretched behind it?

By 1:00 A.M. there were huge roaring flames in the upper stories of the Spreckels house. Across the street the fire had reached Van Ness again in eight or ten different places, and as it spread north it spread back toward the east too, from street to street. By 2:00 A.M. not only Van Ness, but Larkin, Hyde, Leavenworth, Jones, Taylor and Powell were on fire; to those watching from the heights on the other side of Van Ness the streets were flaming bars of light marked in parallel lines against the darkness.

While the fire worked its way north on Van Ness and half a dozen other streets in the face of the wind, it had been going south, with the wind driving it, in the Mission district, spreading its surging flames to east and west as it went. As it had done at Van Ness, it was reaching into building after building on Dolores Street, and like Van Ness, which it nearly equaled in width, Dolores was being made the site of the last desperate fight to turn the fire back. There was no water at all in the mains here. Eleven million gallons had poured out of the College Hill reservoir south of the Mission district early Wednesday morning and left it completely empty—poured out in huge geysers of wasted water through great arterial pipes sheared off as Valencia Street sank between Eighteenth and Nineteenth, in the center of the district which this Thursday evening needed it so badly. There was no alternative but a hand-to-hand battle for thousands of soldiers, policemen, firemen, volunteers.

It reached Dolores at Fifteenth Street, rearing up in a wall of flame that seemed bound to leap over and take hold in the little Swedish Church across the street to the west. The fire fighters discovered a pool of water half a block away in an empty lot which had been excavated for a new building; they formed a chain, passing along buckets and milk cans of water while others clung to the roof of the church, soaking blankets and applying them, moving precariously to extinguish flames as they sprang up in new spots. A barn near the pool began to smoke. Hastily long ropes were attached and the barn was pulled down and out of the way before it could catch fire and drive off the bucket brigade.

While they worked to save the Swedish Church at Fifteenth Street, beating back flames four times as they sprang up in the roof, the fire was threatening to cross between Sixteenth and Seventeenth, licking about an old building—so old that, except for one or two buildings at the Presidio, it was San Francisco's oldest—the mission dedicated to San Francisco d'Asís (which gave San Francisco its name but came itself to be known as the Mission Dolores from a nearby lake, long since filled in, called Laguna de Nuestra Señora de los Dolores). The little adobe building was no longer in use. (It had been replaced by a fine brick church, now ruined by the earthquake.) It was of little importance to the Church or the people of the district in these modern times of 1906, but it was important to the fire fighters this Thursday night. The fire must not be allowed to cross here, to spread on through Mission Dolores and the wooden buildings near it to the residences beyond. They fought it with sacks and blankets and buckets of water, while the east side of Dolores became a solid wall of fire that singed their eyebrows and scorched their clothing. Men fell in the street overcome by the heat and were taken to a temporary hospital in Mission High School while others took their places, tearing out doors from buildings to carry as shields against the heat.

Behind Dolores the fire was roaring on to the south, leaping vacant lots and dynamited ruins. With the wind driving it, it seemed certain to spread on into the hills where thousands of refugees waited. Here again it was time for drastic measures; the dynamiting of individual buildings just ahead of the fire or already burning was plainly not enough. At eleven o'clock, when the fire had already reached Seventeenth Street, soldiers raced well ahead and began to lay huge charges in a great block of flats that stood towering above everything else on the north side of Twentieth Street, halfway up Dolores Heights. The buildings disintegrated in one tremendous blast that shook the earth and sent thundering echoes rolling over the countryside. The dynamiters had already moved down Twentieth to lay more charges, clearing a line all the way from Dolores to Mission Street.

Back of that line everything had been sacrificed. The fire crept on through abandoned blocks; over James Phelan's old-fashioned wooden house at Seventeenth and Valencia (empty since the day before; bachelor James Phelan's sister Mollie had spent Wednesday night in Golden Gate Park and today he had managed to find time to drive her to Burlingame). At midnight it had gotten as far as Nineteenth Street and was stalking through the empty rooms of the Youth's Directory. The fire fighters were making hurried preparations to meet it when it reached the long row of demolished buildings at Twentieth Street. Hoses were strung out to the cistern blocks away at Mission and Shotwell.

Some of them knew of water—wells and springs—on the steep slope of Dolores Heights around Twenty-first Street. As a matter of fact, the springs had had a certain fame in the past. Ducks who drank the water were found to have gold in their craws, and the water of at least one well was said to possess curative values, although its popularity diminished sharply after the woman who owned it fell in and drowned. The waters possessed a special curative power this Thursday night, though—if they could be reached. The steep grade was beyond the strength of the exhausted fire horses; fire fighters almost equally exhausted manned ropes attached to the fire engines and with a whoop and hurrah dragged the engines up the hill.

At 1:00 A.M. the fire reached the debris along the north side of Twentieth, and the fire fighters were ready for it, the engines with their steam up, hoses trailing down the side of the hill pumping water into the flames. The fire was beating against a huge front now, all along the west side of Dolores Street as far as Twentieth, along Twentieth as far as Mission, but slowly the fire fighters were winning their battle. Along Twentieth the dynamiting was proving effective, for once; with the engines going and the wind now blowing more from the west than from the north, it was possible to keep the fire in the debris under control and prevent it from crossing Twentieth.

On Dolores Street, too, they were winning. Although it was burning all along Dolores as far as Twentieth, there was little enough, beyond Seventeenth, for it to cross into on the west side: between Seventeenth and Eighteenth, Mission High School with its big yard and playground; from Eighteenth to Twentieth, the old Jewish Cemetery (as Mission Park was still called, although the bodies had been moved to San Mateo County in 1894). And the wind, blowing increasingly strong from the west, began to throw the fire back upon itself. It had already done its own backfiring, burned a strip on the eastern boundary, along lower Howard Street (now South Van Ness Avenue) which it could not cross. Finally they could say confidently that, although within its boundaries twenty blocks still blazed, the fire's progress had halted. At three o'clock Friday morning the Mission fire had been stopped.

.   .   .

North of Market, though, it had not been stopped at 3:00 A.M.—nor would it be for another twenty-four hours. Flames poured out of the Spreckels house at Clay and Van Ness, but this was not the danger point; its sturdy framework was holding them in bounds so that they did not spread. (The house burned until ten o'clock Friday morning and even then its outer appearance remained uncannily the same; only its empty, staring windows showed what had happened inside. With the interior restored the Spreckels mansion lasted until it was torn down in 1927 to make way for a large block of apartments called, appropriately enough, "Spreckels Mansions.")

South of the Spreckels house, in the long ravaged strip between Van Ness and Franklin, all the fury of the fire seemed to be concentrated in the wooden houses in the two narrow blocks between Pine and Bush. The all-night battle was coming to a climax here, and there was, suddenly, the sickening realization that they were about to lose Franklin Street, as they had lost Montgomery, Powell, Van Ness, before it. In spite of every effort, in spite of the fire engines, the tubs of water, the axes, the blankets, the gales of wind from the west, the fire had crossed Franklin Street.

The house on the west side of Franklin, at the corner of Austin Street, was on fire and the one next to it was already smoldering. Caught in a never-ending nightmare in which actions had no meaning, efforts no results, Captain Coleman moved his men another block west to Gough Street. There, between Pine and Bush, there were a vacant lot, two flimsy wooden buildings, and the massive stone Trinity Church. Surveying the situation mechanically, oblivious to all the previous failures, Coleman noted that, if the two wooden buildings were out of the way, that would leave an impenetrable strip two blocks wide ahead of the point where the fire had crossed Franklin. In a few minutes the first of the wooden houses had been blown up and soldiers were setting charges in the other one. But there was no need to continue; before the second house could be demolished firemen ran up shouting that they had put out the fire where it had crossed Franklin. Coleman was needed now at Sutter, where the fire had gotten out of control while firemen were working at Austin. Coleman hurried to Sutter, leaving behind the wreckage of the one wooden house on Gough Street—the only debris from dynamiting during the entire course of the fire, as it turned out, that was not subsequently burned.

At five o'clock Friday morning dynamite had brought the Sutter Street fire under control, and all along the long Van Ness-Franklin frontier the fire was dying down. It was time for Captain Coleman, with more justice than most, to get credit for saving the Western Addition. But for his work, as General Funston saw it, "the entire Western Addition of the city would have been destroyed."

The Western Addition was safe at last—or seemed to be.

FOUR

Friday, April 20, 1906

▲▲▲

"FIRE SITUATION AT 7:00 AM BETTER," Funston telegraphed the War Department Friday morning. "FIRE HAS BEEN STOPPED PRACTICALLY AT FRANKLIN."

San Francisco began to shake off the fear of the long desperate Thursday. People told themselves uneasily, only half believing it, that the fire was over. Food and work kept in the background the nagging anxiety that there might be more to come; people would not let themselves think of this, in spite of the clouds of smoke pouring out of the region between Russian Hill and Telegraph Hill, the miles of fire hose snaking through the streets from a hydrant at Franklin and Broadway toward Russian Hill and from there on to Telegraph Hill.

The most important thing to people this morning was that there was food. "Almost everyone had breakfast this morning," a newspaperman was able to report, although it seldom bore any resemblance to the breakfast menu most people were used to. Five thousand pounds of beef, partially cooked by the fire, had been discovered in the ruins of a wholesale market on Sansome Street. That was distributed as long as it lasted. Out on Fillmore the big California Baking Company was back in operation, turning out thousands of loaves of bread for thousands of people standing in line, and by nine o'clock two smaller bakeries were also in operation.

Supplies were beginning to arrive from other cities. Los Angeles housewives had turned to baking bread, and twelve carloads of provisions and two carloads of barreled mineral water had arrived from San Francisco's erstwhile rival. Stockton had appropriated a thousand dollars of its Fourth of July money and bought 8000 eggs—"hen-fruit" as they were almost invariably referred to in the slang of the day— which were hard-boiled and sent along with four hundred tons, an entire boatload, of other food. Army rations had arrived from Vancouver and were being distributed at the Presidio.

In Golden Gate Park Major McIver, setting up headquarters at the Park Lodge, began the first distribution of food at eight o'clock Friday morning, doling out two cans of goods and a handful of crackers to each applicant, with a can of condensed milk to families with babies. It was at times like these that the enormity of the disaster suddenly became shockingly apparent: there were 200,000 people in the city who had had their belongings so completely destroyed that they did not even have cooking utensils with which to prepare the food that was being distributed. Community frying pans went the rounds and were heated up over makeshift stoves; the most popular man in any gathering was the man who had a can opener.

The estimates of the number of people congregated in Golden Gate Park alone ran as high as 200,000, with another 35,000 on the golf course at the Presidio, and uncounted thousands at Fort Mason and every available park and vacant lot. The disaster had been no respecter of persons. Within a short distance one might see a laborer with his family, a small-time businessman, a Chinese laundryman, a millionaire's wife in her opera cloak from the gay, exciting, now irrevocably far-off evening when Caruso had sung at the opera the night before the earthquake.

The Chinese did not stay long: it was felt that their smell was offensive to decent people and they were quickly segregated into a camp by themselves, although while they were able to stay, Chinese servants had faithfully served their employers and many a Chinese was the only "man in the family" for the family he served so devotedly. Otherwise, rich and poor alike stood in line for food handouts, in a display of democracy that seemed extraordinarily impressive. No matter how gleefully San Francisco might laugh when its gaudy millionaires' clay feet occasionally showed, it had always had a comfortable feeling that rich people were different from ordinary people, that they had only to wave thousand-dollar bills to have all their troubles disappear. Consequently, disregarding the fact that it was practically impossible to buy food in San Francisco, and would be for another ten days, so that anyone who wanted to eat had to stand in line for it, it seemed terribly democratic.

Not everyone was staying in San Francisco, of course. The flood of refugees continued unabated. Exhausted mothers and their children stopped at the Ferry Building to drink milk which had arrived by the thousands of gallons from Oakland, and then continued across the bay, where relief organizations were already at work. Taking care of the thousands of refugees arriving, the relief workers found, was "like taking command after a battle has been turned into a rout." Wan stragglers from the fire found that the relief center in Oakland had been dubbed "Happy Camp." If they did not care for Happy Camp, they could go on from Oakland to any place they chose; both the Southern Pacific and the

Santa Fe Railroads were accepting passengers free of charge. There was only the usual problem of standing in line long enough: there were close to 10,000 people waiting at the Southern Pacific depot.

The majority of people had stayed in San Francisco, though, and now that some food was available, and as the assurance grew that, no matter how bad it had been, the disaster was behind them, they were anxious to get on with the business of living, returning to normal conditions as soon as possible. A committee of bankers had already been out examining the bank and safe-deposit vaults in the ruined financial district, and the results of the examination were reassuring. The committee chairman would be able to report to the bankers that all the vaults were intact; the public would be happy to know that all the papers and money on deposit were safe.

Along their way the bankers and the public in general would find other reassuring signs: here a sign over a little wooden shack being hastily thrown together on a ruined street, "Don't Talk Fire, Talk Business," there a sign on another business already beginning to rebuild,

> "First to shake,
> First to burn,
> First to take
> Another new turn"

and they might find another sign on a gutted ten-story building reassuring if only for its brash refusal to be downhearted at what had taken place: "Forced to move on account of elevator not running."

In the park doctors were hanging out their shingles, a Dr. Lamb, it was noted, not a hundred feet from his traditional fate—Dr. Slaughter. Mailmen were beginning to deliver mail, or as much as could be delivered in a city where 250,000 people had changed their addresses. Outgoing mail was being accepted free by the postal authorities; it was being accumulated in a cardboard box at the YMHA. One man dropped a note in, written on the wrapper from a can of tomatoes: "I am writing this standing in line for food. Everything is all right."

For thousands, the most important task was to reunite scattered families. Fathers went hunting for children, wives for husbands, searching the camps, registering at a desk set up by the Red Cross, a registration bureau opened by the police, or simply scrawling their names and locations on a huge billboard set up at the end of the Panhandle, the long, narrow extension to Golden Gate Park.

The Army was in command. Everywhere one looked, they were there, both reassuring and irritating: Major McIver distributing food in Golden Gate Park, Major Benson and his cavalrymen guarding the ruins of Montgomery Street, soldiers forcing families, generally Italian, to give up their dead, burying the corpses in a trench dug in a vacant lot on Hyde Street. Anyone unwary enough to appear in an automobile might expect to have it seized. Either he gave it up willingly, or he gave it up at gun point. Commandeered cars went hurtling by full of nurses or soldiers or supplies. Cars already commandeered had to carry signs, "Relief Work" or "Courier" or "Ambulance" to keep from being commandeered again. Even so, cars carrying doctors were seized, wagons loaded with milk had the milk dumped and were taken off.

Even with the confusion, impressment and counterimpressment, cars played a tremendously important role in the calamity and its aftermath; it was said that "the automobile came of age" here. This Friday morning, however, there was a vast part of the city where automobiles found it difficult or impossible to go. Streets were piled five and six feet deep with the rubble of fallen walls, crisscrossed with dangling telephone and electric light wires. The Army had begun the job of clearing a narrow path down Market Street, using whatever labor appeared and no excuses accepted. John Barrymore, still in his white tie and tails, was put to work; his uncle, John Drew, said later that "It took a convulsion of nature to get Jack out of bed, and the U. S. Army to put him to work." A newly wed couple, George and Josephine Emerson, were on their way down Market Street this morning, George dragging a trunk with one hand and carrying a heavy suitcase in the other, to take the Ferry to Sausalito for their honeymoon; they had only been married the night before. An Army sergeant took a look at the trunk and told George, "You look husky; let the girl sit on the trunk and you get busy with the bricks." The new bride appealed to the lieutenant in charge. "You wouldn't make George work on his honeymoon?" she wailed. "We were only married last night and we must get to Mill Valley in time for lunch." Sentiment had no effect on the lieutenant. "Can't help it, madame," he told her. "My orders are to put every able-bodied man on the rock pile, and your hubby certainly isn't an invalid." It was five hours before George escaped from the rock pile. He and his bride set out again to catch the ferry, only to be impressed anew and forced to work two hours more as a stevedore.

Not even the press was exempt. San Francisco's newspapers had flung away the unlikely co-operation of the joint *Call-Chronicle-Examiner* which they had put out the previous day. They were back in vigorous competition, amid furious charges and countercharges. According to the *Bulletin*, it had been agreed on the day of the earthquake that the three morning papers (the *Call* did not become an afternoon paper until 1913) and the afternoon *Bulletin* would publish jointly one morning and one afternoon paper, using the presses of the *Oakland Tribune*. They had gotten out the one joint issue of the morning paper and then found out, very much to their surprise, that the era of togetherness was over. Without saying anything to the other newspapers, the *Bulletin* charged, the *Examiner* had made a deal for the exclusive use of the *Tribune's* presses, and its competitors learned they would have to look elsewhere if they hoped to continue in the newspaper business. This left considerable ill-feeling, so much so that the *Bulletin* dropped almost completely its campaign against Mayor Schmitz for the next few weeks, and filled its columns instead with long tirades against the perfidy of the *Oakland Tribune*.

The *Chronicle* was happier, if anything, to resume its rivalry with the *Examiner*. It moved in with the *Oakland Herald* and began a spirited battle to beat the *Examiner* to the streets with the news. By Friday morning an elaborate organization had been set up, a train held waiting as the presses rolled, the papers rushed to the Key Ferry dock and thrown into a launch that waited there, motor running, ready to go. Without a moment's wasted time the launch roared off across the bay, gaining a head start on the *Examiner's* launch, which was just then pulling out from the Broadway dock.

A horse and buggy was waiting at the Ferry Building in San Francisco. They dumped the papers into the buggy and dashed off with a clatter for Fillmore Street, where the *Chronicle* had set up temporary offices. So far they were ahead. Then suddenly an armed soldier stepped forth to flag down the buggy. "Get down off that wagon and start shoveling these bricks," he ordered. The buggy driver protested in vain that the soldier was holding up the press, that he had a clear lead on the other paper, that he would come back and pile bricks some other time. The soldier brought his bayonet up angrily. The driver got out and began to shovel bricks. The *Chronicle* was late Friday morning.

Nowhere was the growing confidence, the determination to forget the fire and get on with the relief and reconstruction more evident than at Franklin Hall on Fillmore Street, where the Committee of Fifty, and thus the government of San Francisco, now had its headquarters. At a little before ten o'clock the Committee chairmen were preparing their reports for the meeting scheduled at 10:30; there had been "most satisfactory progress," they agreed.

Rabbi Voorsanger would have triumphant news of bakeries operating, supplies arriving; the chairman of the Sacramento Relief Committee was waiting to tell the Committee in person that he had brought with him a steamer load and a barge load of provisions. The Housing Committee was making plans to take lumber to various camps, the Transportation Committee was contacting the railroads to build tracks to carry away the debris. The Mayor himself had had a talk with Hermann Schussler, the Superintendent of the Spring Valley Water Company. There was water already in parts of the Western Addition, and there would be more as main repairs continued. In the Mission district, more repairs were being made, new mains being laid on top of the street in some places to eliminate the need for digging. The College Hill reservoir was filling. There would be water in the Mission district Friday afternoon.

The little dance hall was swarming with people, each of the ten subcommittee chairmen at his own table (tables borrowed from a nearby candy store); other Committee members rushing in and out on vital projects; the ubiquitous California Promotion Committee, which had volunteered its services, clattering away at typewriters; crowds of people waiting to see the Mayor. "Everyone had business of life and death," wrote Charles Keeler, one of the Committee members, "demanding instant attention."

Soldiers, police, relief workers, politicians . . . and suddenly, like a specter at the feast, "Boss" Ruef, waiting impatiently to talk to Mayor Schmitz. Boss Ruef had spent Wednesday and Thursday nights on the yacht *Verada* in the bay. Now that he had returned it had taken him only a moment to realize that a great deal had changed in those two nights. He had gone away the undisputed master of San Francisco. He returned this Friday morning very much an outsider.

Ruef strode into the small corner office that Schmitz was occupying and demanded a place on the Committee of Fifty. But for once the genial, handsome, pliable Mayor was equal to the challenge of the steely-eyed master politician who had put him into office. There were no Committee chairmanships, no positions of any importance, and most of all no positions involving supplies or money, available, he informed Ruef. Ruef left the office a member of the Subcommittee on Relocating the Chinese, of which the Rev. Dr. Philben was chairman.

Mayor Schmitz went back to drafting a telegram to President Roosevelt, a message prompted by the news just received that Congress had appropriated a million dollars for the relief of San Francisco. "GENEROUS CONTRIBUTION OF ONE MILLION DOLLARS FROM THE FEDERAL GOVERNMENT FOR RELIEF OF DESTITUTE CITIZENS RECEIVED AND DEEPLY APPRECIATED," he began. "THE PEOPLE OVERWHELMED BY YOUR GENEROSITY." He paused, thinking of the furious political boss who had just left, and then added a self-conscious statement, "ALL OF THIS MONEY WILL BE USED FOR RELIEF PURPOSES."

It was a statement he need not have made. He had not actually received the money, nor would he. None of the money Congress had appropriated Thursday would ever be

available either to Schmitz or to the Citizens Committee.
Roosevelt was perfectly aware of the political situation in
San Francisco. He had visited the city in 1903, and this year,
1906, he had lent his chief investigator, William Burns, to
help the Phelan-Spreckels-*Bulletin* combine prepare its case
against the city's corrupt administration. He had no intention of letting Schmitz and Ruef get their hands on the
money.

Unaware that the Committee of Fifty had taken over the
government of the city and that James Phelan, whom he
knew and trusted, headed its Finance Committee, Roosevelt
had recommended to Congress that its appropriation be entrusted to the War Department. Before Friday was over the
War Department would have spent it all, as a matter of fact,
and would be asking for more. Dr. Edward Devine, a pro-
fessional charity worker—he occupied the chair of Practical Philanthropy at Columbia University, and was said to
have "reduced charity to an exact science"—was already on
his way to take charge of the relief operations. Before he
arrived in San Francisco, President Roosevelt would have
directed the nation to send its contributions not to Mayor
Schmitz, but to Doctor Devine.

None of this news had reached San Francisco, and it
would be several days before it did. Serenely unaware of
how forcefully he and the Citizens Committee were being
elbowed out of the handling of the relief funds, Mayor
Schmitz ended his telegram in a burst of confidence, "WE
ARE DETERMINED TO RESTORE TO THE NATION ITS CHIEF PORT
ON THE PACIFIC," and proceeded to the next matter at hand.

At ten o'clock Friday morning, an Associated Press man
reported, trumpeters were announcing to the thousands assembled in the parks that the fire was at an end. Mayor
Schmitz began to dictate a proclamation of congratulation
and encouragement to the public. "To the Citizens of San

Francisco," he began. "The fire is now under control and all danger is past."

There was only one trouble with the situation Friday morning. The fire was *not* under control. The danger was not past. Not even the Western Addition was safe yet.

The trumpeters' announcement was accurate enough, "generally speaking," the Associated Press reporter continued, although actually the fire was still raging east of Russian Hill. "But no one bothers about that, so long as the fire is confined to North Beach."

The people crowded together in North Beach, understandably enough, took a considerably different view of the progress of the fire. Spreading in the level area between Russian Hill and Telegraph Hill like air rushing into a vacuum, it had pressed them farther and farther north toward the waterfront. All at once there was fire to the right of them, to the left of them, behind them; ahead was the bay. There was no escape. Panic spurted through the crowds, there were screams of terror, people running to and fro in the streets, stopped short in one direction by the awesome advance of the flames, forced back in another, fighting frantically to crowd into a few launches at the waterfront. Captain Coleman was making valiant efforts to stay the progress of the fire with dynamite, destroying two blocks on Lombard Street, falling back, demolishing a block on Chestnut Street, falling back another block to go to work on Francisco Street.

Word reached General Funston of the desperate situation. While the trumpeters were announcing to the people in the parks that the fire was over, he was commandeering every boat on the bay to take the trapped thousands off North Beach. They jammed along the waterfront waiting to go aboard. They were orderly, almost always, but hurrying, hurrying, desperate to get away, oblivious of everything but their own safety. A woman with a child in her arms set foot on the gangplank to go aboard a ship; a burly Swede pushed her out of the way. She and the child fell into the water. Instantly a soldier drove a bayonet into the Swede's back; he was thrown aside and the crowds continued their way up the gangplank.

Every boat on the bay had been pressed into service. Even old relics like the *Wizard,* a tugboat that had lain for years abandoned in the mud of Oakland Creek, had been resurrected. Now the *Wizard* was hurrying to the rescue, commanded by Lieutenant McMillan, the Revenue Service officer who had established his own brand of martial law at gun point on Nob Hill Thursday morning. Today the noisy lieutenant had volunteered to put the *Wizard* into service. It made voyage after voyage back and forth across the bay, harrowing trips hardly less dangerous than the fate it was rescuing people from, with every passenger aboard in "real danger of a skyward cruise."

And while flames swept on through North Beach, heedless of Captain Coleman's efforts to ward them off with dynamite, the rest of the fire was roaring out of control in every direction, snapping at the steep rocky face of Russian Hill on the west, racing back into the still unburned area to the south, lapping at the base of Telegraph Hill on the east. Navy fireboats were waging a constant battle along the waterfront to keep the fire from catching in the piers. The cutter *Golden Gate* had put in at the Lombard Street pier, east of Telegraph Hill. Sailors swarmed ashore dragging thousands of feet of fire hose, fighting to keep the fire back as it spread irresistibly into the area below Telegraph Hill, falling back, dragging the hose farther and farther, until there were five thousand feet of hose stretched through seven blocks from the waterfront.

More sailors began backfiring, setting fire to a line of

buildings stretching from Kearny and Vallejo Streets north-
east toward the bay, in an effort to cut the fire off from
Telegraph Hill. While the hose was turned toward keeping
this under control, fire was rushing back toward the south,
leaping through the ancient, powder-dry buildings that
housed the last of the Barbary Coast's dance halls and "re-
sorts" with quick flashes of fire, working with lightning
speed to destroy everything that remained in this unburned
pocket left over from Wednesday's fire.

The distance between the fire and the area already
burned was gradually decreasing, the belt of unburned
buildings growing narrower and narrower, shrinking finally
into a small island two blocks wide, one and two blocks
deep, where the Appraiser's Building, the Montgomery
Block, and a block of miscellaneous buildings of various uses
including Hotaling's wholesale liquor warehouse stood. Beyond this small area, to east, to west, to south, everything
had already burned on Wednesday.

It had taken heroic, searing, desperate work that day to
save these buildings: a stretch two blocks long dynamited
along the west side of Montgomery Street, more dynamiting across Washington Street from the Appraiser's Building,
wooden buildings pulled down, three fire engines and their
crews borrowed from Oakland, four cisterns emptied into
the flames, the five-thousand-gallon tank on top of the Appraiser's Building supplying a bucket brigade that successfully prevented the fire from catching hold there. Now it
was all to do over again, defending the buildings this time
from fire sweeping in from the north. The cisterns were
empty, the dynamiters and the fire engines were gone, but
at least there had been a day to rest and get prepared; the
fire had not come anywhere near the area Thursday. There
were reinforcements. A company of soldiers had made its
headquarters in the Appraiser's Building, and they had

spent all day Thursday filling empty whisky barrels from Hotaling's warehouse with water that had collected in the excavations for the new Customs House nearby. Colonel Karman's Marines had joined them early this morning for the fight.

Now the time they had prepared for had arrived, the flames closer and closer, surging masses of fire, showering them with storms of cinders and burning embers. Soldiers and Marines were all over the roofs of the Appraiser's Building, the numerous small buildings in the block next to it, the branch post office across the street from that (although the post office had been so badly damaged by the earthquake—a heavy wall falling on it had rammed a huge hole in it—that it was hardly worth saving) using buckets of water, mops, wet sacks, chopping away at cornices as they caught fire, forcing themselves into the suffocating heat, still fighting to save the post office even when roaring flames surrounded three sides of it.

It did not seem possible at noon Friday that these buildings would be saved, and yet they *were* saved before the day was over, the Appraiser's Building, the Montgomery Block, the branch post office, Hotaling's warehouse with its two thousand barrels of whisky. Hotaling's warehouse— San Francisco would draw its own wry moral from that; the fire was hardly over when Charles K. Field's jingle became popular,

> "If as some say, God spanked the town
> For being over frisky
> Why did He burn the churches down
> And save Hotaling's Whisky?"

All the while, the fire had been encroaching on Russian Hill, sweeping in from the west, racing back from the north along the sides and then up toward the crest of the hill.

They had fought all night to save the houses on Russian Hill; they had been successful, temporarily. The flames had been turned back, to burn down to Van Ness Avenue on the west, out to North Beach on the east. Now it was clear that the few remaining houses on top of the hill must go too. They had already been evacuated and they fell now, one by one, the trees withering and then bursting into flames, the houses going up in smoke. The fire raced along Taylor Street toward the square, shingled Eli Sheppard house at the corner of Vallejo, almost the highest point on Russian Hill. Eli Sheppard had already gone, taking his invalid wife to Berkeley earlier in the day. The house was deserted except for an old Civil War comrade of Sheppard's, a man named E. A. Dakin, who lived in an annex.

Dakin had stayed as long as he could. He realized now that the house was doomed and he was preparing to leave, but not without a last gallant gesture. As the flames came charging at the house he got out a large American flag, took it out and ran it up the flagpole in the front yard, dipping it three times in a last farewell. A new company of soldiers just moving in below saw the signal, took it for granted that the house was a military headquarters and rushed up to its defense. They found only a grizzled old Civil War veteran, but once they were there they stayed to fight. There was a bathtub full of water, they discovered; they used that to soak blankets, sand, anything that could be used to smother out the flames as they caught hold. As the fire swept on around to destroy Ina Coolbrith's home— San Francisco's beloved poetess had already gone, turning the key in her door and walking away without ever looking back—the soldiers worked to save the Sheppard house and the remaining houses just above it.

While they worked on Taylor Street, the fire was coming in block by block from the other side, driven faster and faster from the west by the strong wind, until there was a continuous line of fire on Leavenworth Street, along the ridge of the hill, and then sweeping on over to Jones Street. At noon Friday there appeared to be an unbroken series of flaming houses along Jones Street, all the way from Pacific in the declivity between Nob and Russian Hills, up the southern side of Russian Hill and over to Filbert Street. In the smoke and flame it was impossible to tell that there was a break in that line, houses still untouched in a few blocks at the summit of the hill. It was taken for granted that everything on Russian Hill was gone.

Russian Hill had been written off early in the morning. The fact that the last of the homes on it were presumably burning at noon Friday did not change the conviction in the rest of the city that the fire was under control, nor had anything taken place to indicate that the Western Addition was not yet out of danger. The momentum of relief and reconstruction was growing, the importance of the fire fading into the background. Supplies of food were beginning to pour in. Mayor Schmitz, carrying on a sort of "government by proclamation" from his corner office at Franklin Hall, had told the public, "Do not be afraid of famine. There will be abundant food supplied." Four substations had been set up for the distribution of food, soup kitchens were being established, more and more bakeries were turning out bread.

People stood in lines five and six blocks long to receive relief goods, gifts from other cities that often bore an extremely personal touch: a shipment of hard-boiled eggs had the name of a donor on each egg; a man biting into a loaf of bread found a note in it from the woman who had baked it, inquiring about her relatives in San Francisco. A certain amount of black marketing was still going on, furtive offerings of food at advanced prices, water being sold at five cents a glass. The public was instructed to denounce these extortionists to the soldiers.

Water was not moving as fast as expected. The Mayor's earlier confident proclamation predicting early resumption of water service had not told all the story; probably he did not know it himself. It would be days yet—not until May 1 for the Pacific Heights and Fort Mason area, for example— before some sections had any water. Before the fire was over it would have left more than 23,000 household connections open, making it almost impossible to keep the reservoirs filled, and although six hundred laborers from the Ocean Shore Railway were already at work on the sewers, the mixing of water and sewage made it impossible to use what water there was without boiling it or disinfecting it.

One of the first businesses to get going again was the bottling and selling of soda pop—primarily a subterfuge to get around the restrictions on black marketing water, and frequently taking no precautions whatsoever against contamination. Otherwise, San Francisco would still have to depend on tankers of water brought in by the Navy and distributed from water carts, water that itself was so green and full of life that the carts were referred to as "Aquariums."

There were, of course, supplies of water from the separate water system in Golden Gate Park, as well as the lakes there, and from wells and springs in some districts, but it often seemed easier to wait for water to be supplied. The Richmond district, blessed with an excellent natural water supply, put in a request for water; they received a curt reply from the Relief Committee that if they wanted water they could get a bucket and go to the well for it.

Water would be available in one form or another, but Mayor Schmitz was determined that nothing stronger should be. At his request, bars in Oakland had been closed. Friday afternoon the last of the saloons in San Francisco were broken into and the stocks smashed. A man holding even a suspicious looking coffee can was likely to have it bayoneted. There were ways of circumventing the Mayor's order, however. The first speakeasy had already opened. More and more people were finding that whisky was available at the bars just across the San Francisco County line to the south. And at Fourth and Brannan, in the burned-out South of Market district, a crowd had discovered what the California Wine Association had not: as the earthquake and fire destroyed the Association's warehouses there, the contents of thousands of barrels had poured out into the basement. There was a pool of wine six feet deep there now, and many a wino was happily lowering his bucket into it. (What was left of the wine was eventually pumped out, taken to Stockton and distilled into brandy.)

There were other problems. Civic administration during an emergency, the Committee was finding, was exceedingly complex. It presented one dilemma after another to men not especially qualified to handle them. Food was a problem, not for the lack of it any longer, but for means of getting it into the city and from there to distribution points. The officials were aware that with hundreds of thousands of people camping out, sanitation must be provided for, but they had little idea of how to go about it. Those people whose homes remained were alternately exhorted to make their bathrooms available to the public, and not to use their bathrooms under any circumstances. The Committee thought it would be well to begin building barracks in the park—but it had neither transportation to haul the lumber nor qualified people to supervise the work.

Often the only solution to the various problems as they arose seemed to be to dump them onto the Army. Army engineers began constructing barracks. Army launches carried supplies across the bay as they arrived at the rail terminals in Oakland. Soldiers directed the digging of sanitary ditches; Colonel Torney had been detailed as head of the Sanitary Committee and "all his orders must be strictly observed by whomsoever." Many of the Committee members felt that the entire operation should be taken out of their hands and turned over to the Army, although they did not say so to Mayor Schmitz.

For while admitting the indispensability of the Army, Mayor Schmitz was growing increasingly angry at what he felt was the assumption of some of his own prerogatives by General Funston, and with a politician's feeling for the mood of the people, he was aware of the rumbling discontent stirring in the city against the Army's methods and restrictions. He had repeated his order to shoot looters, and yet he was dismayed by the rumors of widespread shooting. He knew that two more "vigilante" groups had been formed, and that they indicated both how precarious the state of order was in the city, and how onerous the people were finding the Army's rule.

Not that the Army alone was responsible; the National Guard, similarly uniformed, had a way of running together with the Army in people's minds, and there were also six hundred University of California cadets now on duty. Nor was the people's resentment even widespread; most people took the troops pretty much for granted. But each new incident—soldiers butting two men down the street for some offense, leaving them with heads bloody and clothes bayonet-torn, for example—served to increase the Mayor's indignation. And most of all, his annoyance grew from a feeling that *he* should not have to consult General Funston, but that General Funston should consult *him*—and this the stubborn, independent little general frequently failed to do.

Consequently Mayor Schmitz continued to issue orders and directions; sometimes General Funston was issuing the same order, or perhaps ordering just the opposite.

GOVERNOR'S OFFICE

Oakland

April 2 1906

PASS MR. Chas Bree

through the lines in SAN FRANCISCO

By order of GEO. C. PARDEE

GOVERNOR OF CALIFORNIA

Adjt. Gen. of Cal

Oakland, California, Public Library

Mayor Schmitz was not alone in his concern over what he felt were dictatorial tendencies, tendencies toward real martial law, on General Funston's part. Several judges talked over the possibility of asking Funston to exempt them from being impressed to clear streets (even a Supreme Court Justice had been caught and put to work throwing bricks out of the way) but decided not to, since by doing so they would be recognizing Funston's authority. They would rather work than admit that he had the right to make them work. Governor Pardee had had some of the same feelings. Thursday he had been issuing passes to enter San Francisco "by authority of Brig. Gen. Funston." This Friday morning he had realized the indignity of the governor of California acknowledging the superior authority of the Army. The passes abruptly began to read "by authority of the Governor of California," and were signed by the Attorney General. It was a

matter of complete indifference to General Funston, as long
as the number of people entering San Francisco was kept
under control.

It did not occur to General Funston, as a matter of fact,
that there was any reason for anyone to be offended by his
actions. He had received a certain basic authority from
Mayor Schmitz. He did not feel it was necessary to consult the Mayor on each new problem that arose; he simply
did whatever he thought necessary to take care of it. It was
obvious that order must be maintained, and under the circumstances and with the limited number of soldiers at his
disposal, restrictions must be severe. The soldiers were well-
disciplined, and the major lapses, although they occurred,
were remarkably few—a fact which the majority of the public (and ultimately the Mayor) realized.

Funston was to insist later that, contrary to rumor, there
was no proof of a single civilian being killed by a soldier
during the fire (although there *was* proof of killings by the
National Guard and the special police, and the absence of
proof did not necessarily exonerate the Army). In the course
of policing the city arrests had been made, however; by Friday soldiers had arrested 160 people for various offenses.
They had been taken first to San Quentin where they were
refused admittance because they had not been sentenced;
after conferring with Governor Pardee, they were distributed in Alameda County jails. The responsibility had also
fallen to the Army to take charge of the prisoners in jails in
San Francisco at the time of the earthquake; they had been
taken to the military prison on Alcatraz. Mayor Schmitz had
had little to say in either case.

It was equally obvious to General Funston that there was
an extraordinary amount of work to be done in San Francisco, and thousands of idle men available. It was logical

that they should be set to doing the work, and they were: clearing streets, digging trenches, unloading supplies, burying bodies.

Burying bodies—that was a heart-rending job, but one that had to be done. Bodies dug out of the ruins, forty bodies from a boarding house on Fifth Street, a mother and child on Turk Street, a whole family on Howard, bodies collected at Lafayette Square, at the Presidio. Forlorn gatherings where any man capable of handling a pick or a shovel was required to work for at least an hour. A representative of the coroner's office counting the bodies, taking the names of as many as could be identified, then bodies with names buried beside nameless bodies that would never be known. Weeping relatives, a priest reading the burial service and pronouncing absolution, curious onlookers, the dirt being shoveled in over the bodies in the shallow graves.

The Army's work went on, dividing the city into districts for administration, undertaking an ever-increasing part of the relief activity. Every effort by the Army in San Francisco was being matched in Washington. Funston had the assurance now that in addition to the trickle that had already arrived, vast quantities of supplies were on the way. The proportions of the disaster and the consequent need had become much clearer in Washington. For the War Department, Thursday had been a day of driving activity to fill those needs; constant telegrams, orders and more orders, scanning replies for indications of progress and hints of delay.

General Geary in Seattle, who advised that his shipment would be made by the 25th, was informed, "THAT DATE ENTIRELY TOO LATE." Queries as to how to ship were impatiently answered, "EXPRESS. ALL SHIPMENTS TO SAN FRANCISCO BY EXPRESS." When Philadelphia seemed to quibble over details, the depot received curt instructions, "CARRY OUT YOUR ORDERS WITH ALL DISPATCH."

They paused to glance at a gratuitous telegram from the Buffalo *Enquirer*, "ESTEEMED SIR: THE ENQUIRER WOULD SUGGEST THAT THE GOVERNMENT AT ONCE SEND TO THE HOMELESS PEOPLE OF STRICKEN SAN FRANCISCO A SUFFICIENT NUMBER OF ARMY TENTS TO TEMPORARILY SHELTER THE NEEDY." It did not merit a reply, only a weary murmur, "What does he *think* we're doing?" Five carloads of medical supplies ordered from one depot, 170,000 tent pins from another. Tents for a hundred thousand people. Nine hundred thousand rations. Blankets, mattresses, bed sacks, cots.

By Thursday night telegrams had begun to come back that the shipments were going forward. From New York, "ALL WILL GO BY WELLS FARGO 8:30 TONIGHT." From St. Louis, ". . . STOVE PIPE ORDERED TO SAN FRANCISCO SHIPPED VIA WELLS FARGO EXPRESS TONIGHT." From Philadelphia, ". . . SUPPLIES FOR SAN FRANCISCO WILL BE SENT OUT IN TWO SOLID TRAINS, ONE VIA ADAMS EXPRESS, THE OTHER VIA UNITED STATES EXPRESS." From Omaha, "THREE BAGGAGE CARS LEFT HERE 5:20 PM BY PACIFIC EXPRESS." Every Army Command was making shipments. By Friday morning Funston had been informed that every item of supplies not already in the hands of troops was on its way to San Francisco. The effort still continued, contractors urged to boost deliveries of duck, the Philadelphia Depot instructed to *push* the manufacture of tents.

Theodore Roosevelt had devoted his entire cabinet meeting Friday morning to San Francisco and its needs, listening carefully to the recommendations of Secretary of Commerce Metcalf, who was from Oakland; making up his mind to send Metcalf west as his personal representative in San Francisco. He had also taken note of the offers of aid from other countries—from Canada, from Germany, from

the Dowager Empress of China, and from many others—
and he had made a decision which was to anger San Francisco greatly: no foreign aid would be accepted. The United
States would take care of its own, and it would be generous.
When, Friday afternoon, the War Department informed the
President that it had already exceeded the one million dollars which Congress had appropriated, and requested an additional million, Roosevelt forwarded the request to Congress with the recommendation that not one million, but a
million and a half be added.

But that was of small matter on Russian Hill, as time crept
on into Friday afternoon. There had been no letup in the
sturdy, stubborn fight. Soldiers and civilians were strung
out in the few blocks remaining, surrounded by flames,
sweltering in the heat sweeping up all around them, ob-
scured by dense clouds of smoke. They lost one house, but
only after a terrific struggle; then another house. It was
"some of the hottest work men have ever been called upon
to do"; it saved, on the summit of Russian Hill when the
fighting was finally over, five houses.

Once more seemingly indifferent to the strong west wind,
the fire was bearing down with terrible intensity on Van
Ness Avenue too, building up speed, gathering momentum
in a torrent of crackling, menacing flames. It seemed certain
to leap across Van Ness Avenue; if it did, a whole day and
night of desperate work would have bought only a morning's
safety and the remainder of San Francisco would go after
all. Fire engines were lined up on Van Ness, pumping from
one to another all the way from where a Navy fireboat stood
by at Fort Mason, pumping from the bay.

Captain Coleman had reported to General Funston at
Fort Mason. Funston, who had invariably left the decisions
as to dynamiting to the civil authorities, instructed Coleman

to report to Schmitz. Schmitz was at Van Ness and Green. That point had been the northern boundary of the fire on Van Ness up to now, but it could not be for long. When the fire dipped down to Van Ness again they must be there ahead of it, ready for it, to keep it from crossing. "Blow up everything else on this side of Van Ness," Schmitz told Coleman.

In another spot the fire was making equally disastrous progress. At 2:00 o'clock Friday afternoon fire burst out at the waterfront on the north, surging into the hollow opposite Meiggs Wharf, leaping across East Street, spreading with lightning fury through the warehouses along the sea wall. The waterfront had not been in danger since Wednesday morning. Today, Friday, the Western Addition had been considered safe. Now suddenly that had all changed. The Western Addition, the last major part of the city, was once more at the point of being destroyed, and the docks, the last means of supplying the city, were likely to go too. The city was faced with final, total destruction.

Now the fire reached Van Ness Avenue again, springing up rapidly in the ruins of the house Coleman had just demolished at the southeast corner of Union Street, spreading out in a fiery line a block wide between Green and Union. The last remaining strength of firemen and volunteers was being called on here, concentrated effort against fire stretching back half a dozen blocks deep up the side of the hill. Ignoring the heat, the tottering, flame-riven walls, they took their hoses right into the curb, to force the salt bay water into the flames. A wall fell, crushing a fireman. He was carried off while the fight went on, volunteers rushing in to help carry the hoses, holding up wet sheets to protect the firemen from the heat.

At the same time the fire was roaring through the waterfront, eating into the lumberyards, exploding into a towering column of flame as the gasworks at the foot of Powell Street caught fire, surging back to the east past one dynamited barrier after another. Army tugs were busy once more bringing supplies from Oakland, but suddenly food was no longer important; every available boat was diverted to fight the fire. Soon the coast was jammed with tugs, steamers, destroyers, fireboats pouring water into the fire.

Still it swept on around the sea wall, headed straight for the piers and the Ferry Building. At three o'clock Friday afternoon the warning came to the branch post office at the Ferry Building that the waterfront would soon be ablaze; looking out toward the north at the clouds of smoke approaching, the danger seemed already close at hand. Hasty preparations began to save the mail. The post office was packed with people sending messages to the outside world. Without any warning the windows slammed shut in their faces, soldiers began to herd them out, the doors closed behind them.

In the heat of the fire on Van Ness Avenue at three o'clock Friday afternoon paint was beginning to peel on the houses on the west side of the street, cornices to flicker up in little patches of fire. Throughout the Western Addition, at the Presidio, at Golden Gate Park, rumor was beginning to scurry from person to person that Van Ness had been breached again, that the Western Addition was doomed. Volunteers, soldiers, National Guardsmen were racing to each new danger point to stamp out burning firebrands, dampen smoldering wood, smother pockets of fire. On the east side of the street, firemen and volunteers manned the hoses, more men taking the places of those felled by the heat, forcing the bay water into the flames.

Then—there was no water. Somewhere in the long chain of fire engines pumping from one to another from the bay, one engine had broken down, thereby halting the flow of water altogether. Without wasting a moment the fireman at the next engine in line ripped off a manhole cover in the street, dipped the hose into the sewer running below. The flow resumed until the break in the chain could be restored. Gradually they were bringing the fire under control, buckets and wet blankets were doing their work across the street, the fire had met its match in the block from Green to Union. There was a sudden cheer from the crowd. It was the only one, a volunteer fire fighter said, that he heard during all the days of the fire.

Perhaps the reason people seldom cheered was that the battle was never really won; a stalemate at one point was followed immediately by danger at another. Now, a short distance up the hill, the fire had crossed Union Street to the north and was coming back to Van Ness again, outflanking the fire fighters, leapfrogging a block ahead of them. Captain Coleman began to lay dynamite charges at the next house on Van Ness, across Union Street, to block the fire off when it reached Van Ness again. He stepped back, ready to set off the charge, but as people waited there was no explosion. They saw him talking angrily to firemen and other Army officers.

If the house was to be blown up, the time was *now*, before the fire reached it. Instead, an automobile with a group of officers in it suddenly made a wild dash up Union Street, ignoring flames on both sides of the street, left a charge of dynamite at a house two blocks up, turned with frantic haste to get away as the house exploded behind them, scattering the fire it was meant to check. For half an hour firemen and officers argued in the street, while the fire spread above them; then the hose was carried up the hill, straight into the fire.

It was impossible to stay, hopeless to think of checking it here; there was a shout to drop the hose and run. The moment they reached safety, the house on Van Ness, where Captain Coleman had already laid his dynamite charges, was set off. Volunteer fire fighters, rushing in to keep the fire under control as it darted into the ruined building, speculated as to why the house had not been blown up in the first place as it should have been, why such spectacular efforts had been made to save one house when a hundred finer houses had been sacrificed. It was rumored that the house belonged to an Army officer who was determined not to have it dynamited. Whether or not this was true, no one knew. Captain Coleman discreetly did not mention the incident at all in his official report on the Army dynamiting.

Up the hill the fire was moving ever farther north, crossing one street, then another, sweeping out toward Fort Mason, tearing around to join the fire on the north and east sides of Russian Hill, raging as far as Lombard Street. In the northwest corner of the intersection of Lombard and Hyde there was an odd building, more like a Scottish castle than a house. It was the home of Mrs. Robert Louis Stevenson; attached to it, facing on Lombard Street, was the home of her son, Lloyd Osborne. Stevenson had died in Samoa more than a decade before; he had never lived in this house at all. But his memory was still bright, and his widow beloved in San Francisco. Now as the flames menaced her house, members of the Bohemian Club—writers, artists, newspapermen —gathered almost by instinct to fend off the fire from the Scottish castle. The block-square reservoir above them had been drained in the earlier efforts to halt the fire; they snatched at the trickle that remained to fill buckets, wet blankets. The fences and outbuildings of the reservoir burned, the fire worked its way up the east side of Hyde Street until the homes there lay in ruins, but the Bohemians were able to save the Stevenson house.

This was one block in an arc of fire that stretched from

Van Ness Avenue on the west to Telegraph Hill on the east. Earlier in the morning backfiring and dynamiting and water from the bay had held the fire back momentarily from the southern face of Telegraph Hill. Now, at four o'clock Friday afternoon, it was coming farther up the western and northern sides of the hill. Sailors had stretched out a mile of hose from the bay, but the fire was coming on in a rush of flames now, so fast that suddenly it was ahead of them, surrounding them with fire. They dropped the hose and made a dash for safety, leaving thousands of feet of hose behind.

On the steep slope of Telegraph Hill above, up in the "eaves of the city," crowded the shanties of the Italian Quarter, jammed against each other on slopes so steep that one went up by ladder from one house to another. It had been a district of warmth and confusion, dirt, noise, and lighthearted, carefree people; it was, of all the areas in San Francisco, perhaps the least defensible against fire. These Italians were determined to defend it, though. The men had taken their wives and children down early in the morning. They had come back to wait as the fire grew closer, turning the warehouses at the foot of the hill on the north into furnaces, sweeping around on the western side, overrunning all the barriers, coming up the hill. There was a cistern on the hill; buckets were dipped into it, burlap sacks soaked. Little stilted houses clinging to the hillside began to smoke; ropes were attached to pull them down out of the way, ax brigades formed to chop them down, while more buckets of water were applied to keep others from catching.

At five o'clock the fire was roaring below them into the lumberyards at the base of the hill. On one side of the yards were the docks, stretching along the waterfront from here to the Ferry Building and beyond as far as South San Francisco. On the other, hundreds of freight cars were drawn up on the siding. If the fire spread into either, the entire water-front was doomed. A Navy tug, two fire-patrol boats and more than a dozen other tugs were massed here, their lines of hose laid into the heart of the fire, pumping from the bay to the limit of their capacity. Even that was not enough; they were barely holding their own, the fire ready to spread beyond control into the piers. Major Devol raced down East Street in his commandeered automobile to the Folsom Street pier, where the *Slocum* and the *General MacDowell,* just arrived from Oakland, were unloading supplies, and ordered them to move to the danger point immediately for fire-fighting service.

At the other side of the fire zone, the fire was roaring down Russian Hill toward Van Ness Avenue with such intensity that it was inevitable that it would cross. Three Navy dynamiters, Captain MacBride and two gunners, had arrived from Mare Island with a ton and a half of gun cotton. While they continued the dynamiting on the east side of Van Ness, Mayor Schmitz ordered Captain Coleman to get ready to dynamite the west side. Amid the blasts of Captain MacBride's gun cotton from one side of the street, Captain Coleman went to work on the other, laying dynamite, connecting wires, making ready for another last-ditch attempt, as he had done on Thursday between Sutter and Clay, to establish an uncrossable barrier against the fire.

At seven o'clock Friday evening the fire was forcing the fire fighters on Telegraph Hill slowly back toward the top. At the base of the hill it was spreading into new warehouses in spite of everything the fireboats could do. From there back to the incandescent gas tanks at the foot of Powell Street it was a holocaust that spread over fifty acres of the waterfront, growing in fury, surging masses of flames that lit up the sky and set off in stark light and shadow the tugs crowded together throwing water into the inferno.

At Powell Street it turned back in a diagonal line across Russian Hill to Union Street, a line that was meeting every defense an exhausted army of fighters could offer: the constant explosions of dynamite, the fire engines pumping mightily—defenses so insignificant in the face of this fire that reporters, taking it for granted that they would fail, were already writing stories that the fire had claimed hundreds of victims, that it had crossed Van Ness and was raging out toward the Presidio. These would be scare headlines in Saturday morning's papers.

THE PRICE OF THE TRIBUNE IS FIVE CENTS

150 MEN, WOMEN AND CHILDREN BURNED TO DEATH LAST NIGHT

San Francisco, April 21.--It is estimated that more than 150 people were burned to death last night in the vicinity of Telegraph and Russian Hills and on Union Street. While the fire was raging the people were cut off from retreat. In twenty buildings bodies have been recovered. Two babes were found where they had been dropped in mad flight.

EXTRA Oakland Tribune. EXTRA

VOL. LXV   OAKLAND, CALIFORNIA, SATURDAY EVENING APRIL 21, 1906   16 Pages   NO. 52

It was against this flaming background, with what was left of San Francisco—its piers and the Western Addition— at the brink of destruction, that the Citizens' Committee met again at 8:00 Friday night. For the first time Mayor Schmitz, who had been a figure of encouragement and assurance to the people of San Francisco from the very beginning, began to doubt if he could hold the city together any longer. Earlier in the day, when James Phelan had expressed the opinion that lights seemed necessary at night to prevent disorder, Schmitz had snapped that there was perfect order in the city and there would continue to be; he had refused to allow the risk of fire that candles and lan-

terns would be. But now that confidence was gone, like all
the other confidences of the morning. The situation was so
dangerous that he had decided to swear in and arm a thousand special policemen, and he appointed one Julian Sonntag chairman of the "Protection Committee." Rifles for the
policemen would be obtained from the Army.

Half-heartedly then, preoccupied with disaster, overwhelmed with problems far beyond the experience of law-
yers and publishers and real-estate men, the Committee
chairmen began to make their reports, small meaningless
items of progress, brave plans: the dynamiting of walls left
standing in the ruined area to begin Monday; a meeting of
bankers announced to inform people when business would
be resumed. They spoke of the gratifying arrival of food:
twenty trainloads of food at Oakland; five carloads of flour
at Vallejo.

Small comfort, those carloads of food at Oakland, the
flour at Vallejo; every boat on the bay that might have
brought food to San Francisco was busy fighting the fire.
What was worse, the quantities of food that had already arrived in San Francisco lay useless at the Folsom Street pier
for lack of transportation to move them. Every fire horse was
dead on its feet, every city team engaged in hospital work.
Carriages waited in front of fine homes in Pacific Heights to
take their owners to safety when the fire crossed Van Ness
again, but though many of their owners were members of
the Committee, their teams were not available for relief
work.

The Committee was, as the *Chronicle* put it, "in a quan-
dary." But for once a problem had met its match. Up
jumped a young lawyer, William Denman. He was everything the situation demanded: rough, determined, afraid of
nothing. Give him two Regular Army soldiers, he demanded,
and he would supply the transportation the Committee

needed. With a sergeant and a private drafted to help him, he set off down Sacramento Street from Franklin Hall, commandeering teams at gun point, roaring at their owners, dumping loads of furniture or other effects on the side- walk, rooting out teams sequestered in stables, lining them up with himself at the head, the private in the middle, the sergeant at the end, in a string of oddly assorted vehi- cles, fine carriages and dray wagons, that grew longer and longer as he proceeded toward the Presidio. "If any driver tries to drop out of this line, shoot him," he told the soldiers.

Mayor Schmitz was not having so much success arming his special police. The arms must come from General Funs- ton, but when the application was made, the general refused. He did not believe it was wise to swear in more special po- licemen; he had no authority to hand out Army rifles to civilians. (Nor had he had the authority to hand out any Army supplies, although he had done so, liberally.) Mayor Schmitz insisted; Funston would agree to no more than to leave it up to the Secretary of War. While Schmitz fumed, Funston sent a telegram to Taft relaying the Mayor's re- quest, and there the matter stood.

It was 8:30 Friday evening. Flushed and disheveled, the stubborn little general was busy with more important things at the moment—specifically, the defense of Fort Mason. Plans had been made the night before to meet the fire when it reached the refugee-choked post, and now these plans were going into effect. Fire engines had been obtained, a fireboat borrowed from the Navy. (It was this fireboat, standing off Fort Mason since one o'clock Friday morning, that had pumped water all afternoon to the fire engines along Van Ness.) Now sailors were chopping down the wooden fence around the fort, tearing away outbuildings in the glaring light of the fire up above them; soldiers were on roof tops, manning pre-arranged defense lines, casting

frightened glances at the powder magazine, waiting for the
fire to reach them. "FORT MASON MAY GO," Funston advised
Secretary Taft, "BUT WE WILL KNOW IN AN HOUR."

At the other end of the fire at the base of Telegraph Hill
opposite the Lombard Street piers, the tugs and fireboats,
augmented now by the *General MacDowell* and the huge
pumps of the *Slocum,* were slowly losing ground. At nine
o'clock Governor Pardee received word at the Mayor's office in Oakland (he had been Mayor of Oakland before being elected Governor, and had slipped quite naturally into
his old office) that the piers and the ferry were doomed.

There was nothing Pardee could do; nothing Mayor
Schmitz and Police Chief Dinan, who had now arrived on
the scene (there is no record of where Acting Fire Chief John
Dougherty was Friday night) could do. It was in the hands
of the fireboats and the pale, sleepless men who guided the
hoses into the fire and held them until they dropped from
exhaustion and were replaced by other volunteers—or, if
there were no volunteers, unwilling men summoned rudely
at gun point. One shabby, middle-aged man, a Mexican or
an Italian—no one ever knew, because no one ever knew
who he was—was ordered by a soldier to help pull hose and,
misunderstanding, failed to obey. The soldier stabbed him
in the back with his bayonet. When he turned to defend
himself, another man, one Ernest Denicke, who had volunteered for duty with the National Guard (although he was
not actually a member of the Guard; he was wearing a uni-
form he had brought home from the Philippines), shot
and killed him. His body was carried out of the way and
the fight went on.

Ten o'clock, eleven o'clock, the hours stretched out in a
never-ending battle. The unwelcome wind from the northwest had begun again, growing in strength as it was sucked
in by the rising volume of superheated air until it reached

gale force. As it grew the fire exploded in more fury than
ever. On the waterfront it was so hot that on the *Slocum*,
in a slip surrounded by fire, the walls of the cabin and the
sides of the vessel itself were beginning to smoke. Streams
of water were diverted to keep it from catching fire. Up
above them the fire moved steadily up Telegraph Hill, forcing the sturdy defenders toward the top.

Making his way, in his endless, sleepless rounds, back to
Van Ness, Mayor Schmitz found the one heartening factor
of the night: the fire had not reached Van Ness again, and
now that the wind was blowing so strongly against it, it did
not seem likely that it would. It had gone no farther north
on Van Ness than Filbert Street, although up the hillside it
had leaped over Filbert to Greenwich, over Greenwich to
Lombard, and there it still burned brightly. He praised
Captain MacBride and his Navy gunners for their work, and
informed Captain Coleman that he did not feel it was necessary now to dynamite the western side of Van Ness as he
had ordered him to do earlier.

Fort Mason was safe, and "AT THIS HOUR, 11 PM," Funston
telegraphed Washington, "REMAINDER OF RESIDENTIAL SEC-
TION KNOWN AS WESTERN ADDITION SEEMS OUT OF DANGER."
The fire was actually over as far as the Western Addition
was concerned, although there was none of the certainty of
that this Friday evening that there had been Friday morning, when the trumpets blew and people slapped each other
on the back in congratulation. In the parks cinders and
sparks still showered down; weary, blackened fire fighters
continued to stumble in, dropping in exhaustion to be rolled
out of the way by troops, while women gave up their blankets to cover them. The carriages, those that had escaped
impressment by William Denman, remained all night in
front of the mansions on Vallejo and Broadway and Pacific,
ready for their owners to flee.

By this time Denman had commandeered twenty-four assorted vehicles, as well as some of the "swell male members of the Burlingame set" and was on his way to the Folsom Street pier. When they reached the pier he dismounted and began triumphantly to count them off, only to find that there were only twenty-three; one had got away. There was a bad moment of anger and the rough side of his tongue but then the ones that were left began to load supplies, and when they were finished Denman went back out into the night to impress more wagons, keeping a sterner watch than ever on them this time.

At Mason word had finally arrived from Secretary Taft, instructing Funston to provide one thousand rifles for the "protection of citizens," with five hundred of these to be issued immediately to Julian Sonntag, the chairman of the Protection Committee. Funston was further directed to "KINDLY DETAIL SOME NON-COMMISSIONED OFFICERS TO INSTRUCT THE CITIZENS SWORN IN TO PROPERLY USE THE RIFLE." This he proceeded glumly to do, and the hundreds of new special police flocking to Sonntag's home on Scott Street in the Western Addition, to be sworn in by Judge Cool, were added to the police, the earlier special police, the Army, the Navy, the Marines, the National Guard, the University of California Cadets, and the various vigilante groups, all maintaining their own brands of order or disorder in the city.

The Western Addition was safe, but the waterfront and the piers and the Ferry Building were not, nor was Telegraph Hill, where, cut off from the world, desperate men were still making last-ditch efforts to beat back the fire. Far beyond the reach of fire hoses or fire engines—even in normal times fire engines had never been able to scale these heights—they continued to chop down houses, and drag them out of the way, swarm over small shanties with wet sacks and buckets of water from the cistern on top of the hill. They worked without letup, beating the fire out, drawing more water from the cistern, wetting down smoking houses, dowsing firebrands—until all the water was gone. Then, legend has it, they turned to wine—500 gallons of it —and used that in the face of the flames. (Such unorthodox fire-fighting methods were nothing new to San Francisco, which had been saved in an earlier fire by 80,000 gallons of vinegar, liberally applied.)

At the Ferry Building the employees were still at their posts, although the information Governor Pardee had received at nine o'clock was that the Ferry Building was being abandoned. They would stay as long as they could, although they were certain now that it was hopeless; the violence of the wind made sure of that. At midnight the few ships remaining at the piers—except for the tugs fighting the fire—were moved out into the bay, to protect them from the fire when it got into the piers, as it must, inevitably. As the fire in the lumber district and the warehouses at the foot of Telegraph Hill raged ever stronger, it was but a matter of time.

San Francisco Chronicle.

VOL. LXXXIII.　　SAN FRANCISCO, CAL., SATURDAY, APRIL 21, 1906.　　NO. 96.

RESIDENCE DISTRICTS OUT OF DANGER

At midnight, last night the fire was out or under control in all parts of the city except at the base of Telegraph Hill. There the flames were eating southward, and it was feared the docks would go.　All vessels were moved into the stream.

One o'clock . . . two o'clock . . . the flames grew steadily worse, scaling the paint off the fireboats in their turbulent fury. At 3:30 Saturday morning, suddenly, the fire was burning in the Pacific Mail dock, the first pier actually to catch fire. Now the desperate moment was at hand when the fate of every pier from there to South San Francisco was at stake. Hastily the cutter *Golden Gate,* close by, had lines of hose out, fighting to save the dock, fighting to keep the fire from sweeping through all the piers.

Gradually, facing blinding, searing flames, they were successful. That was the peak of the fire. From then on it was being beaten back slowly, painfully slowly, but steadily. And on the hillside up above, the wine—and the vacant lots on top of the hill—were doing their work. By four o'clock Saturday morning the fire there could safely be said to be under control.

There were still hours of struggle ahead on the waterfront, still hours when success or failure lay in the balance, before the fire beat itself out against the U. S. Customs warehouse and the grain sheds, long one-story brick buildings with metal roofs and doors, beneath Telegraph Hill. It was broad daylight before Mayor Schmitz, exhausted almost beyond endurance but satisfied now that there was no further danger, turned to make his way slowly back to his temporary office at Franklin Hall.

It was seven o'clock Saturday morning, April 21. The fire was over.

FIVE

"I remember the night of rain and seeing a grown man sitting on a curbstone the morning after, sobbing in the final break-down of bodily endurance . . . the sigh of wind through the windows of desolate walls, the screech and clack of ruined cornices . . ."

—David Starr Jordan

▲▲▲

It was eight o'clock by the time Mayor Schmitz reached Franklin Hall and wearily opened the door to his makeshift office. Fire still smoldered in ruins from North Beach to Twentieth Street in the Mission district, black clouds of smoke still rose from burning oil and coal, but the danger was over at last. Behind him lay the ruins of almost everything that had been fine and beautiful, lighthearted and gay in San Francisco—as well as the ruins of the Chinese ghetto, the bawdy houses of the Barbary Coast, the slums of the South of Market district.

520 blocks of San Francisco had been burned, 28,188 buildings destroyed. Hundreds of thousands had left the city. Of the 261 miles of streetcar and cable lines in the city, not a single mile remained in operation. The banking district, the wholesale district, factories, every retail store of any consequence—450 million dollars in property values— had gone up in smoke. 3400 acres, half again as much as the area of the Chicago fire, stretched out, picked bone clean by the fire and the wind—ruins livid red, pale purple, patches of white lime and the dull brown color of the

earth. Here and there little eddies of lime dust rose in the wind, but there were no ashes; they had been sucked up in the vortex and swept away.

In the residential districts, where buildings had been mostly of wood, the fire had left nothing behind but withered trees and charred telephone poles. Commercial areas were jumbles of piled bricks, twisted steel frames, distorted machinery and snarls of wire. A narrow footpath had been cleared on Market Street; down it passed an endless file of refugees, burdened with what possessions they had managed to save, headed for the ferry.

APRIL, 21st, 1906.

To all Civil and Military Authorities.

Pass bearer *B. F. Brisac*

through all lines to and from points beyond the limits of the City and County of San Francisco for the public good.

E. E. Schmitz

MAYOR.

California Historical Society, San Francisco

Tens of thousands of people in camps, hundreds in the Presidio hospital, sanitation problems beginning to fester, a case of typhoid discovered, a death from smallpox. A city existing under ironclad restrictions where no lights could burn, where in large areas one could not even go from one block to another without a police pass; a city ruled by half a dozen conflicting bodies of police, beset by rapidly proliferating vigilante groups. Now that the fire was over, the city's problems were just beginning.

It had been days since Mayor Schmitz had had any sleep, and on Saturday morning he might well have gone home to bed. Instead he sat listening as a succession of people presented accounts of their progress or their problems. Water was still desperately short, except in Golden Gate Park. In other areas refugee camps had sprung up around such limited supplies as could be found: near wells, at a spring that had begun to trickle forth in front of the Mint, and around the Ferry, where a great camp had gathered to take advantage of the incoming boats bringing not only fresh water but also food and clothing. The distribution of food was moving awkwardly and haphazardly, but at least there *was* food now and thanks to the Army and to William Denman (who was still out commandeering more wagons) some of it was getting to the seven distribution stations which had been established. Seven stations for all the thousands of people—no wonder the lines stretched out block after block, and never seemed to grow any shorter.

Again and again an undercurrent of resentment rose to the surface against restrictions, seizures, impressment for public works, confusion, dissension, the various police bodies in conflict with each other, the Mayor's orders conflicting with General Funston's. Angrily Mayor Schmitz decided that it was time to have things out with General Funston, and so a conference was set up, ostensibly to discuss the policing of the city. This being the case, more than the Army was involved: Chief Dinan and several Committee members accompanied the Mayor; General Lauck, the National Guard Adjutant General, attended; and Funston invited Admiral Goodrich to represent the Navy. The conference was to be held at Fort Mason, a matter which only increased Schmitz' indignation.

But when the haggard men assembled at Fort Mason on Saturday afternoon, it was for an unexpectedly placid meeting. Much to the Mayor's surprise the terrible-tempered General Funston was completely co-operative. He had actually been so from the beginning, Schmitz began to realize; in the major areas of fire fighting, and particularly in the matter of dynamiting, the Army had invariably worked at the direction of the civil authorities (although the Army got all the blame for the damage done). Authority had been delegated to the Army to police the city; where Funston had failed was not in performance, but in diplomacy: quick, energetic, impatient, he had simply gone ahead and done what needed to be done.

What needed to be done now was to eliminate the confusion and friction which had inevitably existed during the fire. It was not necessary to blame anyone, although it was agreed that many deplorable acts had taken place. As a result, at this meeting on Saturday afternoon there was little of the acrimony that was shortly to erupt over the National Guard.

For this very Saturday, the National Guard was perpetrating a number of misdeeds which would infuriate the public. Spring Valley Water Company workers, sent in to make desperately needed repairs on the water mains, were hauled up and sent away from their work; they were not allowed to return until the company officials obtained five hundred passes for them. Shortly before noon Saturday National Guardsmen had gotten into an argument with a young man named Frank Riordan in front of his home on Post Street. Riordan had a pint of whisky in his pocket. When he refused to throw it away, he was shot and killed.

A tannery worker, on his way home to his sick wife, was
fired at; he ran back to his tannery.

If the meeting Saturday afternoon had served to put a
halt to such incidents, they might have been forgiven as
overzealous enforcement of rules still in effect on Saturday.
Unfortunately, the Saturday afternoon agreement had little
effect on the rowdy, undisciplined National Guard. They
continued with a series of flagitious actions which brought
on a worse feud than anything that had involved the Army.
But Saturday's transgressions were still unknown to Mayor
Schmitz, and there was no reason to expect future disorders.
The Mayor merely stated that he felt that "normal conditions should prevail" as soon as possible. It was suggested
that where possible the severe restrictions would be relaxed, and personal liberty and personal property would be
respected.

General Funston quickly agreed. So did General Lauck
for the National Guard. The areas for which each of the
policing entities was to be responsible were defined, including that of the Navy, which, no longer operating under the
Army, would patrol the waterfront. "Vigilante" and self-
appointed "special police" groups would be disbanded and
no more would be recognized. And, since the Army was the
only body sufficiently organized and with adequate equipment available, all relief supplies would be consigned directly to General Funston and would be distributed by the
Army. The meeting came to an end in a spirit of harmony
all the more warm because it was so unexpected.

This left matters more or less as they were, so far as General Funston was concerned: an area somewhat smaller to
police and provide for, but still the largest part of the unburned area, and containing a majority of the people remaining in San Francisco; and the responsibility for han-

dling all the relief supplies, which, as boats and men had been available, the Army had been doing to a large extent anyway. Sunday morning he issued an order to the Army embodying the agreement which had been reached the previous afternoon: passes would no longer be required (except from "suspicious characters") to go from one area to another; automobiles would not be commandeered without a written order from himself or from the Mayor, dated April 23 or later; lights would be permitted to burn until 10 P.M. And if lights *were* found burning after that, sentries would investigate *quietly* and *inform* occupants of the curfew time. Above all, troops must act temperately.

THE PRICE OF "THE EXAMINER" IS FIVE CENTS.

For Latest
Military Regulations
See Page 3

San Francisco Examiner

For information of your
friends and families
See Page 5

SAN FRANCISCO, MONDAY, APRIL 23, 1906

FUNSTON RELAXES THE RIGOR OF MARTIAL LAW

Mayor Schmitz was eminently pleased at the satisfactory arrangements and the dispatch with which General Funston issued orders to implement the agreements, so pleased that he was able to persuade himself that there had never been any dissension at all. He was slightly concerned to have the newspapers report Sunday morning that the meeting had "served to clear the air"; that made it look as though he had been quarreling with the city's benefactors—an attitude not only ungrateful but likely to affect further government largess. His concern grew to consternation when Secretary Taft sent a telegram to Funston demanding an explanation of the friction reported to exist between the two.

So far as Funston was concerned, there had never been any friction; he brushed the report off as the "excited imagination of some overworked newspaper correspondent." Schmitz, always on the defensive, telegraphed Taft, "REPORTS OF CONFLICT BETWEEN GENERAL FUNSTON AND MYSELF ABSOLUTELY WITHOUT FOUNDATION. WE ARE NOT ONLY WITHOUT DIFFICULTIES BUT ARE COOPERATING IN THE UTMOST FRIENDSHIP AND HARMONY. Then he brooded about it overnight and on Monday sent another telegram expressing indignition at the "REMARKABLY MALICIOUS AND DECIDEDLY UNTRUTHFUL SUGGESTION" that any conflict existed. And, as a matter of fact, no conflict did exist; henceforth Schmitz reserved his indignation for the National Guard.

Sunday was a day of sudden alarms, tragic accidents, unhappiness and forced cheerfulness, the tentative beginnings of the "return to normal conditions" the Mayor was so hopeful for. It had turned severely cold; perhaps it seemed even colder than it actually was in contrast with the violent heat of the fire. Women shivered over small fires in the park while men went to look for more wood. Policemen began to knock on the doors of undamaged homes, demanding blankets for the refugees. It was hard to believe that the fire was over; there was a wave of panic in the camps at the rumor, later disproved, that fire had sprung up again on Union Street in the Western Addition.

Church services were held throughout the city and the people of San Francisco, not ordinarily a church-going city, filled to overflowing the chapel at the Presidio, turned out by the thousands for Methodist services, Presbyterian, Baptist, masses said in the ruins of St. Dominic's. Thousands wept as Archbishop Montgomery, holding mass on the steps of St. Mary's Cathedral, told them that Fire Chief Dennis Sullivan, mortally injured in the earthquake Wednesday and unconscious since then, had died at 1:10 A.M. this Sunday morning. While eastern sermonizers, drawing morals from San Francisco's plight, were thundering from their pulpits that "the Sodom of the west has been punished," vast crowds, destitute and homeless, were gathering to worship in Golden Gate Park before a pulpit made of two upright stakes and a wooden crosspiece. A man played a cornet, while the crowd sang,

> "Other refuge have I none, hangs my helpless
>   soul on thee;
> Leave, oh leave me not alone; still support and
>   comfort me."

There was a brief disturbance, noisy shouting and confusion in the driveway where soldiers were "herding a squad of gesticulating, jabbering Chinamen as men herd sheep." The Chinese were soon dealt with. The shouting died away and the services resumed, the minister's voice rising and falling over the shivering worshipers.

Thousands of people continued to leave the city, taking advantage of the railroads' offer of free transportation. Many of them simply headed blindly away from San Francisco, with no idea of where they were going. Butte, Montana, became a favorite dumping ground for dazed, hungry refugees. Children and babies, unaccompanied and unidentified, dropped off the trains in Oregon. There were pitiful cases: a man with burned hands; a newly widowed woman, frightened and alone. There were also frauds: a group of three men and a woman traveling together, and one of the men refusing work at $5 a day because he "didn't want to break up the crowd."

In San Francisco many people whose homes were undamaged but who had moved to the park for fear the fire would spread or new earthquakes would come began returning home. There they still shared a major discomfort with the homeless, the necessity of cooking out on improvised stoves. Mindful of the "Ham and Eggs Fire" which had started from a defective chimney, fires were forbidden in every remaining building in the city, until chimneys could be inspected. In front of every house stoves began to appear, at first such simple affairs as a piece of sheet iron on bricks; later elaborate fireplaces, heating stoves, huge iron cooking ranges moved from the kitchen to the front sidewalk. Soon fifty thousand of these cook-outs were in use, kitchens often surrounded by screens made of window shutters, billboards, or frames covered with cloth, where meals were prepared and carried in the house to be eaten in the dining room—or in the real kitchen. "About all San Francisco needs now is a cookbook," said the *Chronicle*.

The sidewalk kitchens provided still another opportunity for San Francisco to hang up its signs: "Little America," "Bon-Ton Beanery" or "Skiddoo Cafe—Wanted, a boy to brush flies off guests" or, on a shack of corrugated iron sheets, "Villa de Ironclad." Some people mockingly hung up the names of famous restaurants, such as "Tait's" or "Zink-and's." Ironically enough, when real restaurants began to struggle back into existence some time later, they too would have to cook in the street: one sat in the restaurant and studied the menu in the usual way, then waited while the waiter went out to the sidewalk to give the order to the chef.

In spite of all the people who had left the city or who were returning to their homes, there were still perhaps a hundred thousand people camped out at Golden Gate Park Sunday, twenty to thirty thousand at the Presidio, and many thousands elsewhere. The Army had begun to stabilize half a dozen locations into more or less permanent camps. Army engineers were beginning to build barracks, and soldiers, no longer impressing men for work, were digging sanitation trenches. Few of the idle thousands looking on offered to help as the soldiers worked in an emergency attempt to ward off smallpox and typhoid epidemics. Already three more cases of typhoid and two of smallpox had been discovered and taken to the Presidio hospital. These were from infections which had occurred before the fire, but combined with a lack of sanitation, water mixed with sewage in the mains, and exposure, they could be the basis for major outbreaks.

An even more prevalent, though less contagious, epidemic was the number of births occurring in the camps. Triplets had been born at the Presidio, and many a child would later be told, with more than a grain of truth, that his mother had found him under a bush in Golden Gate Park. All of which led to serious rivalry in later years over the definition of a "true San Franciscan"—between those born in the Park and those born nine months later to parents who had camped in the Park.

There were births, there were epidemics, or the beginnings of them; on Sunday the city began to calculate its deaths, too, those that had resulted from the disaster. Coroner Walsh was busy reorganizing his office in a vacant store and setting up a morgue; he estimated a thousand dead, but there was no way of knowing. Bodies had been buried by soldiers and the National Guard in parks and vacant lots near where they were found; bodies had burned, never to be found. There was no sign of those who had met death in the earthquake or the flames; only here and there a disconsolate group in front of a ruined building—the silent, aching evidence that a relative had met death there.

But for the most part San Francisco simply stood still on Sunday, shocked beyond movement at the enormity of the disaster, uncertain as to the future. Governor Pardee had declared Monday a legal holiday throughout California, so that banks need not open and contracts need not be met.

He would continue to call such holidays, he said, until a special session of the legislature met to cope with the various legal difficulties arising from the fire. He did not know when the legislature would meet. He was too busy to call it.

No one knew when there would be money from the banks; it was equally uncertain when the insurance companies would begin to pay their claims—if, indeed, some of them ever would. The Board of Underwriters of San Francisco had stated confidently on April 18 that its member companies would pay all their losses. But when they met again on Saturday, behind barred and guarded doors at a newly rented headquarters, it was to warn the public flatly that it should not get the impression "that insurance companies had money to throw away, or that any losses would be paid until properly adjusted." This was reasonable enough, but the impression the public actually received when the statement became public on Sunday was that the insurance companies intended to use every possible means to delay or avoid payment. And when James Phelan attempted to get some kind of encouraging statement from the manager of one of the large insurance groups, he met with the same stony refusal: "It is better for those whose spirits are drooping to allow them to droop, rather than to buoy them up with false hopes," he was told.

But if most of San Francisco was standing still, there were, unknown to the public, ominous stirrings of activity and planning for the future from one group. San Francisco's corrupt Board of Supervisors, shunted aside from the government of the city by Mayor Schmitz and the Committee of Fifty, met on Sunday afternoon for the first time since the fire. The City Hall, where they normally met, was destroyed, of course; they met in Supervisor McGushin's saloon. There they angrily considered the situation, and when the meeting was over their spokesman, Supervisor Gallagher, informed

Boss Ruef that they had no intention of "abdicating in favor of the Committee of Fifty." Ruef had no intention of abdicating either, but he was too wise to tangle, or allow his supervisors to tangle, directly with the formidable members of the Committee. Let the Committee do the dirty work and bear the burden of the relief effort, he cautioned; that would divert their attention while the Board of Supervisors quietly pursued its financially remunerative official functions. Ruef engaged Mowry's Hall, in the Western Addition, where they could meet regularly beginning Monday afternoon.

Ruef himself was content, for the moment, with his nominal function on the Committee—that of member of the Subcommittee on Relocation of Chinese. The Committee was determined that the alien Chinese should not be allowed to congregate again on the extremely valuable land on the side of Nob Hill which had been Chinatown. The members thought that a deserted area near Colma, just beyond the southern boundary of the county, would be a suitable place for the Chinese. Pending a move to this permanent location, the military authorities, at the Committee's behest, were this Sunday segregating all Orientals into a separate camp at North Beach.

Food and other supplies were pouring into San Francisco now, and to keep them moving William Denman was still commandeering transportation. By late Sunday afternoon he had impressed 122 vehicles and was preparing to take over the 123rd, a morgue wagon, when he realized it was a "dead wagon" and allowed it to pass. Only then did he unbuckle the belt of his six-shooter, bow to the new order and stop impressing wagons and carriages. "I suppose if I should serve time for what I have done in the past three days," he observed, "I would not get out in ten years." (But when U. S. Court of Appeals Chief Judge William Denman died, by his own hand, in 1959, he was remembered, not for the spectacular days when he had seized private property at gun point and forced men to work against their will, but as "a man who insists on the rights of individuals, and who insists that these rights be enforced." He had also been, however, said Chief Justice Warren, "a rugged man, a straightforward man who never ran from a fight in his life.")

Thus, for all the apathy, doubt and uncertainty that lay over San Francisco, Saturday and Sunday were days that contained the seeds of most of the major problems that would harass the city in the days to come: insurance settlements and financial problems, the Chinese question, relief administration, civic corruption, vigilantes and the National Guard. And as Sunday drew to an end, still another shocking incident involving the "special police" and the National Guard was about to happen.

At Saturday's meeting the National Guard had been assigned to police a large area south of Golden Gate Park and in the Mission district. General Koster had not been present at the meeting. Although much of the area was undeveloped and sparsely populated, he felt incapable of policing it properly with the 1500 National Guardsmen now on duty. Consequently, in spite of the understanding that the special police would be disbanded and vigilante groups would not be authorized, he had undertaken to recognize and arm a "Citizen's Patrol." Members of this patrol were now on duty at nearly every intersection in the National Guard area.

Sunday evening a commission merchant named H. C. Tilden had taken his wife and three children to their summer home in Menlo Park. It was close to midnight when, accompanied by his coachman and an Army lieutenant, he returned to San Francisco. Tilden was a member of the

Committee of Fifty, and his car had been used for Red
Cross work; it bore a Red Cross flag and he himself wore the
Red Cross insignia on his sleeve. When he reached the first
Citizen's Patrol station at the intersection of Twenty-eighth
Street and Guerrero, he called out "Red Cross" and was allowed to pass. At the second station, at Twenty-fifth Street,
the guard gave way as soon as he saw the Red Cross flag. At
the third station, at Twenty-second Street, there were six
men in the middle of the road; they separated when the car
got within fifty feet of them. Tilden continued, expecting to
pass safely as he had through the previous stations. Instead,
one of the men fired. Lieutenant Seaman, in the back seat
of the Tilden car, returned the fire. Two other patrolmen
fired at the car. Tilden stopped the car, shouted, "I am shot,
they have killed me," staggered to the sidewalk and fell
dead.

It had begun to rain heavily. Through the pouring rain,
with the car breaking down over and over again, Tilden's
body was taken to the Central Police Station. Regular Army
soldiers came and arrested the three members of the Citizen's Patrol who had fired at the car.

On and on the rain fell, drenching the guards at their
posts, the thousands of refugees huddled without any protection whatever, extinguishing the cheerful little campfires,
soaking the signs that had been blithely put up, silencing
the pianos that played ragtime tunes with forced gaiety in
the parks, pouring down on the ruined buildings it might
have saved if it had come in time.

SIX

"The cow is in the hammock
The cat is in the lake
The baby in the garbage can
What difference does it make?
There is no water and still less soap
We have no city, but lots of hope."

Sign on a ruined building
on Market Street

∆∆∆

General Adolphus W. Greely, the Commander of the Pacific
Division, returned Monday morning. He had actually arrived late the night before, but, much concerned with ap-
pearances, he had chosen to spend the night on the steamer
Albatross as the guest of the Fish Commissioner and return
to his command at a more seemly hour the following morning. Greely was a man of imposing presence and monu-
mental self-esteem, "one of those 'me-and-God' fellows,"
General Funston's father, E. H. Funston, called him. The
product at 62 of 45 years in the Army (he was the only enlisted man in the Civil War to become a general officer in the
Regular Army), he and Funston were as unlike as two men
could be. Like most Regulars, Greely resented the fact that
Funston had stepped into the Regular Army with the rank
of Brigadier General; he considered the red-headed young
man a publicity-seeking upstart. (Funston maintained a fit-
ting silence regarding his relations with General Greely.
Not so Funston's father, who cracked that the older general
was "very much put out with God Almighty because He
brought down the earthquake upon San Francisco during

General Greely's absence"—as a result of which General Funston had managed the situation and made a good job of it.)

Nevertheless they had a few things in common. Like Funston, Greely himself had a record of extraordinary heroism; he had known the taste of fame and the feeling of having his exploits recounted on the front pages of newspapers around the world. Nor had he hesitated to rush into print with his own account of those exploits; ultimately he wrote five books to Funston's one. But there the resemblance ended. Unlike Funston's daring forays into the face of danger, Greely's heroism had been a matter of grim endurance: he had been marooned for three years in the Arctic and had hung on until a rescue mission came to get him. Only six of the original twenty-five men of the Greely expedition returned. And over them all from then on hung the terrible suspicion of cannibalism.

General Funston was in a state very close to collapse when Greely reached the Pacific Division's temporary headquarters at Fort Mason, but this was a matter of little concern to Greely. He was horrified at the liberties Funston had taken with the Army, at the suggestion of martial law, determined to retreat immediately from the independent and vulnerable position Funston had gotten the Army into. Coldly he took his subordinate to task for his feud with Mayor Schmitz—a feud which, if it had ever actually existed, had now been thoroughly settled. Dismissing Funston, he set about to remedy the situation, sent word to Mayor Schmitz that an office was available for his use at Fort Mason, and assured the Mayor of the Army's "complete subordination to civil power and urgent public need."

That was all very gratifying, the Mayor said perfunctorily; he had, of course, already come to a complete agreement with General Funston. This Monday morning he was

much more concerned with the National Guard. Nothing
that had happened up to now had so infuriated him or the
public as the Tilden murder the night before. Although the
murder had actually been the work of three "special police,"
and the Mayor himself bore a great deal of responsibility
for the special police, the blame for this particular incident
was placed squarely on the National Guard, which had authorized the Citizen's Patrol.

When the Committee of Fifty met Monday morning
there were angry denunciations of the National Guard, and
heated demands for its recall. These were translated, finally,
into a tactfully worded note to Governor Pardee, expressing a vote of thanks to the Governor and the National
Guard for its excellent service, but stating that there were
now enough Federal troops, Marines and Naval forces in
the city to give it all the protection needed. This did not
fool Pardee, who, a long-time member of the National
Guard himself, chose to take personal affront at the request
for its withdrawal. He sent back a flat refusal.

The Mayor sent a second, less tactful letter. Furious
charges began to fly between the embattled camps. "Such
action is absolutely illegal," the Mayor stormed. "There is
no martial law and never has been since the earthquake."

"Such charges are absurd and cowardly," the Governor
retorted. "I have been a member of the National Guard almost continuously since 1872, and I know whereof I speak."
The Committee then requested Governor Pardee to come to
San Francisco for a meeting to discuss the matter. He sent
word he was too busy to come.

In any case, despite his assurances to Schmitz, the Committee had found that it could not count on Greely at all.
When they asked him to undertake the entire relief administration, as Funston had agreed to do on Saturday, and
which was the justification for requesting the withdrawal of

the National Guard, Greely refused; such action was "unwarranted by law." Mayor Schmitz pointed out that according to the newspapers, Congress had authorized the Army to take such action. He was coldly informed that the Army could not be guided by newspaper reports.

Finally, after considerable pressure and pleading, Greely relented enough to agree to undertake the relief administration if he could be convinced that it was the Army's "civic duty to prevent public suffering." He would consider the matter overnight and meet with the Committee again Tuesday morning.

Monday night Dr. Edward Devine arrived to take charge of the relief administration. His reception by General Greely was exceedingly cool. Despite his protestations, Greely fully intended to take over the relief administration himself as soon as he could get someone else to take responsibility for the decision. Devine was assigned a four-by-six-foot cubbyhole at Fort Mason and told that that was all there was available.

Meanwhile, outraged reports of National Guard antics continued to pour in. A dozen or more shots rang out near the German Health Hospital, dogs being killed or run off, people being frightened into putting out lights. Orderly pedestrians were halted in the dark with rifles pointed at short range.

A National Guard private, "while drunk or crazy," stormed into police headquarters and tried to shoot a detective on duty there. Another National Guardsman compelled a policeman, at bayonet point, to hand over his star; his commanding officer had told him to collect all stars, and had made no distinction between special and regular police. Policeman Alpers was fired on, without even being challenged. Police Captain Martin was ordered to put out his lights, although it was well before the 10 P.M. curfew. "For some reason the police are absolutely against us," General Koster was quoted as saying. "They do not make our burden lighter by sympathy and aid."

Tuesday morning San Francisco papers published, and the members of the Committee learned for the first time, the information that Theodore Roosevelt had issued a proclamation entrusting all relief funds (except the Congressional appropriations) to the Red Cross, represented in San Francisco by Dr. Devine, and instructing the public to send their contributions to Dr. Devine. The Mayor and the Committee had been counting heavily on the Congressional appropriations and the public subscriptions swelling across the country. It was a harsh blow to San Francisco's pride to learn that its leaders were excluded from the handling of the money. (Even worse, the Congressional appropriations had been entirely spent by the War Department, without consulting the Committee at all. They did not know that yet.) They arrived at the meeting Tuesday morning in a stormy mood, furious with General Greely for failing to relieve them of the National Guard, furious with Dr. Devine for usurping their handling of the money, and prepared to combat every move either of them made.

Fortunately, Dr. Devine was the first to speak, and fortunately, too, years of charity work had not made him either arrogant or condescending. He was well aware of the sensitive situation this Tuesday. He was full of compliments for the way the relief efforts had already been handled, full of praise for San Francisco's pluck and courage. He had come, he assured the bristling Committee members, not to interfere, but to help.

"We have the situation well in hand," Schmitz told him angrily. "People think it a reflection on San Francisco," said M. H. de Young, publisher of the *Chronicle*. "I think some mistake has been made," Judge Morrow chimed in.

It remained for James Phelan, Schmitz' long-time foe, and the head of the Finance Subcommittee which would have handled the funds, to put his finger on TR's reasons for wanting the money to be handled by the Red Cross. This was, as everyone was well aware, not an affront to the people of San Francisco, but to their Mayor. It was a precaution to keep Schmitz and Ruef from stealing the money. "President Roosevelt is no stranger to us," he said pointedly. "He must have had the good of the state in mind when he took the extraordinary course of recommending that money be deposited in the Subtreasury to the credit of someone other than the local authorities."

This quiet reminder, delivered by perhaps the most respected man at the meeting, brought the Committee up short. Thoughtfully they began to consider what could be done. It was decided to send the President a telegram, "IN VIEW OF YOUR PROCLAMATION WE DESIRE TO SAY THAT THE FINANCE COMMITTEE IS COMPOSED OF . . ." list the names, and ask that the money be entrusted to James Phelan. Then E. H. Harriman, the railroad magnate (who had made all his trains available for relief purposes and had come to San Francisco personally to aid in the relief effort), had a word of caution. Knowing Roosevelt's stubborn nature, it might not be wise to ask him to back down from a position publicly taken—that was too much like asking him to admit that he had made a mistake. The matter could better be handled through Taft: let General Greely send a telegram to Secretary of War Taft; let Dr. Devine also send a telegram to Taft, as head of the National Red Cross. Then Taft could find the proper time and the proper approach to get the President to change his mind. Greely and Devine agreed.

That matter out of the way, the discussion proceeded angrily to the actual physical operation of relief. The Committee members demanded that the Army take it over; Greely appeared to be even more reluctant than he had been on Monday. He had considered the matter, he told the Committee, with his staff officers, including Funston; they had agreed that it would take 5000 men to do the job. He had no hope of getting that many soldiers.

The Committee persisted. It was necessary to feed 350,000 people. Confusion and waste were reaching fantastic proportions. There would undeniably be the public suffering which Greely had said would be the Army's "civic duty" to prevent. At long last Greely agreed to ask for 2500 additional troops, to make the operation entirely military, and to take over in forty-eight hours, at noon on Thursday.

There remained the necessity of making a place for Dr. Devine in the relief effort. Judge Morrow suggested that the Red Cross and Phelan's Finance Subcommittee merge, thus giving both a voice in the administration of funds. This seemed an ideal solution; the details would be worked out at subsequent meetings. With all the problems seemingly settled, the meeting, like Saturday's meeting with Funston, ended in surprising harmony. Greely and Devine went off to lunch together out of tin cans, but not before Mayor Schmitz, still on edge from the President's telegram demanding an explanation of his feud with Funston, had cautioned those present to let no word get out that things were inharmonious.

The following day, Wednesday, the consolidation was effected, with the two organizations becoming the "Finance Committee of Relief and Red Cross Funds." That same day Roosevelt issued a new proclamation, gracefully withdrawing from his previous stand. He paid tribute to the work of the Committee of Fifty and said that it indicated the necessity for working exclusively through the Red Cross had passed. All contributions should henceforth be sent to the Finance Committee. "Dr. Devine will disburse any contributions sent to him through ex-Mayor Phelan, and will work in accord with him in all ways," the proclamation concluded.

Taft shortly thereafter forwarded $300,000 to Phelan. It was assumed that this was part of the $2.5 million Congressional appropriation. On April 29 Phelan inquired as to when the balance would be forthcoming. On May 1, in a telegram from Taft, the Committee learned for the first time the actual conditions of the government aid. The $300,000 had been from Red Cross funds. Very little money remained of the appropriation, as a matter of fact, and what there was would be disbursed by the War Department, not by the Finance Committee. "YOU AND YOUR COMMITTEE," Taft telegraphed Phelan, "EVIDENTLY MISCONCEIVED THE NATURE AND LEGAL LIMITATIONS OF CONGRESSIONAL AID AND DO NOT UNDERSTAND THE FACTS."

That was the final, infuriating blow. There was no way of knowing at this stage that they would eventually receive more than nine million dollars in contributions from the general public; just now it seemed that the most substantial contribution they could have expected had already been spent. The aid which had been so eagerly accepted was now scoffed at and belittled. The War Department had spent a million dollars on rations, another million on tents, blankets and bedding, thousands for medical supplies, more thousands for transportation. These expenditures were angrily dismissed as wasteful, if not fraudulent. That there had been waste, and duplication by the War Department of contributions from the public, was undeniable; that there had been help, at a time when it was vitally needed, was conveniently forgotten for the moment. But right or wrong, the money had been spent.

. . .

Greely's hedging at Tuesday's meeting on the use of soldiers had nettled Schmitz considerably, and it was by no means the last time he would feel this way. Nevertheless, he had been gratified at the final outcome of the meeting; he announced to the public that the Army would take over the relief operations in the entire city at noon April 26. That would bring order out of chaos, stabilize the operation of the city, justify the withdrawal of the National Guard. Unfortunately, the additional soldiers Greely felt were needed did not arrive. Noon of April 26 came and went and the Army did not take over.

Nor was the National Guard withdrawn. Governor Pardee remained as intransigent as ever, although he had made one concession: he had offered to put the National Guard under General Greely's command. Greely refused. "That is none of my affair," he commented icily. He did unbend enough to suggest that the National Guard be sent to Oakland and the Federal troops on duty there be returned to San Francisco in exchange. Pardee did not reply.

The National Guard continued its merry way and there were more incidents, occasionally serious, more often than not merely ridiculous. That a great many of them were doing good work and behaving themselves was largely ignored in the uproar, although General Koster presented a petition for their retention signed by what he said was 75 per cent of the residents of the National Guard area. Koster was fighting an uphill battle. Every time he implored sympathy from the public, reminding them that many of the Militia were disaster victims themselves, on duty in San Francisco at considerable personal sacrifice, a new incident would occur.

A Marine captain arrested a young Militia sentry who, "afraid of his shadow," was shooting at everything that moved. This time he had killed something, he wasn't sure

what. "If I have killed a man, may God bless him," he cried.
(It was a dog.) He was taken to the guardhouse. The newspapers reported mockingly that two National Guardsmen
had "succeeded in killing a tethered horse," and in so doing had startled the whole neighborhood. The men claimed
that they had fired in self-defense. It was dark, and they
saw a figure moving in the shadow of the wall; it was the
horse's head. They challenged the horse. When there was
no response, they fired. The horse "started to come at them
viciously"—or as viciously as it could, since it was lying
down. As it rose, a shower of sparks flew from its hoofs. The
two privates, scared out of their wits, fired over and over
again—in "self-defense."

There were graver incidents. The Chinese Consul General protested that, while his people were forced to remain
in segregated detention centers, a company of the National
Guard, 150 strong, was looting Chinatown, digging up possessions the Chinese had buried before evacuating the area.
Their commanding officer excused this; "they didn't know
what they were doing." In any case, he said, it was no worse
than what many private citizens were doing. Safes were being looted; only a few days before he had found five hundred men, women and children going over the ground occupied by jewelry stores on Kearny and Market Streets and
had had to run them off at bayonet point.

Looters, National Guard and civilian, were one of the
burdens of San Francisco the turbulent week following the
fire, so much so that Mayor Schmitz was seriously considering repeating his order of "Shoot to kill." Those already in
San Francisco were augmented by hordes of tourists who,
now that General Funston's order forbidding entry into the
city had been rescinded, were flooding in, some in search
of their families, most to see the sights and to pour through
the ruins for souvenirs—or anything more valuable that

could be found. Wagonloads of tourists toured the ruins. They came carrying suitcases, telescope baskets and gunny sacks to conceal their loot. In vain did Police Chief Dinan implore the officials of neighboring towns to keep their people at home. The tourists continued to come. It was suggested that they be charged admission—the proceeds would finance the entire reconstruction.

One minor influx of people was halted. William Randolph Hearst, who on his own initiative had undertaken a private and independent relief operation in San Francisco, was prevailed on to stop sending nurses from Los Angeles. "For heaven's sake, don't you think we have enough people to feed here as it is?" the City Health Officer at Oakland shouted at him. "We are not sick, we are hungry."

To a large extent the City Health Officer was correct. The epidemics that had been so feared never materialized. There were cases of pneumonia from exposure, there was heart trouble, insanity, but remarkably few cases of typhoid and smallpox. Stringent measures imposed by Lieutenant Colonel Torney, the Sanitary Officer, even in the confused and unco-ordinated period just after the fire, had their effect. Contagious cases were isolated. Sanitary trenches were dug. Garbage was buried. (Mayor Schmitz had to issue a proclamation to stop the widespread practice of using the manholes of the telephone company's cable system as refuse receptacles.) Both water and milk were required to be boiled before drinking. No camps were quarantined, but Mission Park, which for many years had been more garbage dump than park, was evacuated.

Consequently the number of contagious cases, although it increased, never reached serious epidemic proportions. Thirty cases of typhoid, well above the normal twelve-per-month rate, were discovered in the remainder of April, but none of these could be considered to be due to postfire conditions, since the incubation period had not been long enough. There were fifty-five cases in May, and then the rate dropped sharply to ten in June. Similarly, April produced seventy-four cases of smallpox, May forty-one, June only eight.

But while Colonel Torney was able to make some headway in disease prevention (and even these efforts were tentative and stumbling at first), relief operations in the ten days following the fire grew more chaotic by the hour. Divided authority, bad management, carelessness, poor judgment, all these contributed to an appalling waste. Relief centers were being maintained, with a complete lack of coordination, by the Army and the National Guard (in the areas originally assigned to them to police), by the Red Cross, by William Randolph Hearst (five camps), by John D. Rockefeller, by the Los Angeles Chamber of Commerce, by a committee from Oregon, by Masons, Knights of Pythias, and other fraternal organizations, and by many others. Tremendous quantities of food were being sent to San Francisco, cooked meat, hard-boiled eggs, sandwiches, in response to Governor Pardee's scores of telegrams to western cities on the day of the earthquake. Some of the food reached the distribution centers. Much of it, particularly the perishable items, piled up at the terminals in Oakland to rot.

What did reach San Francisco, in the haphazard system that existed, was frequently hardly usable by refugees who had lost all cooking equipment. At one point on Thursday the Central Supply Depot found itself with 3000 sacks of potatoes, 2000 sacks of flour, but no meat or canned goods. (Hundreds of head of cattle were arriving, but since there were no facilities for either keeping them or butchering them, that was hardly any help.) The Central Supply Depot was jammed with workers, seventy-five on the payroll and close to two hundred volunteers, busy getting into each other's way, sending out supplies with little regard to where they were going or what had been sent before, a total on Thursday of 151 loads averaging three tons each. In spite of this some distribution stations received nothing; some were so oversupplied that at one a persistent beggar was able to accumulate eighteen hams, to be sold subsequently at considerable profit.

Throughout California the word spread of free handouts without regard to quantity or need, and from all over the state tramps and beggars were arriving to join the rascals already in San Francisco ("We never heard that San Francisco lacked anything of having its due equipment of these cattle," sniffed *Harper's Weekly*) and partake of the easy living. "Bums are living better than ever," cried newspaper editorials. As a tramp named "Shifty Bill" put it cheerfully, it sure beat "spending the winter in the county jail."

Not only tramps took advantage of the situation. Now safe from impressment, only a handful of refugees volunteered for the work of building shelters or clearing streets. A contractor, offering work at $2 a day "and found" to five hundred men standing in line for rations, had only three takers. When the Alaska Packers Association offered to hire five hundred men, forty-six applied. Where relief kitchens had been set up it came to be a near-universal custom to work oneself to repletion at the breakfast table, then stretch out on the grounds in front of the kitchens and await the serving of dinner.

Not content to stand in line, hundreds were engaged in looting supplies. Wearing spurious Red Cross armbands, thieves took over whole wagonloads of relief goods. Unscrupulous teamsters volunteered at the docks to carry supplies, which never reached their intended destination. Men representing themselves to be from fraternal orders were

soliciting funds "for the refugees"—which no refugee
would ever receive the benefit of. Even those willing to
stand in line were becoming disdainful and demanding. A
woman refused a blouse at one relief station because she
did not like the color. As it turned out, she already had on
five blouses, collected at other relief stations, under her
"sacque." Those handing out supplies were often equally
indifferent and impatient. At a station where hundreds were
waiting in line to be issued blankets, the man in charge shut
the door in their faces at 6 P.M. That was the end of his
working day, regardless of who went cold that night.

All in all, Dr. Devine, who had heretofore been able to
reduce charity to an "exact science," was finding that in
San Francisco, where results must be achieved through the
prestigious, but inept (so far as relief operations were concerned) Committee of Fifty, the maddeningly unpredicta-
ble General Greely, and well-intentioned meddlers intent
on running their own operations, the science was not so easily come by. Still he strove manfully to cope with the situation from his crowded office at Fort Mason, now filled to
overflowing with assistants and packing-box desks. (Not until nearly three months later, when they moved to the
Hamilton Grammar School on Geary Street, did Dr. Devine
and his staff have anything like adequate accommodations.)
He had already established a Department of Registration,
which was intended to facilitate the work of distribution.
One hundred and fifty college students and professors were
making a house-to-house survey, registering all those deserv-
ing of aid. Masses of cards were accumulating, giving the
name of the head of family visited, his present and former
address, his occupation, race and religion. On the basis of this
useful information supplies were to be requisitioned by the
various distribution centers.

Unfortunately there was very little relationship between

the supplies requisitioned, the supplies delivered, and the supplies actually required for distribution. As it became apparent that the Army was not going to take over the relief operation on Thursday, as General Greely had promised, and as the newspapers began to raise a hue and cry about the mounting waste, Dr. Devine decided to issue a card to each individual. When he had drawn his ration for the day the holder's card would be stamped on the back or punched with a pencil. Within a few days, he assured everyone, the difficulties and duplications would be eliminated.

In spite of the waste and confusion, and irritation with General Greely as noon Thursday passed with no move from the Army to take over, Dr. Devine was getting along famously with Mayor Schmitz and the Citizens Relief Committee. He kept up a steady stream of happy messages back to Washington and in reply Taft wired Friday morning, "PLEASE SAY TO MAYOR SCHMITZ AND MR. PHELAN HOW GRATIFIED THE PRESIDENT AND I ARE AT THE HARMONY WHICH IS PREVAILING IN THE MANAGEMENT OF THE IMMENSE WORK WHICH HAS BEEN DONE IN SAN FRANCISCO."

This gratifying harmony did not include Governor Pardee and the National Guard, although Thursday afternoon the Governor was finally prevailed on to come to San Francisco for the first time since the fire. He visited the National Guard camps and found them good. He expressed satisfaction with the way they were handling matters, and then repaired to Fort Mason for a conference with General Greely, Mayor Schmitz, and Dr. Devine. It was not a happy meeting. The Governor lashed out at the Mayor and the Committee for requesting the Guard's withdrawal; he considered it a reflection on a "well organized and highly efficient body." He had earlier said that he wished "those who are cowardly enough to besmirch the reputation of our citizen-soldiery were half as good men"; he said it again, with embellishments.

In his best "Who, me?" manner, Schmitz immediately insisted that no charges had been made. On the contrary, he reminded the Governor, he and the Committee had commended the National Guard and thanked the Governor for its services. If there had been any charges, they must have been made by irresponsible outsiders. The request for withdrawal was solely in order to concentrate control of the city in the Federal troops and prevent misunderstanding and conflict of orders.

The Governor said he had no intention of withdrawing the National Guard.

General Greely suggested once more that the Federal troops in Oakland be exchanged for the National Guard in San Francisco. Pardee refused. He repeated his offer, however, to put the National Guard under General Greely's command. Greely refused.

When the sullen controversy was over the only thing anyone had been able to agree on was that General Greely would make available to General Koster a copy of every General Order issued to the Army. The Governor assured him that General Koster would, on receipt of the orders, issue identical orders to the National Guard. What Koster did with them was no concern of General Greely's; he intended to follow, he repeated firmly, the "strictest policy of non-interference with the status or duties of the National Guard." Pardee went back to Oakland publicly damning those who criticized the National Guard, and reiterating his intention to leave the Militia in San Francisco indefinitely.

Although the meeting had been something less than a success, it nevertheless marked for all practical purposes the end of the National Guard controversy. Whether due to Greely's orders, which General Koster faithfully relayed to his troops, or to the simple fact that as they gained more experience the young, untrained men became better soldiers, there were few further troubles with them. They did their work, they fed and cared for 25-30,000 people a day in their area and, in spite of occasional boisterousness, by and large they behaved themselves. (And one observer pointed out that they'd never been able to shoot straight enough to be any serious danger, anyway.)

They stayed until May 31, when they were suddenly paid their wages for April, at the rate of $2 per day, and withdrawn without explanation, leaving behind $300,000 in claims for supplies they had seized and labor they had forced civilians to perform (and taking with them a claim for their own May wages). Leaving San Francisco was an occasion for celebration throughout the National Guard camps. In one of the more spectacular observances, a Cavalry troop stationed in Portsmouth Square held a mock funeral with such solemnity that, until they looked closer, sight-seers thought it was the real thing. The citizen-soldiery gathered up all the empty bottles in their camp, placed them on a stretcher, and with a bugler playing a funeral dirge, marched two-by-two all around the square. The bottles were then laid to rest in a deep grave dug on the Washington Street side of the square, and covered with dirt, while a guardsman pronounced benediction.

The Thursday afternoon conference was not, however, the end of the harried Mayor's difficulties with General Greely. The very next day Greely tossed a new bombshell by informing the Mayor, by letter, that he intended to withdraw the Army altogether from San Francisco. "The War Department looks with doubt," he wrote, "on the continued use of the Army in policing San Francisco, and also the operation and supervision of relief measures, subsistance, sanitation . . ." Once again, though, Greely left the door open: the Army would stay if he could be convinced that it was really necessary. Mayor Schmitz thought he knew the petulant general pretty well by now; what Greely really wanted, he told the Committee of Fifty, was to be coaxed to stay.

It was more serious than that. To do General Greely justice, there *was* considerable anxiety in Washington over the Army's position; the "constitutional cranks" Secretary Taft had anticipated were beginning to raise a clamor over the "martial law" in San Francisco. There was a flurry of conferences, hasty telegrams back and forth to Washington. Secretary Taft suggested a loophole, although not a very comfortable one, considering the present strained relations with Governor Pardee. There was no alternative, however, and Pardee was beseeched to do as Taft suggested. As a result, Friday found Governor Pardee, only the day before at loggerheads with every official in San Francisco over the military forces in the city, sending a telegram to Washington, asking the War Department to assign U. S. Army troops to San Francisco. And this, ignoring the fact that the troops were already there, and had been for several days, the War Department proceeded to do.

The Army was now in San Francisco legally, Greely had been authorized to take over relief administration and, although he had no more soldiers now than he had had before, he did so on Saturday. It was not a day too soon.

Greely found on taking over that the waste had reached proportions which "threatened to exhaust the treasury and deplete the storehouse within a very brief period." Food had been given out at the rate of 1,400,000 pounds a day, far more than was needed to feed the people still in San Francisco. The operation of many relief stations was in complete chaos. The one at Hamilton Square was typical. There a man named Kolinsky, acting on a card issued by Mrs. Merrill, the San Francisco Red Cross chairman, was reported to be issuing supplies "in a wholesale and reckless manner";

about twenty persons were giving orders and "thousands of dollars worth of supplies were wasted and getting worse every hour." Poor harried Mrs. Merrill, who had given her entire time to the relief effort, with selfless devotion and disregard for her own welfare, said she would send a policeman to bring Kolinsky in and he would be prosecuted.

Mrs. Merrill would have been the first to admit that the distribution of supplies was in a bad state. "We are suffering for lack of transportation facilities," she said—although when the Army took over it was able to cut the amount of transportation used enough to save $5000 a day. "There is no bread at the relief stations, and there is much wasting and rioting," she went on. No bread at the relief stations: that very day tons of it were being dumped into the bay at Oakland, along with five to seven carloads of other perishable supplies and oranges. "Stop sending oranges," the Los Angeles Relief Committee was told irritably. ("Also," it was informed, "there is no present or pressing need of any more souvenir postal cards from the ostrich farm," the contribution of one woman.) Fortunately Los Angeles was not deterred by the little thanks it was getting for its efforts. "It would be disastrous," the *Times* told its readers, "for Los Angeles to stop sending food on the supposition none is required."

With the Army assuming control, order began to appear immediately in the distribution of relief goods. There remained the serious bottleneck at the rail terminals in Oakland. By Monday, April 30, the Southern Pacific alone had brought in 1099 carloads of supplies. Without supervision and for lack of locomotive equipment to shunt the cars, fully one third of these supplies never got any farther than the Oakland railhead. The situation was so bad that on Monday Mayor Schmitz was forced to tell the Committee that San Francisco faced a serious shortage of food. His words evoked a "feeling of consternation" in the Committee; the members had been confident that generosity had placed the city beyond want for a long time to come. What was there to do? Ask the Army to take over the Oakland Terminal also. The Army did so a few days later.

```
   1   2   3   4   5   6   7   8   9  10  11  12  13  14  15  16  17

First California Issue Station, No...............
      MILK and BREAD    DEPARTMENT,
No,.....1703........ Date.................................

              W. E. Webber
              123 Castro

Adults.....2..........          Children.....2.........
       Signature.....................................

  18   19  20  21   22   23  24  25   26  27   28  29  30  31
```

California Historical Society, San Francisco

That was the end of any real difficulties in relief operation. Using a force that grew to 64 officers and about 500 enlisted men (still far short of the 1500 Greely had finally asked for) the Army manned 177 stations in the day-to-day distribution of relief. The city was divided into six sections (later eight, which were in turn the basis for seven civil relief districts) with an Army officer and a paid, competent civilian designated by the Red Cross in charge of each. The National Guard faithfully copied the Army's action and divided its area into eleven districts, although it did not allow representatives of the Red Cross, which, it said, "had sought to get control." Five general supply depots were established for the receipt of goods from the two central depots and distribution to relief stations; lines of relief districts were straightened out, overlapping districts eliminated. Independent relief stations were either taken over by the Army, as in the case of Hearst's camps, the Los Angeles Chamber of Commerce camp, and others, or abolished.

At the same time, the Army continued a certain amount of police activity, although soldiers had long since been ordered to refrain from interfering with private business or restricting personal liberty. They were, however, authorized to arrest those guilty of personal assault, robbery, looting or other serious offenses, persons so arrested to be turned over immediately to the nearest police authority. And, "where the moral force of Federal authority was felt desirable," Greely issued joint proclamations with Schmitz on such matters as building of fires, use of chimneys, economizing in the use of water, operating streetcars, and many others.

Altogether it was a tremendous undertaking. About 150 carloads of supplies were now arriving daily; the Army was eventually to handle more than 50,000 tons of stores. 313,000 were fed on the first day of the Army's operation; two weeks later there were still 225,000 standing in line for food. Greely made it clear from the outset that those who would not work would not eat. Men began to be "found unworthy" and taken out of line, amid hoots and jeers; it was an indication that the days of comfort and ease for bums were over. (Schmitz was quick to assure the public that "those who work will be paid," however; there would be none of the forced free labor at gun point of the days immediately after the fire.)

Greely was equally determined to stop the looting of supply wagons. An armed soldier was detailed to accompany each truck, with orders to shoot if anything was touched. The Committee of Fifty was outraged. "You can't do that," they told the general. "The food belongs to the people of San Francisco."

They were about to find that, once in charge, Greely was in charge with a vengeance. "No," he told them, "it belongs to the *distressed* people of San Francisco, and it is my place to say who is distressed."

"Someone will be shot," one of the members protested.

"Gentlemen," Greely told them coldly, "when the first man is shot, come to me and I will consider rescinding the order."

FINANCE COMMITTEE
of the
RELIEF AND RED CROSS FUNDS.

———

MEAL TICKET.

[May 16,06]

California Historical Society, San Francisco

There were also loud complaints when the direct distribution of uncooked rations was abandoned and a civilian contractor, Dan Desmond (the first of several), designated to provide cooked meals at refugee kitchens. A charge of ten cents was made for these meals, improperly, some felt, since the food had been *given* to the people of San Francisco. But Greely felt that absolute charity was harmful; it was better for people to pay for the meals if they could. The Red Cross handed out thousands of free meal tickets to those who could not. There was a good deal of grousing about the distance of the kitchens from the camps, and about the inconvenience, and from those who simply did not like eating in relief kitchens—many of these took their hand-outs of cooked food back home to eat.

But most of all there were complaints about the quality of the food. The residents of the Jefferson Square camp—always one of the most congested and uncomfortable of the refugee centers—finally held a mass protest meeting, orderly enough, despite the efforts of some on the outskirts of the meeting to start a riot by shouting "Tear down the soup house!" and "Burn the bean barrel!" Lieutenant Colonel Febiger, supervising the contractors furnishing meals, admitted that the food hadn't been very good, and promised that it would be better. The Red Cross began to issue additional 5-cent coupons to indigent women and children. This made up in quantity, presumably, for the lack of quality, for the meals never really improved very much. Prefire San Francisco had been known all over the world for its fine food, but no chefs made their reputations in the relief kitchens.

There were minor skirmishes with those who contributed to San Francisco relief, too. Many of the items sent were consigned to individuals, but with the welter of supplies arriving, the Army could not make individual delivery. The goods were simply combined with the general relief supplies, to the indignation of the senders, some of whom—a man who had sent eight bread pans to a friend, for example—threatened to file suit. The city of Minneapolis, which contributed thirty car-loads of flour, was incensed when the flour was sold to bakeries, and demanded that it be given to individuals. Greely told them that if they didn't like the way he was handling the flour, they could have it back. There was far more than was needed, anyway, he added ungraciously.

Considering the size of the operation, however, the Army's administration was relatively uneventful. On July 1, with the task largely finished, what remained to be done was

turned over to the Red Cross and the Army withdrew—but
not without a parting dig from Greely. After that date, he
notified Mayor Schmitz, the Army would no longer furnish
"free labor" for San Francisco. There were plenty of unem-
ployed people in the city, he pointed out—firemen, for example. Let them do the work.

With the Army assuming direct relief operations on April
29, James Phelan's "Finance Committee of Relief and Red
Cross Funds" had been able to devote itself to long-range
efforts at rehabilitation. In spite of the War Department's
having spent the entire $2.5 million government aid, there
were ample funds available; they poured in from all over the
country, from celebrities and from ordinary people alike.
Mansfield and Sarah Bernhardt gave benefit performances.
The Metropolitan Opera not only gave a benefit performance, but refunded the unused tickets for the balance of its
season in San Francisco as well. (But it was forty-two
years before it would give another performance in San Francisco.)

Marie Dressler sold benefit tickets on street corners. An
actor in New York sold newspapers; for a $100 contribution
he would break into song. Chorus girls sold smiles at a dollar a smile. Heavyweight champion James J. Jeffries sold
oranges at $20 an orange. A box of California cherries was
auctioned off, one by one, in Philadelphia: the first brought
$105, the last 50¢—a total of $2440 for the box. Tessie Oelrichs, forgetting her own losses, arranged a benefit at the
Hippodrome that raised $31,000. The State of Massachu-
setts voted $500,000. Millionaires gave checks for $100,000,
bootblacks emptied their pockets of nickels and dimes.

A subscription department began tallying subscription
data, recording letters and telegrams as they mounted up,

scouring local and eastern newspapers for information of new commitments. Contributors were remarkably faithful to their promises: of 4917 subscriptions noted by the Committee, all but 31 were fulfilled.

Since banks were not open, funds as they were received were deposited with the San Francisco Subtreasury, and the Committee drew checks directly on the Subtreasury until May 31. With business not getting started again as quickly as had been predicted, the Finance Committee's assistance was an important element in getting people back on their feet. The emphasis from the beginning was on the "little man," individuals who, by returning to useful occupations could themselves make a contribution to the recovery. Advances were made to provide tools for bricklayers and other artisans to enable them to resume their trades. Women of various callings—boarding-house keepers, laundry women, seamstresses—were re-established. Most of these grants, although vitally helpful, were quite small: of 444 made by July 4, more than half were for less than $25.

This work continued, and mounted in volume. Assistance was given in all to more than 900 individuals, ranging from grocers to sheetmetal workers to a Chinese cigar maker, to return them to their callings. Small cash grants—more than 28,000, amounting to $3,020,000—were made to buy furniture, sewing machines, to tide needy families over. When the Army withdrew on July 1, there were still about 25,000 in camps and about 20,000 being fed. Many were aged and infirm. Many others could supply their own food but not pay rent or buy furniture; about 2000 families had no prospects of obtaining furnished quarters. Large amounts would be needed to solve these problems. At the outset $150,000 was allocated for a winter home for the aged, $500,000 for a fund to enable working people to rebuild their homes, and

$2.5 million to build four-to-six room cottages—not cheap construction, either, but "ornate little homes of varied design."

To proceed to put these plans into effect, the Ingleside Race Track stables were transformed with whitewash and hot and cold running water into a home for about 1000 aged and infirm, which would be maintained for a year and a half and cost eventually about a quarter of a million dollars. The "ornate little cottages" did not materialize. Instead, the Relief Corporation built, in several closely crowded groups, 5610 two- and three-room buildings, universally referred to as "refugee shacks," at a cost of $100 and $150 each, which it rented to worthy applicants. These were later sold to the tenants, who then moved them to their own lots. (Perhaps a hundred or more, now much remodeled, are still being occupied in San Francisco.) Another $600,000 was spent matching the investment of 1400 individuals building new homes throughout the city, and $500,000 to give a bonus of one third of the cost to anyone who rebuilt his home in the burned area.

Altogether the cash contributions received by the Finance Committee and its successor organizations, including cash realized from the sale of surplus supplies, amounted to $9,254,000. With the amounts received from miscellaneous sources (interest, sale of gas to tenants of refugee cottages, sale of the cottages themselves, etc.) the Finance Committee would receive and spend in all, over a period of several years, $9,723,000.

Before the fire was over Boss Ruef had made it clear to his protégé, Mayor Schmitz, that he had no intention of remaining in the background of affairs. The mayor resisted, but not for long; his new-found determination to do what was best for the city, without taint of political corruption, weakened and finally collapsed altogether. With the Army taking over relief operations, and with the Finance Subcommittee, headed by James Phelan, merging with the Red Cross, there was no further excuse for the balance of the Committee of Fifty's existence. They thankfully disbanded on May 3, having proved, the Russell Sage Foundation found in a later study, "an excellent illustration of the futility of trying to effect an elaborate organization before the measure of disaster is taken or means for recovery learned." The Committee of Fifty was replaced by the "Committee of Forty on Reconstruction" and on this committee Ruef held no such minor position as member of the subcommittee on Relocating the Chinese. The Committee of Forty was Ruef's own creation; he controlled it by being chairman of the Committee on Committees.

Not that Ruef had waited for the Mayor's acquiescence or the dissolution of the Committee of Fifty to get on with his own plans; far from it. The stones were not even cold in the city's ruins before he resumed his corrupt negotiations. A month before the earthquake he and his hand-picked Board of Supervisors had received and divided the initial $25,000 of an agreed $125,000 fee from the Home Telephone Company to insure its being successful when it bid for the telephone franchise in San Francisco. April 23 had been set as the date for the bidding. In the meantime the disaster occurred. Governor Pardee declared April 23 a legal holiday, as he did every day until the legislature met in June. The same day the judges of the Superior Court met and ruled that all executions were stayed, all returns of process or order to show cause extended, and that "the status of all matters in all cases pending in this court shall remain as it was upon the 17th of April, 1906."

With all legal processes ground to a halt it did not occur to anyone, except Ruef and the Home Telephone Company, that the legal date set for the competitive bidding would be observed. At noon, April 23, Ruef stole down to the ruins of the City Hall and set up a small sign notifying the public that bids for the telephone franchise would be received that afternoon at 3:00 o'clock by the Board of Supervisors, meeting at Mowry Hall. The Home Telephone Company was the only bidder. It received the franchise for $25,000. A competitor, trying later to set aside the award, indicated that it would have bid a million dollars.

That matter triumphantly disposed of, Ruef moved on to the next, the much-opposed application of the United Railroads, the city's public transportation system, to convert its cable lines to overhead trolleys. The ownership and management of the United Railroads had begun first with an effort to win over the public. Its carbarns were opened to refugees and it began the distribution of food and clothing. Its trolleys ran a short distance on Market Street for a few hours Sunday evening, April 22, until ruled unsafe, in a gesture that did much for San Francisco's morale. It finally resumed actual operation on Friday, April 27, when, with Mayor Schmitz himself at the controls, and delighted, cheering people jumping on all along the way to ride for a few blocks, it made a much-publicized trip through Fillmore Street, out to Broadway and then downtown. There was no charge; part of its contribution to the rehabilitation of San Francisco, the trolley line grandly stated, would be free rides for all. (A limited contribution, considering how little of its system was in operation.)

Such gestures were doing much to win over the public, but the UR intended to be absolutely sure. Boss Ruef took to having lunch, at the company's invitation, in its comfortably appointed dining salon. A figure of $200,000 had been mentioned to him several months before; the subject was discreetly brought up again. Ruef would take care of it, and he did, although there was unexpected opposition from the *Examiner*, which began to run articles with such headlines as "UR Would Try to Loot Stricken City" and "Sneak Thieves Among Ruins And Sentries Who Turn Their Backs." (Curiously enough the *Bulletin*, which had banded with Phelan and Spreckels before the fire to attack Ruef and Schmitz, made no objection. It was spending all its energy attacking the *Oakland Tribune*.)

Ruef said, "To hell with the *Examiner*, no public man can afford to swallow that paper. This thing will go through on Monday. It is all settled." On Monday, May 21, the Board of Supervisors passed the ordinance permitting the UR to equip its entire system with overhead trolleys. The UR had what it wanted and Ruef, Schmitz and the Supervisors (except for Supervisor Rea, who was inconveniently honest and thus not included) shared the $200,000.

Other promising deals followed. $15,000 from the developers of the Parkside subdivision to expedite a profitable franchise for them. Negotiations that promised a million dollars if the franchise to furnish San Francisco's water could be delivered to the Bay Cities Water Co. It was all coming true, as Ruef had hoped and planned, and as he had told Mayor Schmitz the day of the earthquake that it would: the reconstruction period was proving a golden era of bribery, theft and corruption.

Although Ruef was busy with his own schemes from the outset, it could not be said that he neglected his duties on the Committee of Fifty during the two weeks that body remained in existence after the fire. The Subcommittee on Relocating the Chinese, of which he was a member, had swung into action without delay. It had been taken for granted from the first that the Chinese would not be allowed to return to the desirable area that Chinatown had occupied on the side of Nob Hill. Where they should go was another matter; probably to Colma, just beyond the county line. Meanwhile, on Sunday, April 22, the Chinese had been segregated into a camp at North Beach.

By Monday Theodore Roosevelt had already received reports of particularly severe suffering among the Chinese. Mindful of prejudices in San Francisco—and already *persona non grata* here because, three years before, he had forced the integration of Japanese children into the public schools—he warned Taft that Red Cross aid must be given wholly without respect to color. Given it might be, and San Francisco insisted that it was. Where and how was something the Committee would decide for itself. (The bulk of aid to the city's Orientals actually came from their own communities and, despite Roosevelt's refusal of foreign aid, from the Dowager Empress of China, who contributed $40,000, and the Japanese Red Cross, which contributed nearly $245,000.)

The following day, Tuesday, it was announced that Chinatown would be located at Hunter's Point, at the county line. Pending that move, Police Chief Dinan was directed to herd all Chinese remaining in the city to warehouses near Fort Mason until a camp could be laid out and tents erected for them on the sand lots bounded by Octavia, Franklin, Chestnut and Mason Streets, near the foot of Van Ness Avenue.

On Wednesday, however, when Reverend Philben, the subcommittee chairman, reported the plan to concentrate the Chinese here temporarily, the move met with strenuous objections, most notably from James Phelan, who pointed out that wherever the Chinese were concentrated now was where they would be likely to stay. No one wanted them to stay at the foot of Van Ness Avenue. Phelan insisted that they be moved to Hunter's Point without any further delay. This move, however, was objected to by Gavin McNab, manager of the city's Republican Party. Being just on the county line, there was danger of losing the Chinese's poll tax to neighboring San Mateo County. Nobody wanted to run that risk. The Chinese went back to the temporary camp at North Beach.

On Thursday an ideal solution was found. The Chinese were moved to the golf course at the Presidio. There was no danger of them establishing themselves permanently there, after all.

On Friday one Charles S. Wheeler, heading a delegation of residents and property owners, called on the military authorities to object to the establishment of the Chinese at the Presidio, so close to their homes. "The summer zephyrs," he said, "would blow the odors of Chinatown to their front doors," and that, it was generally agreed, was enough to drive a white man into the bay. The Chinese were hurriedly moved again, this time to the Parade Ground above Fort Point, at the eastern edge of the Presidio. Of the nearly 25,000 Chinese in San Francisco before the fire, less than a hundred now remained in the city to make this move.

While they were being moved hither and yon, such possessions as remained were being stolen. Consul General Ching Pao-Hsi went to Oakland to protest to Governor Pardee that Italians were looting Chinatown; he went again to protest that the National Guard was stripping everything of value there. Both protests were brushed off. Looters continued, working all day, carrying off "bushels of bronzes, brasses and partly melted jewelry" from the bazaars. Regulations had been relaxed; there was no shooting, no one made any effort to stop them.

The Chinese gave the appearance of being a docile, tractable people. It had not occurred to anyone that they would have ideas of their own about where they should go; there were not enough Chinese left in San Francisco to make themselves felt anyway. Now, however, a clamor slowly began to rise, from the Chinese spread throughout the state, from the Chinese ambassador in Washington, from others who felt the injustice being done San Francisco's Celestial residents. It would seem to have come as a complete surprise to most of the Committee of Fifty. Gavin McNab wanted to know what all the fuss was about. "What has been done to ruffle the temper of the Chinese?" he asked, puzzled. They had been well treated, the Reverend Philben stated, although he did admit that "the Chinese have been hustled from one temporary camp to another without ceremony." Certainly the intention had never been to harass them, Ruef insisted.

Unsettling news came from Los Angeles, too. San Francisco's hated rival was making the Chinese welcome there; it had already begun to boast that it would take Chinatown away from San Francisco. When the Committee met Monday, April 30, it was to scoff at the idea of Los Angeles taking anything away from San Francisco. Nevertheless, suppose the Chinese did move to Los Angeles? It would mean the loss of a great deal of taxes, the Oriental trade, the tourist business . . . It was something to worry about.

Not for another ten days, however, did the subcommittee, which continued as part of the new Committee on Reconstruction, get around to hearing the Chinese views on the matter. On May 10 Reverend Philben, Ruef, James Phelan and a few others met with representatives of the Chinese community. The Chinese were bland and polite. They must be near white trade in order to live, they explained. Hunter's Point would not be suitable. They did not intend to go to Los Angeles or Seattle. They were going right back to Chinatown. One third of the land in Chinatown was owned outright by the Chinese. The balance was owned by absentee landlords who did not care who occupied it as long as the rent was paid. There was nothing anyone could do to stop them.

And that was that. There was nothing to do but accept it and be philosophical about it. "Let the Chinese locate where they please," Phelan said. "If they prove obnoxious to whites they can gradually be driven to a certain section by strict enforcement of anti-gambling and other city laws." If the new Chinatown was but a replica of the old, he counseled, the fault would be the city government's. The matter came to an end, finally, on July 8. That day the Committee on Relocation of the Chinese submitted a final report admitting inability to drive the Chinese from their former site, and asking to be discharged. The Chinese were already rebuilding.

While the authorities wrangled among themselves over the relief administration, while Ruef and his gang of grafters connived to put their schemes into effect, and while the Chinese were being shuttled back and forth at the whim of the Committee, the general public was making the best of post-disaster life, performing those tasks that had to be done. The city was slowly dragging itself back into existence.

Life in San Francisco just after the fire, said one observer, was like the Wild West without saloons, or like life in a new mining town. There were the same crowds of people, the hastily built, unpainted wooden buildings, sidewalk vendors doing a rushing business in sandwiches at 5¢, soft drinks 5¢, hard-boiled eggs, three for 10¢. Souvenir-postcard salesmen were already hawking crudely printed pictures of the fire. A pawnbroker had set up a lemonade stand on top of his safe, until it could be safely opened. Around the Mint and the Post Office "at least forty fakers" were selling souvenirs of the ruins to tourists too lazy to go and dig for their own. Shabby Fillmore Street, in the Western Addition, blossomed temporarily as the new main thoroughfare of San Francisco. There, at what had been a cigar stand, Raphael Weill's fine store, The White House, was beginning all over again. The Emporium, the largest department store in the west, had taken over a former soda fountain, now roughly partitioned into a front space 14 feet by 16 feet, which was used as an office, and to the rear, a "retiring room to which the executives go for frijoles and coffee warmed over an alcohol lamp." A sawmill that had employed 4000 men before the fire now had an office in a hall bedroom that had once rented for a dollar a week. A bakery that had employed 300 was operating from a former hand laundry once run by three women. (Fillmore Street's prosperity was brief, however; it was soon superseded by Van Ness Avenue which, no longer fashionable and elegant, was to become the commercial center of San Francisco during the reconstruction. The White House and The Emporium reopened for business on Van Ness. Stores and business firms took over the fine residences that remained on the western side of the street, others built new temporary wooden buildings on the east side.)

The three telegraph companies, Western Union, Postal Telegraph, and Commercial, were back in limited operation, thanks to materials and technicians supplied by the Army. (There was a backlog that could never be caught up with by ordinary means; on Monday following the fire 12,000 telegrams arrived by train.) The Pacific Telephone Company, hastening to resume operations before its competitor, the Home Telephone Company, could move in, announced that it was ready to supply service to 18-19,000 subscribers. The Spring Valley Water Company, in an even more vulnerable position than the Pacific Telephone Company—critics were already charging that the inadequacies of its water system had been a major cause of the disaster—was hurrying to replace mains and resume service, although water would have to be boiled for another two months. Sewers were being repaired; by Wednesday, April 25, it was reported that they were "now in shape to carry off another winter's rains."

Homeowners faced the first of an interminable series of inspectors, condemning chimneys and forbidding their use, shutting off gas, disconnecting water mains. Weeks, or months, later there would be a whole new series of inspectors to turn on the water and gas and pronounce judgment on the repaired chimneys. Those chimneys: there were 50,000 of them to repair or rebuild; to be a skilled bricklayer was like owning a gold mine.

FINAL NOTICE

All Chimneys in this house having been put in order, permission is given to use them until further notice.

Jackson Street   Number   *3712*

Dated *Sept 8* , 1906-   **PERCY M. LEVI,**   Inspector.

Any person removing, altering or destroying this Notice will be punished according to law.

California Historical Society, San Francisco

Many people left their homes and moved back to the park, either because they had rented their homes to others at substantial rents, or because it was inconvenient to live in houses at this time, with gas and water disconnected and indoor cooking forbidden, or to be closer to the uncertain

and irregular supply of relief goods—or simply for the lark
of it. The Army had built wooden barracks in Golden Gate
Park and was building more, but they were half empty and
destined to remain so; perversely enough, people preferred
to choose their own sites for camping out.

Life in the Wild West without saloons it might seem, but
there was never at any time any real difficulty in getting
whisky. While prohibition continued for two and a half
months after the fire, speak-easies had been in existence
since the day of the earthquake; every so often the authorities would come on unmistakable evidence of another
one in operation. Policeman Dowd began to get suspicious
of an endless chain of men quietly wending their way into a
flat on Dolores Street and reeling out later, much the worse
for wear. He finally went in to investigate and, sure enough,
there were four barrels of whisky, one of brandy, and a
demijohn of gin, all in good working condition. Patrolman
Moffitt saw a number of drunks staggering out of William
Reed's store on Larkin Street; he "arrived at the conclusion
that the Mayor's prohibition mandate was being violated
therein." Three times medical attachés were called to pump
whisky out of one Amelia Freiman; they said they wouldn't
pump her out again to save her life.

Speak-easies in Oakland, which also had prohibition of a
sort, operated more or less openly, under the guise of soft-
drink parlors. Drunks arriving from Oakland were returned there. Saloons in Daly City, just across the county line
to the south, made no pretense whatsoever. They operated
full blast night and day, sending a steady stream of inebri-
ates back to San Francisco. General Greely finally became so
incensed that he sent a company of soldiers across the line
and peremptorily closed them down.

There was plenty of whisky, but there *were* shortages
that hurt. San Francisco's numerous opium fiends were hav-

ing a desperate time getting opium, and its even more numerous peroxide blonds were finding peroxide completely unobtainable. And sex—it was a time when people stood in line for everything, and sex was no exception. At the houses of prostitution in Oakland, men stood in lines a block long, waiting their turn. There were alternatives: the Clerk's office did a land-office business in marriage licenses, often sold on credit. Among the pages and pages of classified ads in all the newspapers, seeking the whereabouts of relatives ("Byron J. Maxim, if you are living come home; your mother is crazy; bring May, Bessie and boys; mother will shelter them. Mrs. Kate Maxim"), there began to appear ads of a more romantic nature ("Gentleman, aged 33, whom the fire separated from friends, etc., desires to meet lady similarly situated; object, matrimony. Address Box 6527, Call office, Oakland").

Slowly retail trade of a more important nature than speakeasies and souvenir stands began to open, too. The confusion and disorder surrounding the relief distribution were a spur that within a week had produced twenty-eight grocery stores, eleven meat markets, seven produce stores, nine bakeries and four restaurants. Wholesale grocers had established a base of supplies in Oakland; eggs were to be sold at 20¢ a dozen, butter 20¢ a pound. Those who had money were urged to buy food. Disgusted by the shambles the relief operations had become, most of those few who did have money needed little urging.

Certain specialized businesses were prospering. Junk dealers were beginning to arrive for the greatest junk pile of all time. The earthquake and fire had left eleven million cubic yards of debris. Much of it was worthless, but a great deal was still valuable: an estimated 400 thousand tons of cast iron, worth $8-$10 per ton, for example. All in all the junk pile was estimated to be worth $20 million.

The real-estate business was thriving too, at least in the less damaged outlying towns around San Francisco. Real-estate agents were not above placing half-page ads in the papers reading "To the Homeless: When you build yourself a new home—if only a simple cottage—why not build in the safest suburb around the bay? Don't build among a crowd of houses where fire is a constant danger." (This from an Oakland firm.)

There were several hundred people who would never have to worry about the shortages of whisky, or food, or the danger of their houses burning again. On Wednesday, April 25, the Coroner's office began to remove their bodies, the bodies of dead earthquake and fire victims, from their temporary burial grounds in parks and vacant lots, to a final resting place at Laurel Hill Cemetery. It was slow and dreadful work, the stench so bad that the crew of diggers was quickly overcome; another crew was impressed from onlookers to continue the work. By 2:00 o'clock the Coroner's assistants in charge were in such a state of collapse that the effort had to be abandoned for the day.

Coroner Walsh kept careful records of the number of bodies discovered. Whether these were all the victims, no one will ever know. As to the number of casualties resulting from the disaster, there are at least two sets of statistics, either of which might be considered reliable were it not for the other: the Army reckoned 498 dead and 415 injured in San Francisco (plus 51 dead in Santa Rosa and 25 in San Jose). The Committee on the Reconstruction's Subcommittee on Statistics counted 322 known dead, 352 missing and not accounted for. "Many have stated to the committee that the loss of life was greater," their report added, "but such statements are founded on *belief*, not fact."

• • •

There were, perhaps, some encouraging signs of recovery within a few days after the fire: a few stores opening for business; streetcars running again, if only on a very limited route; raw, temporary, unpainted wooden buildings springing up; 800 of 1100 prefire street lights burning again April 30. But actually these beginnings were so small as to be insignificant; the grocery stores reopened (including those untouched by the fire) did not amount to 2 per cent of those in operation before the fire, the streetcar line not 5 per cent of its prefire route. Some businesses had announced plans to rebuild. The Bank of California would rebuild on its old site. The Mutual Life Building would be rebuilt. Tom Magee announced plans for a new twelve-story building. New presses had been ordered for the *Examiner*, new stocks for the City of Paris. But these were things yet to come, and few enough of them.

For all practical purposes, San Francisco remained at a standstill, uncertain as to the future, making no plans beyond getting through the day at hand. The vast burned area stretched out virtually untouched, its streets still piled high with rubble and impassable. For all the "Don't talk fire, talk business," and "First to shake, first to burn, first to take another new turn," signs, about the only real activity in the ruins (aside from the invasion of junk dealers, tourists and thieves) was that the Army had begun to dynamite dangerous standing walls. There were, as usual, widespread protests. Property owners claimed that what was left of their own buildings would be damaged, threatened to sue, demanded that donkey engines be used instead.

There were several reasons for the stagnation and indecision. The shock of the disaster and the difficulties that even the barest living now presented were reasons in themselves. There was perhaps a certain validity to General

Greely's caustic comment that free handouts were pauperizing San Francisco. The confusion and uncertainty, and the obvious mismanagement of most matters by the city's leaders, was communicating itself to the people. More than anything else, though, two major obstacles stood between San Francisco and the future: the uncertainty as to when banks would reopen, and when insurance companies would pay their claims.

The San Francisco Mint was back in operation the Monday following the fire. Oakland banks reopened for limited business (withdrawals up to $30) on Wednesday, April 25. But for the San Francisco banks, their buildings ruined, their records in many cases destroyed, their vaults unsafe to open (and soldiers guarding them to see that they were not), the problems were formidable. Governor Pardee indicated that he would continue to call legal holidays for at least thirty days to give the banks time to organize and prepare for all emergencies. What means would be used for determining prefire balances, no one knew.

There was, of course, little to pay cash for these days in San Francisco, and the banks, set up in temporary offices along Laguna Street, between Sacramento and Jackson, did make a certain number of loans to more substantial clients. But as long as they remained closed for general business, and expected to remain closed, it was a severe deterrent to the resumption of normal conditions. (The Metropolitan Life Insurance Company, for example, had to send to Los Angeles for coins in order to do business.)

Bankers were meeting daily to try to map out a means of resuming business, however, and they were making progress. It is to their endless credit that they were back in business again long before anyone expected them to be. To be sure, their means of operation resembled normal banking very little, and there were severe limits. Even so, the fact that on

May 1 "the cash line . . . supplanted the bread line" (the bread line would actually continue until August 1) was a powerful factor in getting the city back into action.

Permit the bearer Mr. *J. T. Willard* at *122 Mark. St.* to open safe and remove contents.

Jno Stafford

Major 20th. Infantry.

Oakland, California Public Library

Toward the end of April it began to be possible to open vaults safely. (Like the junk dealers, safe crackers enjoyed a disaster-bred boom. There was an "incredible" number of them, said the *Chronicle:* every post, every fragment of wall bore a sign advertising a safe-cracker's services.) The contents of many safes had fared badly. Those in Chinatown had been almost entirely destroyed. Records of cases pending and other papers in the District Attorney's office in the Hall of Justice were lost. Of 576 safes opened in the Market-Powell area the last three days in April, less than 60 per cent were intact. Fortunately the bank vaults had been more substantial than most; many, though not all, of their vital records remained. The banks then arranged to have large sums of money transferred from New York and other cities to their credit with the San Francisco Subtreasury. Banding together into one "Clearing House Bank," with headquarters in the Cashier's office at the Mint, and with $2 million in coin (not small change, but gold coins and silver dollars, primarily) and tellers standing ready with their signature lists, they opened at 11:30 Tuesday morning, May 1.

A line had begun to form before 9:00 o'clock that morning; by the time the Clearing House Bank opened it stretched all the way around the corner and down Fifth

Street. Customers were allowed to draw *notes* for as much as
$500, which were guaranteed by the individual's bank and
then presented for cashing at the Clearing House Bank. It
would still be a long time before normal banking began. As
an intermediate step, new accounts were set up, separate
and distinct from prefire accounts; it was possible to deposit
in these and withdraw to the limit of the account without
restriction.

The situation of the insurance companies, and the course
they followed after the fire, was altogether different. Although there were several hundred dead, the life-insurance
companies were not particularly severely hit; most casualties
had been in the poorer districts and such policies as existed
were for small amounts. The life-insurance companies' greatest difficulties came, actually, from the decline in security
values as fire-insurance companies began to cash in their assets. Accident-insurance companies, too, although there
were innumerable claims, had not suffered unduly severe
losses. Worse hit were credit-insurance companies, which in-
sured jobbers and wholesalers against bad debts. As months
went by and San Francisco merchants were unable to meet
their obligations, these insurance companies suffered tremendous losses. But it was the fire-insurance companies
which had suffered losses from which many of them would
never recover. The problem was much more than just that
their offices had been destroyed and their vaults could not
be opened. The two San Francisco companies had lost almost their entire assets; many others had suffered losses far
beyond their total resources.

To the average fire underwriter anywhere else, one insurance man pointed out, San Francisco would have been considered uninsurable. It was built almost entirely of wood;
even many of its downtown buildings, five and six stories
high, were wooden. Its hills made risks difficult of access; it

had almost no secondary water system in case its vulnerable main system was damaged by earthquake. Nevertheless, for more than a quarter of a century luck had held and in spite of low rates loss ratios had never exceeded 25 per cent and companies had continued to make a very comfortable underwriting profit. Although the city had six times been destroyed by fire in its early days, insurers convinced themselves that, with the winter rains and the summer fogs, buildings never really dried out enough to be dangerous and that, in any case, the San Francisco Fire Department, with its excellent reputation, was sufficient protection.

Throwing caution to the winds, they had forgotten principles which they themselves practiced in safer cities than San Francisco. They underwrote huge amounts in congested districts, where numerous risks might be subject to a single fire. Today insurance companies protect themselves by reinsuring a large percentage of almost every risk they undertake, but in 1906 the reinsurance market was little developed. Some companies had not reinsured at all; others had made the mistake of reinsuring with smaller companies even more heavily obligated in San Francisco. Nor were today's stringent regulations on insurance companies in effect in 1906. The amount of insurance a company could sell bore no relationship to the amount it could pay if it had to. The Trader's Insurance Company, for example, with $1.8 million capital and surplus, had insurance in effect amounting to $160 million, with $4,640,000 in San Francisco alone. It promptly went into receivership.

Fire insurance companies had plunged, and they had made money. Year after year income had been high: in 1905 the total premium had been $2,985,540. There were 108 insurance companies doing business in the city, extending themselves farther and farther. European insurance companies which did business nowhere else in the United States had found it worthwhile to make the necessary deposit in order to do business in California, primarily in San Francisco. The deposit, $100,000, was nowhere near the risk undertaken. One of these companies, the Rhine & Moselle, completely unheard of in the rest of the United States, was, with $4,768,000 insurance in effect, the eighth largest insurer in San Francisco.

There were close to 100,000 policies, representing approximately $239,000,000 worth of fire insurance, in effect in San Francisco on April 18, 1906, in the area that was to be destroyed by fire. The fire, in three days, wiped out *all* the underwriting profits that *all* the insurance companies in the United States had made in the past fifty years. (A generous estimate of premium income during that period being $6 billion, and an equally generous estimate of the profits thereon, $180 million. Aside from underwriting profits, of course, insurance companies make a substantial part of their income from investments.)

The insurance in force in San Francisco was $50 million more than that in effect in Chicago at the time of the great Chicago fire. The Chicago disaster had forced forty-six companies out of business, and only 50 per cent of the insurance claims resulting from that fire were ever paid. The prospects in San Francisco were grim indeed.

Only *six* of all the 108 insurance companies represented in San Francisco paid promptly and in full.

Some delayed in honest efforts to meet the crisis, others with the intention of forcing reduced settlement or avoiding payment altogether. (And even some of those who did pay promptly were not above taking advantage of the situation by making very sharp, tricky settlements.) Insurance rates went up all over the country. To raise funds several companies increased their capital stock; many others assessed their stockholders for the necessary amounts. Companies on the brink of ruin began to notify their agents to stop writing business. One by one, insurance companies failed. Three German companies and one Austrian company denied all responsibility and withdrew from doing business in the United States, leaving behind claims that would be the subject of fruitless litigation in international courts for decades to come.

Unscrupulous insurers demanded large discounts, as much as 40 to 60 per cent, for "cash" settlements. Altogether, fifty-five companies—more than half—performed so badly, with anywhere from a 5 to 10 per cent deduction to complete default, that they were rated "Poor" by the National Credit Men's Association. Worst of all were the German companies: even the three that did not withdraw altogether treated their claimants badly, paid only after long delays, and then only after taking substantial discounts. The Hamburg-Bremen Fire Insurance Company, for example, was singled out by the Credit Men's Association for its "insulting and discourteous treatment" of policyholders and because, while it was settling its $4,448,000 in claims at discounts of 20 to 25 per cent, it displayed in its New York office "a misleading notice to the effect that it was pleased to inform its friends and patrons that funds had been sent over from Hamburg for the purpose of promptly paying its San Francisco losses." (It was particularly galling to remember that Theodore Roosevelt had turned down the offer of a $25,000 contribution from another German firm, the Hamburg-American Line.)

On the other hand, no companies had more outstanding records than the two San Francisco companies, the California Fire Insurance Company and the Fireman's Fund Insurance Company, particularly in view of the fact that many of their assets were invested in San Francisco bonds and mortgages, now impossible to realize on. The California Fire

Insurance Company, with claims of $2,550,000 against assets of $450,000, assessed its stockholders and paid off all its claims in full—and was one of the six to pay immediately. The Fireman's Fund, even more heavily involved—its claims exceeded its assets by $4.5 million—took another course. The company was dissolved and a new company, debt free, founded to take its place. Policyholders were paid 56½ per cent in cash and 50 per cent in stock in the new company on their claims. It showed, the Policy Holders League felt, "admirable pluck and fair dealing"; it was, in fact, "a splendid victory—honorable to both the company and to the community—over tremendously adverse circumstances."

THE PRICE OF "THE EXAMINER" IS FIVE CENTS.

 News of Your Family or Friends on Page 5

 San Francisco Examiner

List of TELEGRAMS Uncalled for on Page 5

SAN FRANCISCO, FRIDAY, APRIL 27, 1906

CALIFORNIA INSURANCE COMPANY WILL PAY IN FULL

PUNISHMENT SURE FOR ALL DEALERS AND OTHERS WHO OVERCHARGE CUSTOMERS

BOTH WHOLESALE AND RETAIL BUSINESS IS NOW BEING RESUMED UPON A FORMER BASIS. THE DESIRE OF THE LARGER MAJORITY SEEMS TO BE TO CONDUCT THEIR BUSINESS UPON THE SAME PLANS AS THOSE EXISTING BEFORE THE FIRE TOOK PLACE. A FEW SMALL RETAILERS, HOWEVER, WHO ARE SO MERCILESS AND DISREPUTABLE THAT THEY WISH TO MAKE BIG PROFIT OUT OF THE MISFORTUNE OF THE PEOPLE AT THIS TIME, ARE CHARGING MORE THAN THE MARKET PRICE FOR THEIR GOODS. I HAVE BEEN INFORMED THAT A NUMBER OF EXPRESSMEN ALSO ARE DOING THE SAME THING—OVERCHARGING THE PUBLIC—AND I WISH, THEREFORE, TO PUBLICLY ANNOUNCE THAT NO OVERCHARGE WILL BE TOLERATED, AND THE MERCHANTS OR THOSE ENGAGED IN THE TRANSPORTATION OF GOODS OR FURNITURE FOR THE PEOPLE AT LARGE WHO OVERCHARGE THE PUBLIC BE SUMMARILY DEALT WITH, UNDER CONDITIONS LIKE THOSE THAT OBTAIN IN SAN FRANCISCO AT THE PRESENT TIME IT IS A HEINOUS CRIME TO OVERCHARGE THE PUBLIC FOR ANYTHING WHATSOEVER. THE GENERAL PUBLIC IS HEREBY REQUESTED TO NOTIFY ME OF ANY OVERCHARGE WHICH COMES TO THEIR ATTENTION, AND STEPS WILL BE TAKEN IMMEDIATELY TO PUNISH THE OFFENDERS. E. E. SCHMITZ, MAYOR CITY AND COUNTY OF SAN FRANCISCO.
FORT MASON, CAL., APRIL 26, 1906.

There were, unfortunately, more who followed the course of the German companies than that of the San Francisco companies. As the weeks passed, every pressure possible was brought on the laggard companies to settle. "Let them therefore deliver what we have bought," newspapers demanded. The Policy Holders League was formed to fight for its members' rights. Claimants against individual companies banded together to battle those particular companies. The Credit Men's Association and the Chamber of Commerce pressed for settlements. The state legislature, called to special session June 2, passed a law compelling insurance companies to give their policyholders the information necessary to make proper proof of loss. The State Insurance Commissioner ordered a full list of policies to be furnished by all insurance companies, and threatened receivership for those who failed to comply.

Gradually companies which had delayed payments by reason of agreements with other companies—"agreements 'suggested by prudent business reasons' but which are really for protection of smaller and weaker companies"—began to repudiate those agreements and settle their claims. A Fire Underwriters Adjustment Bureau was formed to handle claims which involved six or more companies; in these community-adjusted claims the companies found it much more difficult to employ the sharp practices they used when the losses were settled individually and privately.

The Bureau was a very substantial factor in insurance settlements. By the end of November it had adjusted 1149 claims (representing several thousand policies) amounting to $88,379,000 and had only nine claims remaining unsettled. Including individual settlements privately made, insurance companies had paid altogether by this time about $150,000,000 on the $239,000,000 in policies in the burned area. Ultimately the total payments would amount to about 80 per cent—not a good record, perhaps, but far better than the 50 per cent payment on losses in the Chicago fire, and in any case a larger sum than insurance companies had ever paid before. Twelve companies, all American, failed as a result of the San Francisco fire.

There was one other factor which had a certain effect in delaying the rebuilding of San Francisco, even after banks had opened and insurance companies had begun to pay. That was the question of *how* the city should be rebuilt. "Now will come the city beautiful," said the *Overland*

Monthly. "The mistakes of the past are to be remedied in the future." And it did seem that the destruction had given San Francisco the never-expected opportunity to rearrange its inconvenient street system, reorganize the city and, in fact, to put into effect the highly visionary "Burnham Plan" which had been drawn up the year before at the behest of the "Association for Improvement and Adornment of San Francisco."

"Think no small thoughts," had been the motto of Daniel Burnham. Architect of the Union Station in Washington, the Flatiron Building in New York, "father of the sky-scraper," he had been invited by the Association in 1904 to draw up a comprehensive plan for rebuilding San Francisco. Installed in a bungalow built for him on a spur of Twin Peaks, commanding a panoramic view of the city, he had set to work on a plan "designed not only for the present but for all time to come."

Drawing his inspiration from the radial plan of the city of Paris, he envisioned a broad boulevard, to which all streets would lead, embracing the city. Each hill or succession of hills would be circumscribed at its base by a circuit road, repeated at intervals and connected by easy inclines. Streets would be widened, Mission to 250 feet, others to 150 feet. A "great Central Place," a civic center, would be the focal point of the city, with radiating streets to the outskirts. Other subcenters would be located "at the intersection of the radial arteries with the perimeter of distribution." An underground rapid transit system would be installed. No detail was overlooked: parks, amphitheaters, monuments, trees in the streets were itemized; an art commission, hospitals, almshouses, cemeteries provided for.

Even Burnham had admitted that such a plan could only be executed by degrees; opening the diagonal streets alone would be the work of a generation. Now, with so much

of the city obliterated by the fire and to be entirely rebuilt, it seemed to the Association for the Improvement and
Adornment of San Francisco that almost the entire plan
could be put into effect—the great Central Place, the radiating arterial streets, the circumscribed hills, the broad
boulevards, all of it.

They had not reckoned with the property owners of San
Francisco, however, who would have none of the Burnham
Plan. By and large they were interested only in their own
individual projects, unwilling to give an inch, impatient of
"master plans," furious as consideration of the plan delayed
building permits. Pressure groups were organized to force
abandonment of the plan, to protest to the legislature, when
it met, to defeat efforts to widen streets and make other im-
provements.

City planning was in its infancy; the city had no authority to force condemnation of property, and little money to
do it with, anyway. Gradually the great opportunity was
lost, and the plan faded into the background. When Burnham
died in Heidelburg in 1912, only a few of his recommendations had been put into effect, or ever would be: Market
Street and a few others widened, Rincon Hill lowered, a
civic center, the "great Central Place" where city, state and
Federal buildings faced each other across a central plaza—
but without the radiating streets that gave his plan meaning.
Decades later the Burnham Plan would still be wistfully
spoken of as "San Francisco's golden asset" but it was one
that would never materialize.

In spite of every obstacle and delay, however, the city did
rebuild. Early in May the Southern Pacific and Ocean
Shore Railways began to lay spur tracks into the wreckage,
and the debris slowly melted away. Aided by the Relief
Corporation and the increasing insurance payments, new

homes began to appear, new business buildings more substantial than those first "frontier town" wooden buildings. From month to month the momentum increased. In the three-month period of June, July and August, $8,000,000 in building permits were issued; for the next three months, the figures leaped to more than $26,000,000.

In other ways, too, the situation slowly began to return to normal. The legislature met, finally, June 2, ending the long series of legal holidays. (The legal holidays had not actually brought everything to a halt. Shortly after the fire Tax Collector Barber notified the public that taxes became delinquent on April 30, legal holidays or no; checks would be accepted, provided the banks honored them within thirty days. And the Attorney General explained that there was nothing to prevent the voluntary resumption of business. Obligations might be met and contracts entered into "with entire security.") It began the vast amount of legislation necessary to meet special situations caused by the fire, to coerce procrastinating insurance companies, to protect banks, to reconstruct all the legal papers that had been destroyed. Provisions were made for burned bonds and stock certificates, lost articles of incorporation, duplicate marriage licenses.

People began to return to the city in large numbers. The population had sunk to a low of 110,000 by Army census early in June (causing the Los Angeles *Herald* to crow that Los Angeles was now "the undisputed metropolis of the two-thirds of the United States between the Missouri River and the Pacific") but it quickly swelled again as refugees—many of them wives and children who had been waiting for homes to be rebuilt—came back, so that by the time the Army withdrew on July 1, Greely estimated that there were at least 375,000 people in the city. On July 5 Mayor Schmitz felt it was safe to allow saloons to reopen, from 8 A.M. to

6 P.M. for the first thirty days, then all night if the police commissioners saw fit.

Every new statistic was an indication of how the city was hastening to recovery. 11,000,000 passengers carried on streetcars in July. $46,000,000 in bank clearings the first week in September, an increase of 25 per cent over the same week in the previous year. By the end of the year the city was in the midst of a building boom so tremendous that every cement factory was working a double shift, building trades men worked 18-hour days, and lumber camps as far north as British Columbia were busy supplying the demand. (This brought about, incidentally, a subsidiary boom in growing eucalyptus for timber which collapsed in 1909, a total loss for those who had hoped to get rich quick from it. Author Jack London, for one, lost the $40,000 he had invested in planting eucalyptus at his home in Santa Rosa.)

By December there was sufficient confidence for the city to resume the plans conceived in 1905 to hold a giant World's Fair in 1915. It was a project that might have daunted a city undamaged by fire and earthquake, and one that under the circumstances might justifiably have been postponed. Instead it was pressed through to fulfillment in the San Francisco Exposition of 1915. By the time it opened, hardly a trace of the ravages the city had suffered remained.

What of the men who loomed so large in the city's affairs during the crisis? The clouds were already forming over Mayor Schmitz, and the era of corruption was coming to an end. As conditions returned to normal James Phelan, Rudolph Spreckels and *Bulletin* editor Fremont Older—no longer preoccupied with his feud with the *Oakland Tribune* —found time once more for their campaign against Boss Ruef and Mayor Schmitz and the Board of Supervisors.

With the co-operation of District Attorney Langdon the prosecution began again, and Schmitz and Ruef were arraigned for bribery and extortion on December 6, 1906.

It was the beginning of months of lurid trials. Grasping at every straw, Boss Ruef would have District Attorney Langdon removed and himself installed as District Attorney, only to withdraw at the Supreme Court's ultimatum. Fremont Older would be kidnaped and the house of the prosecution's chief witness bombed. Francis Heney, the special prosecutor, would be shot, and his would-be assassin would commit suicide—or perhaps be murdered to keep him quiet—in jail. The assassin's jailer would commit suicide, and the last man to see the jailer alive would go mad, screaming, "I don't know what happened to him."

Schmitz would be convicted of extortion and sentenced to five years in jail, but the conviction would be set aside on a technicality, and only one man—Abe Ruef—would ever serve in the penitentiary for his crimes. Indeed, Schmitz, branded guilty beyond question but immensely popular as a result of his leadership during the fire, would run again for Mayor, draw a tremendous number of votes (although not enough to elect him) and ultimately serve two terms on the Board of Supervisors.

Mayor Schmitz' chief opponent, James Phelan, had labored long and hard for San Francisco at the time of the fire, and to protect it from people like Schmitz, and in many other civic causes. He had the city's respect, perhaps, as a reward, but never the love and adulation that Schmitz evoked. He served as Senator from California from 1914 to 1920, but he never again held office in San Francisco.

General Greely retired shortly after the Army withdrew from administering relief operations in San Francisco, and went to Washington, D.C., to live. As the years passed he came to be an institution—and one of the oldest—in Washington. Herbert Hoover once said that there were always two things he was certain to see when he returned to the city: the Washington monument and General Greely. He died, at 91, in 1935.

General Funston, on the other hand, had a bare eleven years left, but they were to be full years, in the typical Funston pattern. On Greely's retirement he became temporarily commander of the Pacific Division. In the years that followed, he saw service in Hawaii and again in the Philippines and then became Military Governor of Vera Cruz in 1914, with service so outstanding that he was promoted to Major General. He spent his last year leading the hunt for Pancho Villa along the Mexican border, only to die, ironically enough, sitting in an armchair in a hotel lobby in San Antonio, Texas, waiting for dinner. (He was succeeded, as he had been once many years before in the Philippines, by John J. Pershing.)

And San Francisco? In the words of the *Overland Monthly*, "Possibly the new San Francisco will not be so joyous a place to the unregenerate nor so painful a spot to the pious as formerly, but even of this it is not well to be too positive."

BIBLIOGRAPHY

▲▲▲

Much of the material in this book was derived from the California newspapers of the time, particularly the San Francisco *Bulletin, Call, Chronicle, Daily News* and *Examiner;* the San Jose *Mercury* and *News;* the Sacramento *Bee;* the Oakland *Herald, Tribune,* and *Enquirer;* and the Los Angeles *Herald* and *Times;* and from the California periodicals *Argonaut, Overland Monthly,* and *Sunset.* Reference was also made to *Harper's Weekly* and *Cosmopolitan.*

In addition, the following are cited in the text or were referred to in its preparation:

Aitken, Frank W., and Hilton, Edward, *A History of the Earthquake and Fire in San Francisco.* 1906.
Altrocchi, Julia Cooley, *The Spectacular San Franciscans.* 1949.
Asbury, Herbert, *The Barbary Coast: An Informal History of the San Francisco Underworld.* 1933.
Atherton, Gertrude, *California, An Intimate History.* 1914.
———, *Golden Gate Country.* 1945.
Bean, Walter, *Boss Ruef's San Francisco.* 1952.

Blake, Evarts I., Editor, *San Francisco: A Brief Biographical Sketch of Some of the Most Prominent Men Who Will Preside Over Her Destiny for at Least Two Years.* 1902.

Boden, Charles R., "San Francisco's Cisterns." Reprinted from *California Historical Society Quarterly*, Vol. XV, No. 4. 1937.

Bowlen, Frederick, "San Francisco Fire Department History." San Francisco *Chronicle*, May 14-July 13, 1939.

Burnham, Daniel H., assisted by Edward H. Bennett, *Report on a Plan for San Francisco.* 1905.

Carnahan, Melissa Stewart McKee, *Personal Experiences of the San Francisco Earthquake of April, 1906.* 1908.

Complete Story of the San Francisco Horror. "By the Survivors and Rescuers." 1906.

Davis, Robert, as told to John M. Connor, "Incidents in the Life of Major General Frederick Funston, U.S.A." (Manuscript, California State Library, Sacramento). 1949.

Department Reports of the San Francisco Relief and Red Cross Funds (A Corporation). 1907.

Everett, Marshall, *Complete Story of the San Francisco Earthquake.* 1906.

Funston, Frederick, *Memories of Two Wars.* 1911.

———, "How the Army Worked to Save San Francisco." *Cosmopolitan Magazine*, Vol. XLI, No. 3. July 1906.

Greely, Adolphus W., *Earthquake in California, April 18, 1906. Special Report of Major General Adolphus W. Greely, U.S.A.* 1906.

Himmelwright, A. L. A., *The San Francisco Earthquake and Fire.* (n.d.)

House Documents, 59th Congress, 1st Session. Volume 49. 1906.

Irwin, Will, *The City That Was.* 1906.

Jones, Idwal, *Ark of Empire.* 1951.

Jordan, David Starr, Editor, *The California Earthquake of 1906.* 1907.

Keeler, Charles, *San Francisco and Thereabouts.* 1906.

———, *San Francisco Through Earthquake and Fire.* 1906.

Key, Pierre U. R., in collaboration with Bruno Zirato, *Enrico Caruso, A Biography.* 1922.

Lane, Franklin K., *The Letters of Franklin K. Lane,* edited by Anne W. Lane and Louise Herrick Wall. 1922.

Lewis, Oscar, and Hall, Carroll D., *Bonanza Inn, America's First Luxury Hotel.* 1939.

Maxwell, Elsa, *R.S.V.P., Elsa Maxwell's Own Story.* 1954.

Mitchell, William, *General Greely, The Story of a Great American.* 1936.

Morrow, William W., *The Earthquake of April 18, 1906, and the Great Fire in San Francisco on that and succeeding days— Personal Experiences, Inauguration of Red Cross and General Relief Work.* (1906.)

Reed, S. Albert, *The San Francisco Conflagration of April, 1906. Special Report to the National Board of Fire Underwriters Committee of Twenty.* 1907.

Report of Marsden Manson to the Mayor and Committee on Reconstruction on Those Portions of the Burnham Plan Which Meet Our Commercial Necessities. 1906.

Report of the Board of Trustees of the Relief and Red Cross Funds to The American National Red Cross, covering the period from Feb. 4, 1909 to July, 1917. 1917.

Report, the Sub-Committee on Statistics to the Chairman and Committee on Reconstruction. 1907.

Ruef, Abraham, "The Road I Traveled. An Autobiographic Account of my Career from University to Prison, with an Intimate Recital of the Corrupt Alliance Between Big Business and Politics in San Francisco." San Francisco *Bulletin,* April 6, and May 21 to September 5, 1912.

San Francisco Municipal Reports for the Fiscal Years 1905-1906 and 1906-1907, Ended June 30, 1907. 1908.

San Francisco Municipal Reports for the Fiscal Year 1907-1908, Ended June 30, 1908. 1909.

San Francisco Relief Survey, The Organization and Methods of Relief Used After the Earthquake and Fire of April 18, 1906, compiled from studies by Charles J. O'Connor, Francis H. McLean, Helen Swett Artieda, James M. Motley, Jessica Peixotto, Mary Roberts Coolidge. 1913.

Schussler, Hermann, *The Water Supply of San Francisco Before, During, and After the Earthquake of April 18, 1906, and the Subsequent Conflagration*. 1906.

Stetson, James B., *San Francisco During the Eventful Days of April, 1906*. 1906.

Ziegler, Wilbur Gleason, *Story of the Earthquake and Fire*. 1906.

INDEX

The Call=Chro

SAN FRANCISCO, T

EARTHQUAKI
SAN FRANCIS

DEATH AND DESTRUCTION HAVE BEEN THE FATE OF SAN FRANCISCO. SHAKI
AND SCOURGED BY FLAMES THAT RAGED DIAMETRICALLY IN ALL DIRECTIONS, THE
INGLY PLAYING WITH INCREASED VIGOR, THREATENED TO DESTROY SUCH SECTIO
PATH IN A TRIANGUAR CIRCUIT FROM THE START IN THE EARLY MORNING, THEY JC
VASTATED, AND SKIPPED IN A DOZEN DIRECTIONS TO THE RESIDENCE PORTIONS.
SPRINGING ANEW TO THE SOUTH THEY REACHED OUT ALONG THE SHIPPING SECT
STREETS. WAREHOUSES, WHOLESALE HOUSES AND MANUFACTURING CONCERNS F
AS THE "SOUTH OF MARKET STREET." HOW FAR THEY ARE REACHING TO THE SO
SAN FRANCISCO PAPERS.

AFTER DARKNESS,THOUSANDS OF THE HOMELESS WERE MAKING THEIR WA
FIND SHELTER. THOSE IN THE HOMES ON THE HILLS JUST NORTH OF THE HAYES
ONS AND AUTOMOBILES WERE HAULING THE THINGS AWAY TO THE SPARSELY SI
BELIEF IS FIRM THAT SAN FRANCISCO WILL BE TOTALLY DESTROYED

DOWNTOWN EVERYTHING IS RUIN. NOT A BUSINESS HOUSE STANDS. THEATRES
THEIR FORMER SITES. ALL OF THE NEWSPAPER PLANTS HAVE BEEN RENDERED USI
ROOMS ON STEVENSON STREET BEING ENTIRELY DESTROYED.

IT IS ESTIMATED THAT THE LOSS IN SAN FRANCISCO WILL REACH FROM $15
PARTIAL ACCOUNTING IS TAKEN.

ON EVERY SIDE THERE WAS DEATH AND SUFFERING YESTERDAY. HUNDREDS
INGS AND ONE OF TEN DIED WHILE ON THE OPOPERATING TABLE AT MECHANI
THE NUMBER OF DEAD IS NOT KNOWN BUT IT IS ESTIMATED THAT AT LEAST 500 ME

AT NINE O'CLOCK, UNDER A SPECIAL MESSAGE FROM PRESIDENT ROOSEVELT,
AND DROVE THE CROWDS BACK, WHILE HUNDREDS MORE WERE SET AT WORK ASSI
TRUE MILITARY SPIRIT THE SOLDIERS OBEYED DURING THE AFTERNOON THREE
WERE DRIVEN BACK AT THE BREASTS OF THE HORSES THAT THE CAVALRYMEN ROD
YOND TO THE NORTH

THE WATER SUPPLY WAS ENTIRELY CUT OFF, AND MAY BE IT WAS JUST AS V
STAGE. ASSISTANT CHIEF DOUGHERTY SUPERVISED THE WORK OF HIS MEN AND E.
IN EFFORT TO CHECK THE FLAMES BY THE USE OF DYNAMITE. DURING THE DAY A B
INGS NOT DESTROYED BY FIRE WERE BLOWN TO ATOMS. BUT THROUGH THE GAPS I
LICE FIREMEN AND SOLDIERS WERE AT TIMES SICKENING, THE WORK WAS CONTIN
TER. MEN WORKED LIKE FIENDS TO COMBAT THE LAUGHING, ROARING, ONRUSHIN